THE UNITED STATES AND THE POLITICIZATION OF THE WORLD BANK

A PUBLICATION OF THE GRADUATE INSTITUTE OF INTERNATIONAL STUDIES, GENEVA

THE UNITED STATES AND THE POLITICIZATION OF THE WORLD BANK

Issues of international law and policy

Bartram S. Brown

KEGAN PAUL INTERNATIONAL
London and New York

First published in 1992 by
Kegan Paul International Ltd
PO Box 256, London WC1B 3SW, England

Distributed by
John Wiley & Sons Ltd
Southern Cross Trading Estate
1 Oldlands Way, Bognor Regis
West Sussex, PO22 9SA, England

Routledge, Chapman & Hall Inc
29 West 35th Street
New York, NY 10001, USA

Typeset in Palatino by
Input Typesetting Ltd, London
Printed in Great Britain by
T. J. Press

British Library Cataloguing in Publication Data
Brown, Bartram Stewart
The United States and the politicization of the World Bank: issues of international law and policy. (A Publication of the Graduate Institute of International Studies, Geneva)
1. World Bank
I. Title. II. Series
332.1532

ISBN 0–7103–0424–2

Library of Congress Cataloging-in-Publication Data
Brown, Bartram Stewart
The United States and the politicization of the World Bank: issues of international law and policy / Bartram Stewart Brown.
295p. 23.4cm. – (A Publication of the Graduate Institute of International Studies, Geneva)
Includes bibliographical references (p.275).
ISBN 0–7103–0424–2
1. World Bank. 2. World Bank – United States 3. Development banks – law and legislation – United States. 4. Development banks – Political aspects – United States. I. Title. II. Series: Publications de l'Institut universitaire de hautes études internationales. Genève.
K4451.B76 1991
341.7′51—dc20

To my parents,
Russell W. Brown and
Susie H. Brown

CONTENTS

ACRONYMS AND OTHER ABBREVIATED FORMS USED

ADB	Asian Development Bank
AfDB	African Development Bank
AfDF	African Development Fund
Bank	International Bank for Reconstruction and Development
Council	National Advisory Council on International Monetary and Financial Policies
ECOSOC	Economic and Social Council
EDs	Executive Directors
ESCOR	Economic and Social Council Official Records
GATT	General Agreement on Tariffs and Trade
GAOR	General Assembly Official Records
IBRD	International Bank for Reconstruction and Development
ICJ	International Court of Justice
IDA	International Development Association
IDB	Inter-American Development Bank
IFIs	International Financial Institutions
IGO	Intergovernmental Organization
ILO	International Labour Organization
IMF	International Monetary Fund
MDBs	Multilateral Development Banks
ODA	Official Development Assistance
UN	United Nations
UNCTAD	United Nations Conference on Trade and Development

UNESCO	United Nations Economic Social and Cultural Organization
USC	United States Code
UNGA	United Nations General Assembly
UNSC	United Nations Security Council
US	United States

ACKNOWLEDGEMENTS

I wish to express my thanks to the faculty members at the Graduate Institute of International Studies in Geneva, Switzerland who helped me in the preparation of the doctoral thesis which was eventually transformed into this book. These include the members of my thesis committee – Stuart Robinson, Huu-Tru Nguyen, and the late Michel Virally – as well as Lucius Caflisch who also provided support and encouragement. Special thanks go to Georges Abi-Saab, my thesis director, for his advice and guidance on this and other matters.

I am most grateful to the College of William and Mary and my colleagues there who provided important support for the preparation and publication of the final manuscript.

Many other people helped in the realization of this book, either through their comments, criticisms and suggestions or through other types of support provided to me during its preparation. It would be impossible for me to mention them all by name here, but I would nonetheless like to offer them this general expression of my thanks. As much as others may have contributed to this book, I alone am responsible for any shortcomings.

Bartram S. Brown
Williamsburg, Virginia
June 1991

1

INTRODUCTION

In recent years there has been a great deal of controversy and polemic concerning what is often referred to as the "politicization" of international organizations. The United States government invoked politicization as one of the justifications for its temporary withdrawal from the International Labor Organization from 1977 to 1980.[1] A similar logic contributed to the decision of the US to withdraw from the United Nations Economic Scientific and Cultural Organization (UNESCO) at the end of 1984.[2]

It would be quite unrealistic to expect international organizations such as these to be totally non-political. Their budgetary resources as well as the fact that they owe their existence to the desire of states to cooperate, ensure that there must be some political side to their activities. What basis is there then for objecting to their "politicization"? This book is an investigation of the legal and practical implications of a certain type of politicization in the context of two of the institutions which comprise the World Bank Group, i.e., the International Bank for Reconstruction and Development (IBRD) and its soft loan affiliate the

1 See *Department of State Bulletin*, Vol. 30, No. 2037, April 1980, at pp. 65–66, and Letter dated 5 November, 1975 from Henry Kissinger, Secretary of State of the United States of America, to Francis Blanchard, Director General of the ILO, containing notice of intent to withdraw from the ILO, in *International Legal Materials*, Vol. XIV, No. 6, November 1975, at pp. 1582–1584.

2 See *Department of State Bulletin*, Vol. 84, No. 2083, February 1984, at pp. 41–42.

International Development Association (IDA).[3] It focuses upon the use by the United States of its voting power in these organizations in order to serve political purposes unilaterally determined by the US Congress.

This book is not so much about what the World Bank does, but rather is about the internal constitutional structure of the World Bank, the relations between its members, and the political consensus which is the basis for the cooperation of states within that organization. In particular, it examines the role of international law in structuring this cooperation. Before focusing upon these issues it is important to consider the role of international economic organizations in the global economic order.

A. INTERNATIONAL ORGANIZATIONS AND THE WORLD ECONOMIC ORDER

The development of the present system of multilateral economic institutions after World War II may ultimately prove to be one of the most significant international political developments of the 20th century. The period preceding that war had been characterized by protectionist high tariffs, exchange rate manipulations and other "beggar thy neighbor" economic policies. During that time the pursuit of economic policies reflecting a narrowly nationalistic perspective had led to a choking off of international trade and contributed to global economic stagnation. Remembering the international economic chaos which had preceded the war, the victorious Allied Powers, under American leadership, decided to construct a postwar system of international economic organizations which would structure international economic relations along more positive and cooperative lines. Their proposed system has sometimes been likened to a three-legged stool, each of whose legs was to

3 The IBRD is commonly referred to as the World Bank, and the cluster of affiliated organizations centered around the IBRD is often referred to as the World Bank Group. Throughout this work, the terms "Bank" and "World Bank" will be used to refer to both the IBRD and the IDA except where the two are specifically differentiated or referred to separately.

correspond to a separate specialized agency affiliated with the United Nations (UN).

One leg of the stool was to be a strong International Trade Organization (ITO) based on a treaty (the Havana Charter) which would have as its mandate the elimination of most barriers to trade. Although the proposed ITO was largely an American initiative, in the end the US Senate refused to ratify the treaty which would have brought it into being. Since the US was indisputably the preeminent economic power in the world at the time, the dream of an ITO could not survive without American support. The less ambitious framework of the General Agreement on Tariffs and Trade (GATT) was all that could be agreed to at the time. Although the GATT had originally been created as an interim arrangement, it was left to take on an expanded role as a permanent multilateral trade mechanism.

The other two legs of the stool were completed more or less as planned, pursuant to agreements reached at the Bretton Woods Monetary and Financial Conference of 1944. Two key international economic institutions were negotiated at that Conference, the International Monetary Fund (IMF) and the International Bank for Reconstruction and Development (IBRD). Each of them plays an important role in the international economic order today.

The IMF was created to promote international monetary cooperation. It was to concern itself with maintaining exchange rate stability, helping its members to deal with short term balance of payments disequilibria and in general with establishing a reliable international payments system. The task of the IMF has evolved quite a bit since it was founded, and today it plays an especially important role in helping developing countries and their creditors to manage the international debt crisis. The Fund allows debtor countries to draw upon its financial resources only if they comply with IMF "conditionality". In practice this means that it makes financing available to debtors only if they promise to comply with conditions it sets concerning their national economic policies and performance. After initial approval it continues to act as a sort of international financial policeman monitoring compliance with the promises it has exacted from debtor countries, and giving a creditworthiness green light to the international financial community.[4]

The IBRD, the central institution in the World Bank Group, was established in 1945 in order to finance the reconstruction of countries devastated by World War II as well as to finance the development of more traditionally impoverished areas of the world. The Marshall Plan, introduced in June of 1947, eventually assumed the burden of financing reconstruction in Europe leaving the Bank free to devote its resources to the development task.

IBRD members finance that organization through subscriptions to its capital stock, but only 10% of each member's subscription is actually paid into the Bank. Most of the money lent (90%) is raised by IBRD borrowing in private capital markets. This corresponds to the portion of each member's capital subscription which is payable only in the event that the Bank needs the additional funds to meet its financial commitments to borrowers ("callable capital").

In essence IBRD loans recycle funds borrowed in private capital markets, and because of this that institution must charge a rate of interest for its loans which corresponds to market conditions. It must also pay close attention to the ability of its borrowers to repay the money borrowed.[5] Many developing countries cannot afford to borrow on the terms offered by the IBRD, and thus in 1960 the IDA was created as the "soft loan" affiliate of the Bank.[6] The IDA's resources come almost entirely from voluntary contributions made by donor governments. The funds contributed at any given time don't last very long, and so there is a need for additional contributions called "replenishments" every few years. To the extent of its limited resources

4 For more on the IMF role in dealing with the international debt crisis see ROBICHEK, E.W., "The International Monetary Fund: An Arbiter in the Debt Restructuring Process", *Columbia Journal of Transnational Law*, Vol. 23, No. 1, (1984), pp. 143–154.

5 Attention to the creditworthiness of potential borrowers is required by Article III, Section 4(v) of the IBRD Charter.

6 Another Bank affiliate, the International Finance Corporation (IFC) had been created in 1956. Unlike the IBRD and the IDA, the IFC purchases an equity interest in selected ventures in developing countries as a means of promoting development. Yet another new member of the World Bank Group is the Multilateral Investment Guarantee Agency (MIGA) which began operating in 1988. Each of these organizations operates very differently from multilateral development banks (MDBs) like the IBRD and the IDA, and this study will not directly deal with either of them.

the IDA makes development financing available to the most impoverished of the developing countries on very favorable terms.[7]

The Bank's role goes beyond providing development financing, since it has always provided borrowers with advice on development as well. There can be a fine line at times between giving advice on development and giving general advice on economic policy, and the Bank now shares with the IMF responsibility for inducing debtor countries to make much needed macroeconomic reforms.[8] Continuing problems with international debt have made the Bank more important that ever to the functioning of the international economic order.

B. DECISION-MAKING IN THE WORLD BANK

The Bank and the IDA are organized along the same lines. All powers are vested in a Board of Governors consisting of one governor and one alternate appointed by each member. The actual voting power of each member country is related to shareholding so that in the IBRD each country has 250 votes and one additional vote for each share of stock held.[9] The formula for voting in the IDA is somewhat different but follows the same principle of "weighting" the vote of each member state so that it corresponds to the financial contribution it makes to the organization.[10]

In practice, most of the powers of the Board of Governors

7 IDA development financing comes on very favorable terms. No interest rate as such applies although there is a nominal 0.75% "service charge". The terms of IDA credits are also distinguished from IBRD loans by especially long grace and repayment periods (typically 10 years before any payments are due, and from 35 to 50 years to repay).

8 Some resist the idea that the World Bank can impose conditionality on its borrowers as well as the IMF can. In September of 1988 the Bank agreed to make a large loan to Argentina in exchange for a "Letter of Development Policy" in which that country pledged to undertake major macroeconomic reforms. The IMF had been negotiating with Argentina for over six months concerning many of the same policies, and some IMF officials were skeptical that the Bank would be able to enforce the reforms. Such enforcement has traditionally been left to the IMF but Argentina preferred to deal with the Bank, probably because the reforms requested by the Bank were somewhat less stringent than those of the IMF. See, "World Bank Agrees to $1.25 Billion in Loans to Argentina", *The Washington Post*, Monday September 26, 1988, p. A12.

9 Articles of Agreement of the IBRD, Article V, section 3.

10 Articles of Agreement of the IDA, Article VI, section 3.

are delegated to the Board of Executive Directors (EDs). The relative economic strength of the various member countries is reflected in the composition and voting of the Executive Board in much the same way as in the Board of Governors. Each of the five members of the Bank having the largest number of shares of Bank stock is allowed to appoint an ED. The other EDs (presently 17) are elected by the Governors from those member states not appointing one of the above five EDs.[11]

The Executive Board functions in continuous session and makes most of the Bank's decisions. Within the Board each ED is entitled to cast in a block the total votes of the member country (or countries) who selected him. Those members who appoint their own EDs are thus in a position to exert a very direct influence within the Bank.[12] Given the fact that those five countries have over 40% of the total voting power in the Bank their influence is as strong as it is direct.[13]

The Bank's weighted voting formula has never been very popular with the developing countries since, in effect, it institutionalizes within the Bank the inequality between the economically strong countries and the economically weak ones. The desire of these latter countries for greater equality has led to the adoption by UNCTAD and the UN General Assembly of resolutions calling for the reform of the decision-making procedures in international economic and financial institutions.[14]

The weighted voting procedure may seem to conflict with notions of "sovereign equality"[15] but it has the virtue of being

11 See IBRD Articles, Art. V, Sec. 4. The number of EDs was originally set at 12 by the IBRD Articles of Agreement, but has been expanded to 20, and more recently to 22.

12 These members have a special position within the IDA as well as in the IBRD since the IBRD's EDs serve as the IDA's EDs.

13 The percentage of total voting power in the IBRD for each of the five is presently as follows: US: 18.22%, Japan: 9.27%, Federal Republic of Germany: 7.14%, UK: 6.18%, France: 3.92%. In February of 1988 the Bank's Board of Governors unanimously approved a general capital increase of US $75 Billion. The reluctance of the US Congress to contribute funds to that increase raised the theoretical possibility that the US share of the Bank's voting power could plummet to as little as 11% by 1993. See, COSTELLO, J.H., "Increase in World Bank Capital: A Test of US Leadership", *Christian Science Monitor*, Thursday October 13, 1988, at p. 11.

14 See, for example, Article 10 of the "Charter of Economic Rights and Duties of States", adopted by the UN General Assembly as Resolution 3281 (XXIX) on 12 December 1974.

15 Article 2 (1) of the UN Charter states that "The Organization is based on the principle of sovereign equality of all its Members."

a practical solution to a very real problem. The major contributors to the Bank and the IDA are naturally concerned about how the funds they contribute are used. They are also concerned about their potential liability should the Bank ever face losses due to defaulting borrowers. Weighted voting answers these concerns and thereby assures the participation of donor countries. This system does not actually violate the principle of sovereign equality but it does recognize the economic inequality between member states, something which in this context cannot realistically be ignored.

While weighted voting within the Bank is arguably both justifiable and unavoidable, that system is subject to abuse. It concentrates a great deal of power over the Bank's policies in the hands of the principal contributor countries, especially the US. The possibility exists that this power could be used for purposes unrelated to the Bank's goals, and should that occur it would constitute a politicization of the Bank. One important question to be answered is whether it might also be seen as a violation of any binding international legal norm.

C. THE OBJECT OF THIS STUDY

The unequal distribution of economic power among the nations of the world and the use of that economic power as a weapon in interstate relations are both facts of life in today's world. A number of existing studies have argued that a state's right to apply economic pressure in an attempt to coerce another state is limited under international law. One preliminary thesis of this book is that international law places even greater limits upon the use of World Bank voting power as an instrument of economic pressure to be used in the pursuit of unilateral political interests. These limits can be related to the issue of politicization as it occurs in the UN specialized agencies.

One central thesis of this study is that this politicization can be defined not only as a political phenomenon, but as a legal phenomenon as well. While a number of difficulties are involved in determining whether legally significant politicization has occurred, this study argues that in certain cases such a determination can indeed be made. More specifically, it concludes that to a limited but troubling extent, US national legislation concerning the World Bank has impermissibly compromised the international and independent character of that institution by politicizing it over issues unrelated to its stated purposes.

The politicization phenomenon is a serious threat to the effectiveness of the UN specialized agencies. Those political issues which impinge upon the activities of international organizations are often quite important, but they also tend to be difficult to resolve. If they cannot be to some extent insulated from political controversy, the specialized agencies may not be able to function at all. The danger is that if a trend towards politicization develops, and if every issue is discussed in every international forum, then it might even be possible for one particularly difficult political problem to preoccupy and paralyze all of the specialized agencies. In the light of this danger there is a need to explore both the legal and the policy aspects of the politicization problem. An examination of the situation in one specific context, that of the World Bank, may contribute to the development of a more general understanding of the issues involved.

It is hoped that this study will help to clarify the state of existing law governing the use of World Bank voting power for political purposes. Some policy makers in the US apparently believe that no rule of international law can limit a country's right to use its voting power in the World Bank as it may please. But a number of arguments can be advanced in support of the proposition that this power cannot be used to advance "political" objectives without violating the obligations of the United States under the Bank's Articles of Agreement.

The existence of conflicting views concerning the "permissible" uses of voting power in the Bank suggests that the existing law on the subject is unclear. What then can be done? A cautious attempt has been made to go beyond an analysis of existing law in order to determine whether there is a need for a change in, or development of, the law on the subject; and to identify principles, *de lege ferenda,* which could be applied to the question and which would be desirable from the point of view of international public policy.

The specific focus is upon certain legislation passed by the US Congress which may be inconsistent with the Bank's need to function as an independent international agency. This legislation is important since it purports to set the terms of US participation in the Bank, and the US is the single actor-country pre-eminent in the area of international financial aid to developing countries.[16]

This book explores an important but, as yet, unanswered question in the field of international law and organization, i.e., what is the legal significance of the politicization phenomenon in the UN specialized agencies? Can there be any legal grounds for opposing this politicization? The issue is of fundamental importance not only to the World Bank but to all of the specialized agencies. In spite of its importance the literature on the subject is quite thin.[17] This may be due to a certain reluctance on the part of the international officials most concerned to confront publicly the serious lack of consensus among governments on this issue. One scholar who has devoted considerable attention to analyzing the politicization of the UN specialized agencies is Victor-Yves Ghébali, but his work on the subject, while quite valuable, does not explore the legal issues involved.[18] This book explores new aspects of the politicization phenomenon both by seeking to evaluate the legal significance of the politicization phenomenon and by focusing specifically on the World Bank.

Although the existing literature on the related subject of economic coercion is extensive, very little has been written about the normative aspects of using World Bank voting power coercively for unilateral political purposes.[19] Sidney Weintraub has edited a very thoughtful book on economic coercion and US foreign policy, but he limits the scope of his study with the statement that:

16 See WILKINS, J. R., "Legal Norms and International Economic Development: The Case of the Cuba Shipping Restriction in the US Foreign Assistance Act", *California Law Review*, Vol. 55, No. 4, (1967) at page 980. Wilkins suggests that the US as the "pre-eminent" donor country may be in a position to determine by its practices the future development of international aid doctrines just as in earlier centuries the "pre-eminence" of the British navy allowed Great Britain to exercise a decisive influence on the development of the traditional law of the sea.

17 Very brief but useful legal discussions of the politicization issue appear in KAY, D., *The Functioning and Effectiveness of Selected United Nations System Programs*, American Society of International Law, (1980), (Studies in Transnational Legal Policy; no. 18), at p. 7, and in ORSONI, G. "Le retrait des Etats Unis et la crise de le B.I.T.", *Révue Générale de Droit International Public*, Vol. 83, No. 3, (1979), pp. 689–746.

18 See GHEBALI, V., "The Politicisation of UN Specialized Agencies: A Preliminary Analysis", *Millennium*, Vol. 14, No. 3, (1985), pp. 317–334.

19 One rather thought-provoking article has been found which directly raises the issue, see YOKOTA, Y., "Nonpolitical Character of the World Bank," *Japanese Annual of International Law*, No. 20, pages 39–64 (1976).

> "Aid on a true multilateral basis is provided by donor governments through international institutions like the World Bank, the regional development banks, and the United Nations Development Program. Since this [Weintraub's] study is concerned with *unilateral economic coercion*, the examination of aid as an instrument will not consider multilateral aid."[20]

While this is a perfectly appropriate way for him to limit his study, the language quoted seems to be based on the false assumption that unilateral economic coercion (initiated by one sender state acting alone) cannot be exercised through institutions such as the multilateral development banks (MDBs). The case studies examined in Chapter VI demonstrate that the large financial contribution which the United States makes to the MDBs and the weighted voting systems upon which they are based, have at times permitted the US to exert unilateral economic pressure through the use of its power within them. The US government has used this capability in the past to block multilateral loans to countries which it has targeted for political reasons, and at present there is US legislation in effect which requires the US to make further political use of this power within the Bank.[21] While focusing on that legislation and its compatibility with the values, principles and rules of the modern international system, this study builds upon the literature on international law and institutions and relates it to the literature on economic coercion.[22]

The politicization of the specialized agencies raises a number of issues of public international law and of international politics

20 WEINTRAUB, S. (ed.) *Economic Coercion and US Foreign Policy: Implications of Case Studies from the Johnson Administration*, Boulder, Colorado, Westview Press, 1982, at p. 12 (emphasis and bracketed clarification added).

21 See Chapter VII, *infra*, and Annex B to this study for details on this legislation.

22 A number of studies and articles have been published concerning this US legislation, but none found so far examine the compatibility of that legislation with international legal principles. Usually, the focus has been upon the effectiveness of that legislation in promoting its objectives or upon the desirability, from the point of view of US foreign policy of "politicizing" the Bank. See for example US Policy and the Multilateral Banks: Politicization and Effectiveness; Staff Report to the Subcommittee on Foreign Assistance of the Committee on Foreign Relations, US Senate, Washington, US Government Printing Office, (1977), 33 p; and SCHOULTZ, L., "Politics, Economics and US Participation in Multilateral Development Banks", *International Organization*, Vol. 36, No. 3, (1982), pp 537–574.

and this book does not attempt to resolve or even to discuss them all. The next chapter after this introduction consists of a discussion of many such general issues, but for the most part only the more specific topic of politicization of the World Bank will be addressed.

While this work focuses on the World Bank, it is not a critique of that institution nor of its policies. The focus is upon the decision-making criteria which are part of the agreed terms of cooperation within the Bank; and in particular upon certain policies of the US as a member acting within the Bank. Accordingly, the issue of whether international financial institutions such as the Bank should comply with United Nations General Assembly resolutions calling for the cessation of loans to certain countries (such as South Africa) is not of primary importance, although the possible relevance of such resolutions to a World Bank member government's voting decision will be briefly considered in Chapter VI.[23]

Chapter II is devoted to the concept of politicization. The uses of the term "politicization" are examined as are the causes of the phenomenon. An effort is also made to distinguish between the use of the term as part of political polemic and the more precise definition which must be given in legal terms. Chapter III introduces various elements of economic coercion analysis as applied to international relations beginning with the actors, the objectives, the methods and the conditions under which such coercion may be possible. It then explores the coercive potential of international financial aid, and the advantages for the recipient of multilateral aid over bilateral aid.

The principle of non-intervention and other international legal rules applicable to international economic coercion outside the context of multilateral aid organizations are the subject of Chapter IV. After concluding that there is a lack of agreement concerning standards in this area, this Chapter then goes on to propose a standard. It also considers whether the coercive use of bilateral aid and aid cutoffs can properly be classified as illegal intervention.

Starting with Chapter V this book turns to the specific legal issues raised by politicized voting within the World Bank. After an initial discussion of the constitutional nature of treaties such

23 On this topic see BLEICHER, S. A., "UN vs IBRD: A Dilemma of Functionalism", *International Organization*, Vol. 24, No. 1 (1970), pp. 31–47.

as the Bank's Charter, Chapter V addresses the question of whether international law could logically be expected to place limits upon the use by member states of their voting power in the Bank. Next there is an examination of the internal legal regime which exists under the Bank's Charter, and an analysis of the significance of Article IV, Section 10 of that Charter which is known as the "political activity prohibition". The possible contributions of general principles of law and of customary law to the institutional law of the Bank are also discussed in this chapter.

In Chapter VI a number of case studies on politics and World Bank decision-making are reviewed. A view emerges of the past practices of the Bank's members, its organs and its staff in interpreting the Bank's political activity prohibition. Over the years there have been efforts to block World Bank loans to one country or another for a variety of political reasons, but the Bank as an institution has consistently resisted inappropriate political pressures, although with varying degrees of success.

Chapter VII and the associated tables (Annexes B and C) are intended to provide a systematic view of the many legislative enactments of the US government which present some risk of politicizing the Bank's decision-making. After setting out a typology of relevant US legislation, that chapter examines the legislative evidence before concluding that at times this legislation has indeed resulted in the illegal use of US voting power in the Bank.

The more general conclusions of this study are presented in Chapter VIII. After some additional comments on the nature of the politicization phenomenon this chapter formulates the rather "minimal" legal standard applicable to politicized voting which can definitely be said to command consensus support among the World Bank's members. It then catalogs some of the obstacles which have so far prevented the development of more effective legal standards and of mechanisms capable of limiting the politicization of that organization. The issue of how seriously politicized the Bank has become is then discussed. After a number of observations concerning international cooperation and the international legal system the chapter ends with a discussion of US foreign policy interests within the Bank.

2

THE POLITICIZATION PHENOMENON

A . POLITICIZATION AS A GENERAL TERM USED OUTSIDE THE CONTEXT OF INTERNATIONAL ORGANIZATIONS AS WELL AS WITHIN THAT CONTEXT

Although this study will be primarily concerned with politicization as it applies to the activities of international organizations, politicization can occur outside of that context as well. The term is most often associated with changes in the processes for dealing with certain national or international economic or technical issues. Politicization is often said to be increasing, which is meant to suggest that relatively high level political decision-makers are becoming more directly involved in dealing with economic matters which " . . . were once dealt with at a technical level or left entirely to the outcome of market forces".[1]

It would be rather simplistic to assume that politicization merely represents the sudden and inexplicable intrusion of politicians into matters best left to technocrats or market forces. Political factors are often responsible for determining the structure of relations within which economic and other supposedly "non-political" activities take place.[2] This is the case when at sometime in the past a political decision has been made and implemented which has the effect of authoritatively redefining

1 HIRSCH, F., DOYLE, M. and MORSE, E.L., *Alternatives to Monetary Disorder*, 1980's Project/Council on Foreign Relations, New York, McGraw-Hill, 1977, at p. 11. See also pages 11–24 where the authors discuss various different concepts of politicization.

2 See, KEOHANE, R.O. and NYE, J.S., "World Politics and the International Economic System", a chapter in BERGSTEN, C.F., *The Future of the International Economic Order: An Agenda for Research*, Lexington, Massachusetts, Lexington Books, 1973, at p. 116.

a particular issue as technical and therefore somehow above political disputes. While an exhaustive general study of the politicization phenomenon is not possible within the scope of this thesis, some of the principal concepts involved will be discussed below as this chapter explores that phenomenon in the particular context of the UN specialized agencies.

B. THE POLITICIZATION PHENOMENON IN THE UN SPECIALIZED AGENCIES

Throughout this study the term "politicization" will be applied to certain actions[3] of states (or their representatives) within a certain type of intergovernmental organization (IGO).[4] The IGO must be one whose purposes can be characterized as primarily technical or "non-political",[5] while the actions in question must be taken for purposes referred to as "political" because they are considered by some to be unrelated or inadequately related to the purposes and functions of that IGO.

The concept of politicization becomes most clear when it is related to the theory of "functionalism". Functionalism is a theory of international organization which holds that a world community can best be achieved not by attempts at the immediate political union of states, but by the creation of non-political international agencies dealing with specific economic, social,

3 Politicization might also be said to occur in situations where a decision-maker is *inhibited from acting* due to political concerns which, in theory, are not relevant to the technical task at hand. See, LECKIE, S., "The Inter-State Complaint Procedure in International Human Rights Law: Hopeful Prospects or Wishful Thinking?", *Human Rights Quarterly*, Vol. 10, No. 2, 1988, at p. 297.

4 It may also be appropriate to speak of some international *non*governmental organizations becoming politicized. Statements and actions by national Olympic committees would certainly appear to have politicized the International Olympic Committee at various times in the past, especially when boycotts of the Olympic Games have occurred. To the extent that the national Olympic committees function as "representatives" of national governments it will be possible for those governments to politicize the IOC.

5 IGOs dealing with specific economic, social, technical or humanitarian functions are sometimes said to exist for non-political purposes, although it is clear that there can be a political side to all these functions. In any case, the term "politicization" as used in this study cannot be applied in any meaningful way to an organization such as the United Nations whose primary function is political, i.e. the maintenance of international peace and security.

technical, or humanitarian functions.[6] Functionalists assume that economic, social and technical problems can be separated from political problems and insulated from political pressures. Because of the greater difficulties involved in resolving political problems the theory maintains that non-political forms of international cooperation should be given priority, and that only later, after states have developed habits of effective international cooperation concerning such matters, will it be possible to apply the new cooperative skills and habits to high-level political problems.[7] This theory was well known in the years prior to the formation of most of the UN specialized agencies, and Eckart Klein has gone so far as to say that "[t]he conceptual basis of the specialized agencies is functionalism."[8]

While it is indeed arguable that functionalism as a strategy for international cooperation is the conceptual basis of the specialized agencies, it is clear that the theory is neither a rule nor even a principle of international law. The significance of functionalist theory is further called into question by the fact that there are many doubts about the basic assumptions behind the theory.[9] The assumption that economic, social and technical matters can be effectively separated from politics is particularly dubious. With regard to this assumption Inis L. Claude Jr. has asked rhetorically, "Does not this assumption fly in the face of the evidence that a trend toward politicization of all issues is operative in the twentieth century?"[10] In spite of these problems the theory of functionalism helps to explain why certain IGO's are referred to as "non-political", and it also clarifies the link between the defined purposes of an IGO and the notion of politicization.

6 See MITRANY, D., *A Working Peace System*, 4th edition, London, National Peace Council (1946), for the most classic exposition of the theory of functionalism.

7 Inis L. Claude Jr. calls this the "separability-priority" thesis, CLAUDE, I.L. Jr., *Swords Into Plowshares: The Problems and Process of International Organization*, 4th edition, New York, Random House, (1971), at p. 384.

8 KLEIN, E., "United Nations Specialized Agencies", in *Encyclopedia of Public International Law*, Vol. 5, Max Planck Institute, Amsterdam, Elsevier Science Publishers B.V., (1983), at p. 366.

9 See CLAUDE, *op. cit.*, at pp. 385–391.

10 *Ibid.* at p. 388.

1. The Inevitability of Politicization

The point has often been made, and it is both a legitimate and an important observation, that politicization of the specialized agencies is inevitable. Each of these agencies is essentially an institutional framework through which different national governments interact. In theory that interaction should be cooperative, and the purpose and scope of the cooperation involved should be defined in the agency's constitutive instrument. But even though every specialized agency's constitution or charter contains a statement of the organization's purposes, these statements are often vague and subject to varying interpretations. This can make it difficult to determine whether or not a certain type of activity falls within the "agreed" purposes of a given agency. Disagreements between member governments concerning the purposes of these agencies are thus inevitable. This is especially true when one considers the different perspectives which result from the political, economic and cultural diversity among the member governments. The North-South and East-West divisions in international society are well known, and each can contribute to the problem

Furthermore, national governments may disagree and come into conflict within a specialized agency not only about the scope of that agency's mandate, but also about matters which are obviously outside the scope of that mandate. Realistically speaking, there is little that can be done to muzzle a government with a political ax to grind when it is determined to exploit every opportunity to air its grievances on an issue. The fact that those grievances are unrelated to the business of a specialized agency will not always deter a state from raising them in that forum. Gilbert Orsoni, after reviewing the history of the politicization phenomenon within the ILO, has concluded that it has been a more or less permanent feature of that organization since it first hosted political confrontations between fascist and non-fascist member states in 1923. He has ventured his opinion that no ILO member state is completely innocent of contributing to this state of affairs.[11]

Yet even though politicization is to some extent inevitable, it can represent a very real threat to the specialized agencies.

11 ORSONI, G., "Le retrait des Etats-Unis et la crise de l'OIT", *Révue Générale de Droit International Public*, Vol. 83, No. 3, (1979), at pp.725–731.

From a practical point of view politicization can be a threat to the often delicate political consensus which is the basis for both the creation of an IGO and its continued ability to function. The very creation of an IGO requires a political decision by the various participating governments. Those governments must decide whether to participate, and they must also decide what financial and other resources, if any, they are willing to contribute to the organization. Only a political consensus or shared agreement of some kind among future member states can permit such an organization to be successfully instituted. That political consensus finds its legal expression in the constitutive instrument of the organization created, and an essential part of it is the agreement, however vague, concerning the purposes of the agency

How then does the politicization of a specialized agency threaten to destroy that political consensus? By injecting extraneous political considerations into the deliberations and activities of an agency, politicization can alter the costs and benefits of participation for member states and shift the parameters or underlying assumptions of cooperation.

2. Categories of Politicization

The link between the agreed purposes of an IGO and the notion of politicization is of critical importance. The common thread detectable in various definitions of the term seems to be that politicization implies some politically motivated actions tending either to go beyond or to contradict the agreed object and purpose of the agency involved. David Kay identifies three patterns of politicization which provide a good example of this.[12]

12 Kay says the following about the term "politicization", (KAY, D., *The Functioning and Effectiveness of Selected United Nations System Programs*, American Society of International Law, (1980), (Studies in Transnational Legal Policy; no. 18), at p. 7.):

"When this term is used carefully, which is often not the case, it denotes three closely related behavior patterns: first, considering and acting on matters that lie essentially outside the specific functional domain of a given specialized agency or program; secondly, the reaching of decisions on matters within an agency's or program's functional competence through a process that is essentially political and does not reflect technical and scientific factors in the decision process; and thirdly, the taking of specific actions on issues within an agency's or program's competence for the sole purpose of expressing a partisan political position rather than attempting to reach an objective determination of the issues."

The first pattern is essentially a matter of an IGO (or one or more of its organs) which reviews and/or acts on matters not associated with the functional mandate of that agency. The second concerns decisions by an agency which are taken according to a procedure which may be considered flawed because it reflects "political" factors rather than the "technical" or "scientific" factors which are related to the purposes of the agency and are often considered to be its only appropriate concern. The third pattern of politicization which Kay has described may overlap substantially with the second, but it seems to involve the use of an agency's technical decision-making process in order to make political statements.

Kay's three patterns of politicization, like those of at least one other scholar who has written on the subject,[13] appear to be derived from an analysis of the reasons cited by the US government in 1975 as the motivation for its withdrawal from the ILO. The US notice of intent to withdraw from that organization, signed by Henry Kissinger, refers to "four matters of fundamental concern" considered to be problems by the US government. As three of these four items involve politicization of a sort it will be worthwhile to examine each of them individually here.

One of the matters referred to is the "increasing politicization of the organization". The following is the description of this problem contained in the US notice of withdrawal

> "In recent years the ILO has become increasingly and *excessively involved in political issues which are quite beyond the competence and mandate of the organization*. The ILO does have a legitimate and necessary interest in certain issues with political ramifications. It has major responsibility, for example, for international action to promote and protect fundamental human rights, particularly in respect of freedom of association, trade union rights and the abolition of forced labour. But international politics is not the main business of the ILO. Questions of relations between states and proclamations of economic principles should be left to the United Nations and other international agencies where their consideration is more relevant to those organization's responsibilities. Irrelevant political issues divert

13 Williams, D., *The Specialized Agencies and the United Nations: The System in Crisis*, New York, St. Martins Press, (1987), pp. 55–56.

> the attention of the ILO from improving the conditions of workers – that is, from questions on which the tripartite structure of the ILO gives the organization a unique advantage over the other, purely governmental, organizations of the United Nations family."[14] (emphasis added)

The concern here is with the first pattern of behavior described by Kay above, and specifically with the fact that the attention of the ILO was being diverted by "irrelevant political issues", that is to say issues considered by the US government to be irrelevant or inadequately related to the specific functional domain of the ILO.

It has already been noted that Kay's second and third patterns of politicization appear to overlap a great deal. Both seem to entail action or decisions by an agency on matters within its competence or mandate, but according to a process which is politically rather than "technically" or "objectively" determined. One clear distinction between them is that Kay's second category involves "the reaching of decisions" (plural) and thus describes a general pattern of behavior, while his third concerns "the taking of specific actions on issues . . . for the sole purpose of expressing a partisan political position."

Whether one considers the distinction to be a useful one or not, it is fairly evident that the same distinction was made by Henry Kissinger in the US notice of intent to withdraw from the ILO. Complaining of "Selective concern for human rights" as another of the fundamental matters of concern to the US government that letter describes the problem as follows:

> "The ILO Conference for some years now has shown an appallingly selective concern in the application of the ILO's basic conventions on Freedom of Association and Forced Labour. It pursues the violation of human rights in some member states. It grants immunity from such citations to others. This seriously undermines the credibility of the ILO's support of Freedom of Association, which is central to its tripartite structure, and strengthens

14 Letter dated 5 November, 1975 from Henry Kissinger, Secretary of State of the United States of America, to Francis Blanchard, Director General of the ILO, containing notice of intent to withdraw from the ILO, in *International Legal Materials*, Vol. XIV, No. 6, November 1975, at pp. 1582–1584.

> the proposition that these human rights are not universally applicable, but rather are subject to different interpretations for States with different political systems."[15]

This selective concern for human rights is a general pattern of behavior which the US apparently found objectionable in a number of decisions by the ILO Conference. In this way it corresponds to Kay's second category of politicization.

Kissinger's complaint about the alleged "Disregard of due process" by the ILO conference in adopting resolutions corresponds to Kay's third pattern of politicization. Note the language used:

> "The ILO once had an enviable record of objectivity and concern for due process in its examination of alleged violations of basic human rights by its member states. The constitution of the ILO provides for procedures to handle representations and complaints that a member State is not observing a convention that it has ratified. Further, it was the ILO which first established fact-finding and conciliation machinery to respond to allegations of violations of trade union rights. In recent years, however, sessions of the ILO conference increasingly have adopted resolutions *condemning particular member states* which happen to be the political target of the moment, in utter disregard of the established procedures and machinery. This trend is accelerating, and it is gravely damaging the ILO and its capacity to pursue its objectives in the human rights field."[16] (emphasis added)

The reference here to "resolutions condemning particular member States which happen to be the political target of the moment" is more specific than the prior complaint about selective concern for human rights, just as Kay's third pattern of politicization is more specific than is his second. The distinctions between Kay's three patterns of politicization can thus be clarified by reference to the US notice of withdrawal from the ILO.

Victor-Yves Ghebali has linked politicization with six different types of organizational dysfunction which exist within the UN specialized agencies. The first of these he refers to as "extran-

15 *Ibid.*
16 *Ibid.*

eity", i.e. "the systematic insertion of extraneous issues into agendas, debates and work programmes . . . exemplified by the intrusion of the Middle East question into the debates of virtually all the agencies since 1973."[17] The second is concerned with "the erosion of liberal principles embodied in the charters of the various Specialized Agencies", (especially the international financial institutions) in favor of a "statist approach", and the third is referred to as "hyper-confrontation".[18]

The other three types of organizational dysfunction *cum* politicization which Ghebali identifies include what he calls "nomomania", or "the abusive practice of forcing through resolutions of normative content", the "condemnation and excommunication" of member states, and last but not least, "administrative mismanagement and budgetary excess".[19].

These six categories do much to illustrate the problems associated with the politicization phenomenon, but Ghebali's classifications, even more than those of Kay discussed above, substantially overlap with one another. A simpler classification can be reached, it is submitted, by distinguishing between two basic types of politicization using more or less the same criteria mentioned above. One type, essentially identical to what Ghebali refers to as "extraneity",[20] involves an attempt to cause the resources of an international agency (its time, its financial resources, perhaps even its publicity) to be diverted to broad purposes beyond the competence and mandate of the organization. This can be referred to as "positive politicization". Kay's first pattern of politicization and Henry Kissinger's complaint quoted above about the increasing politicization of the ILO would both fall under this rubric. UNESCO's efforts to promote a New World Information Order may also be considered to be an example of this type of politicization. Whether it is seen as such depends primarily upon one's interpretation of what UNESCO's mandate is. We shall see below in Chapters V and VI that reference to an IGO's constitutive instrument does not always dispel doubts about the breadth of its mandate.

17 GHEBALI, V., "The Politicisation of UN Specialized Agencies: A Preliminary Analysis", *Millennium: Journal of International Studies*, Vol. 14, No. 3, (1985), at p. 322.
18 *op. cit.*, at p. 323.
19 *op. cit.*, pp. 323-324.
20 Many of the other "dysfunctions" mentioned by Ghebali might also accompany the positive politicization of a specialized agency.

Another type of politicization, which can be referred to as "negative politicization", occurs when an international specialized agency makes decisions (which may well be within its competence) but makes them according to "politicized" criteria which are unrelated to, or at least not adequately related to, the technical mission of the agency involved. It is negative because it is normally directed against a certain member state, or a group of member states, which have been targeted for political reasons. The result of negative politicization, when it is effective, can be to deprive a member state (the target) of some or all of the benefits of membership in an IGO.[21]

3. Politicization as a Political Phenomenon

Implicit in the very term "politicization" is the suggestion that the phenomenon described is a political one. In fact, it is possible to analyze and attempt to understand politicization both as a political phenomenon and as a legal phenomenon. Some observers, rejecting a legal approach to the question, have noted that it seems to be nothing more than the existence of controversy within an organization which leads to charges by some of the antagonists that the organization has become politicized.[22] It is undeniable that politicization seems to be something that states are quite willing to accuse each other of doing but that they never seem to admit to doing themselves. While states have been known to trade legal as well as political accusations,

21 As we have seen above, the increasing politicization of the ILO was only one of four matters of concern referred to by the US in its notice of withdrawal from that agency. Two of the other problems mentioned were "selective concern for human rights" by the ILO Conference and "disregard of due process" by the organization in its examination of alleged violations of basic human rights by member states. In a sense, both of these involve action directed against a state or states presumably targeted for political reasons, and thus both can be classified as forms of negative politicization. See ILO withdrawal notice, *op. cit.*

22 See LYONS, G. M., BALDWIN, D. A. and MCNEMAR, D. W., "The Politicization Issue in the UN Specialized Agencies", in KAY, D.A. (ed.), *The Changing United Nations, Options for the United States*, New York, Praeger, 1977, at pp. 85–86.

In a discussion of politicization which is not limited to the phenomenon as it occurs within international agencies, Keohane and Nye take a similar view stating that "In the terminology that we will use . . . the system becomes 'politicized' as controversiality increases and depoliticized as it decreases." KEOHANE, R. O. and NYE, J. S., "World Politics and the International Economic System",op. cit. at p. 117.

the use of the term suggests that its primary usage may indeed be political and not legal, and that the actual meaning of the term is unclear.[23]

We shall see below that the legal or "functionalist" approach to the issue is based on the assumption that political and economic or technical relations are fundamentally and rightly separable.[24] This is a view which reflects the Western liberal economic philosophy, and which has to some extent been incorporated into the Charters of many of the specialized agencies including, as we will see, the World Bank. But another approach, which to some extent reflects Marxist thought, assumes that political and economic relations are inextricably linked. This approach has a very real appeal for many in the developing countries who feel that their economic weakness leaves them in a situation of political subordination to the economically stronger industrialized countries. To them politicization "means an open challenging of political relationships previously only implicit in economic activities",[25] and might best be understood as a part of the global bargaining process between rich and poor states.

By asserting their numerical superiority in the specialized agencies the developing countries can draw attention to their problems and grievances.[26] When the grievances in question do not directly concern the business of the agency involved politicization of the agency made be said to occur.

While from a functionalist point of view this type of politicization may be condemned as an evil, it can at least be said that it often has little immediate legal effect. The political decisions of the specialized agencies often take the form of resolutions which do not give rise to legal obligations for the member

23 LYONS, BALDWIN and MCNEMAR put it this way, "The term 'politicization', like 'exploitation', and 'imperialism', is so loaded with pejorative connotations that serious questions arise about its analytic utility", *op. cit.* at pp. 84–85.

24 Cf. also the discussion of functionalism, *supra*.

25 See, HIRSCH, F., DOYLE, M. W. and MORSE, E. L., *Alternatives To Monetary Disorder*, 1980's Project/Council on Foreign Relations, New York, McGraw-Hill, 1977, at p. 16.

26 "Politicisation has always existed, but what is new today is that it operates systematically in favor of the new, non-Western majority of nation-states", GHEBALI, *op. cit.*, at p. 322.

states.[27] The advantage to the developing states as the "politicizers" in such situations is that they are able to state their case in an international forum, and it is in this sense that they may be seen as participating in a negotiating process. The industrialized Western states, who were instrumental in forming the specialized agencies, may reasonably object that the issues involved are being raised in an inappropriate forum. The developing states may feel that they can ill afford to pass up any opportunity to communicate their grievances given their general inability to remedy them.

To the extent that politicization can be seen as part of a global negotiating process between rich and poor states it is both a political phenomenon and, for the time being, an inevitable development. If a broad consensus could be achieved on international economic and political issues across the board, (admittedly a highly unlikely development), then there would be little need for any state or group of states to politicize international agencies in protest over an inability to obtain satisfaction. Thus politicization is linked to the lack of consensus, and is as inevitable within the international agencies as is controversy itself. The politicization phenomenon in the UN specialized agencies is indicative of the present state of development, or underdevelopment, of the international community. There must, as we have seen, be a certain degree of consensus within that community before IGOs (or at least quasi-universal IGOs) can be formed at all; simply because the very existence of these organizations depends upon the concurrence of the member states. On the other hand the differing viewpoints, and more fundamentally, the differing interests of the member states ensure that that consensus can only be a limited one. Viewed as a political phenomenon, the politicization of an IGO is characterized essentially by the controversy which results from the conflicts of interest both within that institutional framework and outside of it.

27 See, OSIEKE, O., "The Legality of Ultra Vires Decisions of International Organizations", *American Journal of International Law*, Vol. 77, No. 2, (1983), at p. 252.

4. Politicization as a Legal Phenomenon

Politicization as a legal phenomenon must be somewhat more carefully defined since (as used in this study) it implies not merely some vaguely and perhaps subjectively defined impropriety, but actual illegality. This raises the question of by what objective and definable criteria one might hope to identify the threshold between politicization as politically and as legally defined. By definition, this latter type of politicization must have legal as well as political implications, i.e. it must affect the rights or the duties of states under international law, and not just their interests as politically defined. More specifically, it should affect the rights and/or duties of states as members of the international organization involved. Membership in an IGO can confer upon member states both rights and duties under international law. The legal significance of politicization results from the effect which it can have upon the balance of such *rights* and *duties* applicable to individual member states.

The legal significance of politicization is most apparent when it substantially and detrimentally affects the legal *rights* of a state as a member of an international organization. Only in the case of effective negative politicization is this likely to occur. If the negative politicization of an agency is ineffective, this means that in spite of that politicization no decision adverse to the target's rights was ultimately taken by the organization. This is a very common result of negative politicization (especially within the World Bank context as we shall see). For political reasons the United States voted against 26 consecutive IDA loans to India between 1974 and 1976, yet every one of those loans was nonetheless approved because other member countries supported them and resisted the politicization of the Bank by the US.[28] Thus the effect of the negative votes was purely

28 These negative votes were cast pursuant to US legislation requiring that within the IDA the US was to oppose financing for any country which developed a nuclear explosive device unless that country was a party to the nuclear non-proliferation treaty. See The Long Amendment to the IDA Fourth Replenishment Act, Public Law (hereinafter "PL" 93-373, Section 3; approved August 14, 1974 adding Section 15 to the International Development Association Act. It was repealed by the International Financial Institutions Act, PL 95-118, Section 702, approved October 3, 1977. (The amendment appeared as 22 USC Sec. 284m.) A more detailed discussion of that legislation appears in Chapter VII, *infra*.

symbolic. Those votes constituted a public condemnation of Indian nuclear arms policy by the US, but without the support of other members they could not actually affect the rights of India within the IDA.

Even if a "politicized" decision directed against a target state is approved by the membership of an IGO the effect may be largely if not entirely symbolic. As Ebere Osieke has noted:

> " . . . many of the political decisions adopted by the plenary organs of the international organizations, particularly on such questions as the apartheid policy of the government of South Africa, are symbolic in character and are, in most cases, self-executing. Their primary objective is normally to condemn the member state concerned, and that objective is fulfilled once a resolution is passed and published . . .
>
> Again, the political decisions of many international organizations, which are adopted in the form of resolutions, do not normally give rise to binding legal obligations for the member states. The resolutions often ask the members not to collaborate with the policies of the condemned government or to give it assistance in the implementation of its policies. Thus, any member that strongly opposes adoption of a non-binding resolution is not under a legal obligation to implement its provisions – a factor that reduces the legal significance of political decisions within international organizations."[29]

Of course any state is sure to resent being the target of negative politicization even if the actual legal effect upon its rights seems to be minimal or even nil. The target may take little comfort from the knowledge that the manner in which it has been condemned is merely symbolic, regardless of whether that condemnation comes in the form of a unilateral statement by one member of an IGO or a resolution endorsed by the plenary organ.

Even a condemnation or other decision by an IGO which detrimentally affects the rights of a member state may be legally justified where the target state is condemned for activities

29 OSIEKE, E., "The Legal Validity of Ultra Vires Decisions of International Organizations", *op. cit.*, at p. 252.

within the purview of the specialized agency concerned. When for political reasons that agency acts selectively against certain members and not others this does raise problems of fairness, and charges of politicization are sure to follow, but this alone cannot invalidate an otherwise valid decision.[30]

Legally significant politicization also occurs whenever a state, acting within the context of an IGO, takes politicizing actions which are in conflict with the constitutive treaty of that organization and which materially violate its *obligations* as a member. In many cases such a material violation is likely to have a direct effect upon the rights of other members, but a material breach is legally significant even where there is no such immediate effect.[31]

It is difficult to say at what point the positive politicization of an IGO could become a legal rather than merely a political phenomenon. When, according to the standard suggested above, are the legal rights of member states "substantially and detrimentally affected" by positive politicization? And when could this form of politicization constitute a material violation of an IGO's constitutive treaty? Positive politicization by definition refers to an attempt to cause the resources of an IGO to be diverted to or used for purposes beyond the competence and mandate of the organization. But who determines what does and what does not fall within that mandate?

It would be convenient to conclude that this is a matter which can be determined solely according to legal principles based on an objective interpretation of the constitutive instrument of the IGO involved. Unfortunately, such a conclusion does not appear to be justified since the charter of an IGO can be very

30 Thus the unfavorable treatment which the government of South Africa receives in many specialized agencies can be justified by the detrimental effects of *apartheid* upon the technical matters dealt with by those agencies. The fact that some other member states with serious human rights problems are not subjected to the same unfavorable treatment does not invalidate the anti-apartheid policies of these agencies.

31 According to the definition found in Article 60(3)(b) of the Vienna Convention on the Law of Treaties, material breach of a treaty can consist in either the unsanctioned repudiation of the treaty or "the violation of a provision essential to the accomplishment of the object and purpose of the treaty." Article 60(2) of that convention also provides that the material breach of a multilateral treaty can in certain circumstances be invoked to justify the suspension of such a treaty.

vague about the scope of its intended mandate. States can and do disagree about how broadly or narrowly the purposes of a given IGO should be interpreted, and when this occurs the dispute is likely to be resolved politically if at all. Of course, if the various member states agree that broader action by an agency is desirable then the issue will not be controversial and no charges of politicization will be raised. All of this suggests that it would be difficult if not impossible to formulate a workable definition of positive politicization as a legal phenomenon.[32]

This is not to say, however, that there is no possible loss to member states from the positive politicization of an international agency. The political interests of a state may be disserved by the (from its point of view) unwelcome expansion of an IGO's field of activities. The US, for example, considered that UNESCO's efforts to promote a New World Information and Communication Order were contrary to the national interest of the US.[33] But international law is concerned with protecting the rights of states and does not necessarily protect their political interests

32 See CLAUDE, I.L. Jr., *The Changing United Nations*, New York, Random House, 1967, at p. xvii, where he asserts that the UN can have no purposes of its own. He goes on to state that " . . . the political process within the organization . . . is, in essence, a continuous struggle between the advocates of conflicting purposes or between those whose conception of the proper order of priorities are different, a struggle to determine which purposes and whose purposes the United Nations will serve. This is what politics is about, and this is the fate of political institutions."

Although Claude expresses this view only with regard to the UN and "political institutions", his point that the purposes of an international organization are determined by the attitudes of its members could be applied to the specialized agencies as well. According to this logic, positive politicization would only be a state of mind, and could not be objectively defined at all.

33 See "Perspectives on the U.S. Withdrawal from UNESCO", an address at Stanford University on October 31, 1984 published in *Department of State Bulletin*, No. 2094, January 1985, at pp.54–55, where Gregory D. Newell, the former Assistant Secretary of State for International Organization Affairs of the US, explaining the motives behind the US withdrawal from that agency stated that:

"UNESCO programs and personnel are heavily freighted with an irresponsible political content and answer to an agenda that is consistently inimical to U.S. interests . . .

"Voluble UNESCO participants are persistently hostile to U.S. political views, values, and interests. Our participation, then, in UNESCO 'consensus' can, on occasion, amount to complicity in vilification of the United States – which is part of everyday life there."

The interests of a member state which does not support the positive politicization of an international agency may be affected in a more tangible manner as well if the agency's funds, a portion of which are normally contributed by each member, are diverted to activities which are seen as going beyond the agreed purposes of the organization. Thus positive politicization may affect the pecuniary interest of member states to the extent that they are required to pay the costs of the activities or programs involved. Disputes between member states about the proper purposes of an IGO can therefore be directly linked with disputes about the budget of the organization.[34]

If positive politicization is fundamentally a political rather than a legal phenomenon, the remedy for this type of problem, from the point of view of a concerned state which objects to the politicization, is likely to be political as well. One political remedy is that course of action pursued by the US to protest what it perceived as the politicization of the ILO in 1975 and of UNESCO more recently. No state can be legally obliged to remain a member of an IGO and this in theory means that they all retain the option of withdrawing. By withdrawing and "voting with their feet"[35] member states can make a very strong and clear statement of their disagreement with what they see as a trend towards politicization in an agency of which they have been a member.

In practice, withdrawal will be a more attractive option for some states than for others. If, for example, a developing country wanted to withdraw from the World Bank to protest the politicization of that agency, it might have a lot to lose by doing so. As a non-member it would no longer be eligible to borrow from the Bank. An industrialized country, which may

34 The case of the recent US withdrawal from UNESCO again provides a convenient example of a situation where one member state, the US, was unhappy both with the scope the organization's activities, which it considered to be excessively broad and with the expansion of the organization's budget. See *loc. cit.*

35 Leo Gross suggests that states serious about preserving the rule of law in international organizations "will have to vote, regretfully perhaps, more often 'with their feet,' as the saying goes, and with the purse, and not merely with the voice and hands." GROSS, L., "On the Degradation of the Constitutional Environment of the United Nations", *American Journal of International Law*, Vol. 77, No. 3, (1983), at p. 583.

make a substantial financial contribution to an IGO without feeling an urgent need for its programs, has less to lose.[36]

36 In 1950 Poland, originally a member of the Bank, withdrew because it became clear that the Bank, which was largely under the influence of the US, was not going to approve any loans to that state as long as it was on the other side of the East-West ideological divide. Czechoslovakia's membership in the Bank followed a similarly troubled course, and was formally terminated in 1954 after a dispute about the unpaid portion of its capital subscription. See MASON, E. S. and ASHER, R. E., *The World Bank Since Bretton Woods*, Washington, Brookings Institution (1973), at pp. 170–171. This demonstrates that withdrawal can be a viable option for target states in cases of negative politicization. After all, a state which has been deprived of all the benefits of membership has little to gain by remaining a member. See also the Poland and Czechoslovakia case study, *infra*. in Chapter VI.

3

SOME ELEMENTS OF ECONOMIC COERCION ANALYSIS

A. PRESSURE AND COERCION

Every state is in a sense subject to "pressure"[1] from the other states with which it must coexist and at times interact in the international system. The very existence of other states in that system constitutes a "constraint of circumstance" which frequently demands attention. This type of pressure would be present even if states did not deliberately attempt to influence each other's policies. Often, however, states do intentionally apply pressure to other states in an attempt to influence (or in some cases punish) them, and this type of pressure is sometimes referred to as "coercion." In this sense pressure is a more general term than coercion

But it is more than just the intentional nature of coercion which distinguishes it from mere pressure. Coercion implies domination through the use of force or threats,[2] a more extreme phenomenon than pressure. In practice defining the threshold between pressure and coercion is quite difficult, particularly where the relations between states are concerned.[3] The subjugation of one state by another, through the threat or use of

1 "Pressure" in the sense of this study has been defined as "the constraint of circumstance" and "the stress of urgency of matters demanding attention." *Webster's Seventh New Collegiate Dictionary*, Springfield, Mass., Merriam Company, 1970.

2 "Coercion" has been defined as "the act process or power of coercing" and to "coerce" as "to restrain or dominate by nullifying individual will", "to compel to an act or choice" or "to enforce by force or threat." Webster's *op. cit*.

3 A recent study on economic coercion (WEINTRAUB, S. (ed.), *Economic Coercion and U.S. Foreign Policy: Implications of Case Studies from the Johnson Administration*, Boulder Colorado, Westview Press, 1982, at p. 4), says only the following about the semantic issue:

force, is a violation of a basic norm of international law,[4] and the threshold between pressure and coercion in interstate relations may correspond to a threshold between legal and illegal behavior.[5]

Myers McDougal and Florentino P. Feliciano have argued that a certain amount and level of coercion is normal and that it is "implicit in and concomitant to the ordinary interaction of states."[6] This they refer to as a form of "permissible coercion."[7] It is clear that states will always attempt to influence each other through "persuasion" as this is the central task of diplomacy.[8] Still, one hesitates to refer to the ordinary conduct of diplomacy as a form of coercion. One commentator has defined international coercion as "the attempt by one independent nation to influence the actions or policies of another by means which extend beyond simple persuasion."[9] Unfortunately, stating that coercion begins when a nation uses means "beyond simple persuasion" does not throw much light upon the question of exactly where one ends and the other begins.

McDougal and Feliciano do not hesitate to acknowledge that

"The use of the word 'coercion' has an imperious connotation – to force a country to take an action it otherwise would avoid. At the extreme, it is clear when coercion is being used – a trade embargo or collective economic sanctions. At other times there may be a fine line between persuasion and pressure, e.g., the withholding of concessional aid unless economic or human rights policies are modified. We do not wish to be diverted by a semantic distinction; the cases speak for themselves about the extent of persuasion, pressure, and coercion being used. The form and degree of pressure chosen by a policy-maker depends greatly upon the nature and severity of the objective."

4 See Chapter VI, *infra*.

5 This point will be discussed again in Chapter IV, *infra*.

6 MCDOUGAL, M. S. and FELICIANO, F. P., "Legal Regulation of Resort to International Coercion: Aggression and Self-Defense in Policy Perspective," *Yale Law Journal*, Vol. 68, (1959) at p. 1061 (hereinafter cited as "Policy perspective").

7 *loc. cit.*

8 As VIRALLY, M., observes ("Panorama du droit international contemporain", *Recueil des Cours*, Vol. 183, (1983,V), at p. 108), "L'action diplomatique d'un état inclut, inévitablement, des pressions exercées sur les autres afin de les amener à tenir compte de ses intérets nationaux . . . "

9 Comment, "The use of nonviolent coercion: A study in legality under Article 2(4) of the Charter of the United Nations," *University of Pennsylvania Law Review*, Vol. 122, (1974), at p. 988 (hereinafter cited as "Use of nonviolent coercion").

diplomacy may have a coercive "impact".[10] In their policy-oriented analysis[11] of international coercion the object is not to be able to distinguish between persuasion and coercion, but to distinguish "permissible" coercion from "nonpermissible" coercion. They make it clear, though, that when they speak of some coercion being permissible they mean only to say that that particular coercion "does not assume the intensity and dimension requiring application of international prescriptions about aggression and self-defense."[12]

There is little reason for considering international coercion to be "permissible" merely because it may not amount to aggression.[13] Not every act of intervention, for example, can be considered an act of aggression, yet intervention is legally impermissible. Accordingly, this study proposes some very different criteria for assessing the permissibility of economic coercion.[14] Nonetheless, certain elements of the analysis of coercion used by McDougal and Feliciano are quite useful. They describe the process of international coercion in terms of:

> " . . . various *participants* applying to each other coercion of alternately accelerating and decelerating degrees of intensity, for a wide range of *objectives*, utilizing *methods* which include the employment of all known distinctive strategies or instruments of policy, under the variable *conditions* of a world arena in continuous flux."[15] (emphasis added)

There may be any number of *participants* in any process of international coercion. The primary participants are "contend-

10 MCDOUGAL, M. S. and FELICIANO, F. P., "International coercion and world public order: The general principles of the Law of War", *Yale Law Journal*, Vol. 67 (1958), at p. 792 (hereinafter cited as "Principles").

11 This approach is developed in three articles published in 1958–59. The three articles, all by MCDOUGAL and FELICIANO, are "Policy perspective" *op. cit.*, "Principles" op. cit., and "The Initiation of Coercion a Multi-temporal Analysis", *American Journal of International Law*, Vol. 52 (1958), pp. 241–259 (hereinafter cited as "Initiation of coercion").

12 "Policy Perspective", *op. cit.* at p. 1124, n. 193.

13 Especially since, as will be discussed below, the UNGA has adopted a Definition of Aggression which describes aggression only in terms of the use of armed force. UN General Assembly Resolution 3314 (XXIX) of 14 December 1974, UN GAOR, Vol. 29, Supplement 31 at p. 142, UN Document A/9631 (1974).

14 See Chapter VI, *infra*.

15 "Initiation of Coercion", *op. cit.* at p. 248.

ing states'' which it is convenient to classify as ''sending'' states[16] (those attempting to exercise a coercive influence), or ''target'' states (those against whom the attempted coercion is directed). At various points during a continuous process of coercion the same state may sometimes play the role of both a sending state and a target state, especially since coercion can provoke a coercive response by the target state.[17] Officials of the contending states may also be important participants in the process of coercion.

The *objectives* of the participants are of great importance in any analysis of coercion. Unlike cases involving the use of force, such an objective is an indispensable element in cases of non-violent coercion. If the objective of a sending state is not to influence the acts or policies of another state (or perhaps to punish it) then its non-violent acts probably do not constitute coercion at all.[18] It will, of course, be necessary to distinguish between the formally stated objectives of states and their actual objectives.

There are a number of *methods* by which states may attempt to pressure or coerce each other including the direct use of military force, the use of propaganda, the fomenting by one state of civil strife in another state and the use of economic pressure. It is the last of these methods which is the subject of this study. This method of coercion is discussed generally in this chapter and in Chapter IV, while Chapters V, VI and VII concentrate first upon the specific method of economic coercion which is available to certain World Bank member countries (i.e., those which have substantial voting power in that institution), and then upon the practice of one such country, the United States, in employing that method.

16 Sending states are also sometimes referred to as ''initiating'' states.

17 MCDOUGAL and FELICIANO stress that given the continuity involved in coercive exchanges between states the determination of ''chronological priority'', i.e., which state resorted first to coercion, is of limited value and should only be one of many factors in determining when coercion should be prohibited. See ''Initiation of Coercion'' *op. cit.* at p. 256. According to the Definition of Aggression *op. cit.*, Article 2, ''[t]he first use of force by a State in contravention of the Charter shall constitute *prima facie* evidence of an act of aggression''; or in other words, the first use of force creates a presumption of aggression which can only be rebutted by a determination of the Security Council.

18 See the discussion *infra* under the heading ''The importance of objectives in the analysis of economic coercion''.

The *conditions* in the world arena constitute the context within which any attempts at international coercion must be viewed. The military balance of power, the distribution of economic power among countries, the type and the extent of interdependence among countries and the extent to which there is or is not a community of values between leaders and peoples of the world are all relevant conditions.[19] Consideration of such conditions should be a factor in any determination concerning the limits of permissible pressure or coercion.

B. ECONOMIC COERCION

Two separate notions of economic coercion are sometimes confused. One involves the use of coercive methods of any type in order to achieve an economic objective. The economic objective may be to gain some economic advantage for the sending state from the target state, to inflict some economic damage upon the target state, or both. The second notion of economic coercion involves the use of economic methods of coercion, sometimes referred to as "economic weapons". The use of economic weapons may properly be classified as economic coercion regardless of the specific objectives pursued. Despite the conceptual distinction between economic methods of coercion and coercion in pursuit of economic objectives, the distinction may not always be clear in practice. The point has been made that "[e]conomic weapons invariably produce economic effects, while an attack upon a nation's economy will often result in undermining its governmental or political structure."[20]

1. Economic methods of coercion

It would be impossible to make an exhaustive list of all of the economic methods of coercion available to states. Obviously different states may have access to different methods of economic coercion.[21] Some of the most common economic methods include a refusal to sell a product or products ("embargo"), a refusal to buy ("boycott"), the manipulation of tariffs and/or

19 See "Policy perspective," *op. cit.* at pp. 1105-1111.
20 "Use of Nonviolent Coercion", *op. cit.*, p. 1004.
21 See the discussion of conditions under which economic pressure can be effectively applied, *infra*.

quotas on imports, and terminating or reducing financial aid flows. In fact, the potential instruments of economic coercion can be conveniently divided into three basic categories: aid, trade and technology, and investment.[22] This study deals only with the first of these categories, although here aid is broadly defined so as to include World Bank loans which could also be seen as a form of investment.[23]

2. The importance of objectives in the analysis of economic coercion: Distinguishing coercion from competition

Derek W. Bowett, in what has been described as a "prophetic article"[24] published in 1972, noted some of the difficulties in defining economic coercion.

> " . . . any measures by State A (the establishment of rival industries for example) may be regarded as coercion by State B in the sense that State B may be forced to take them into account in planning its own economy. In short, economic 'pressure' can assume many forms."[25]

Continuing, Bowett points out that:

> "[since] . . . state economies are competitive promoting one's own economy may well be injurious to others. This suggests that *it will be necessary to characterize unlawful economic measures by their intent rather than their effect.*"[26] (emphasis added)

22 See, WEINTRAUB, *op. cit.* p. 12 where he also reviews alternative, but often similar categories used by some other authors.

23 WEINTRAUB's study defines aid as "grants, concessional loans, and technical and material assistance provided on a grant or concession basis by the donor to a recipient." *loc. cit.* This would exclude the World Bank loans from the definition of aid while including concessional IDA "credits" from the Bank's soft loan affiliate. Weintraub would perhaps classify loans from the Bank itself, which charges a near commercial rate of interest, as "investment" and not aid. This approach may result from an attempt to equate aid with "ODA" (official development assistance). For purposes of the present study, it is more logical and convenient to categorize both hard and soft loans from the MDBs as "aid."

24 LILLICH, R. B., "Economic Coercion and the International Legal Order," *International Affairs*, Vol. 51 (1975), at p. 366.

25 BOWETT, D. W., "Economic Coercion and Reprisals by States", *Virginia Journal of International Law*, Vol. 13 (1972), at p. 3, (hereinafter cited as "Reprisals").

26 *Ibid.* at p. 5.

Setting aside for the moment the question of the legality of economic pressure or coercion, it is clear that unless economic measures are motivated at least to some extent by an intent to influence the actions or policies of another state or to punish it, it would be pointless to consider those measures as coercive.

Complicating analysis, however, is the fact that it can be quite difficult to identify the true objectives of a nation when it takes what may appear to be coercive action. Weintraub suggests an analytically useful distinction between "formal" objectives, which are essentially those communicated by the sender state to the target state; "undisclosed" objectives, which are stated and discussed internally in the sender state but not communicated to the target state; and "implicit" objectives, which seem to be those which are understood within the sender state though they are not explicitly stated even internally.[27]

When it is the formal objective of a state to coerce another, this may be revealed in official statements or elsewhere in the public record. In many if not most cases, we can expect that the coercive objective will not be formally stated anywhere. Where coercion is an undisclosed or implicit objective the evidence of this fact may only be circumstantial and inconclusive.

3. The conditions under which economic coercion can be effective

In order to understand the conditions under which economic pressure can be effectively applied it is necessary to examine the participants and their situations. Unless a sender state has some type of economic power it cannot hope to apply very much economic pressure to another state. Similarly, it would be futile to attempt to place economic pressure upon a state which was not economically vulnerable or susceptible to the type of pressure used.

The question of which states are "vulnerable" or "susceptible" to economic coercion must be answered separately for each separate instrument of coercion. A country may be quite vulnerable to the use of the "trade weapon" but not at all vulnerable to the use of the "aid weapon." In today's world, states are more interdependent economically than they have

27 WEINTRAUB, S. *op. cit.*, at pp. 47–48.

ever been before. As a result, most states are vulnerable today to one or more of the instruments of economic coercion.

C. INTERNATIONAL FINANCIAL AID AS A FORM OF PERSUASION

International financial aid (as variously defined) can take a number of different forms including capital flows, the transfer of technology and even military aid such as weapons transfers and military training. When we speak of aid as a potential instrument of economic coercion we normally refer to government to government financial flows,[28] whether bilateral or (as in the case of the World Bank) multilateral.

International financial aid is a complex phenomenon involving as it does *economic* assistance, transferred as the result of a *political* decision, in any of several different *legal* forms. All three of these aspects must be considered in evaluating the coercive potential of aid.

D. THE COERCIVE POTENTIAL OF AID

1. The Need of Recipients for Aid: A Primary Economic Factor

The economic gap between rich and poor countries and the many foreign aid programs (both bilateral and multilateral) which now exist have "added a new dimension to the realm of international economic persuasion."[29] Clearly aid is a more effective instrument of coercion against some countries than against others. It is a form of persuasion which economically powerful states can use against poor and economically vulnerable states.[30] As Knorr observes:

"It may be added that, ultimately, it is not poverty per se

28 KNORR, (*The Power of Nations: The Political Economy of International Relations*, New York, Basic Books, (1975) at p. 168), defines aid as "a concessionary transfer of resources from one government to another." This definition (like that of Weintraub discussed in a prior footnote) seems unnecessarily narrow as it excludes non-concessional loans even though these loans are necessary tools of development for many countries. For purposes of this study non-concessional loans will also be considered to be aid.

29 "Use of nonviolent coercion", *op. cit.* p. 991.

30 See EL KADIRI, A. K. "Réflexions sur la contrainte économique dans la société internationale," *Revue Juridique Politique et Economique du Maroc*, No. 7, (1980), at p. 11. KNORR, (*op. cit.* at p. 176).

> which makes the aid recipient the weaker party to the transaction. Until two centuries ago, there was no such international economic aid, and the poor countries – and nearly all countries were more or less poor – were not dependent upon it. Their present dependence on aid results from the facts [sic] that some countries are very wealthy, that these differences are generally known, and that the poor want the differences to disappear."[31]

While it is hard to dispute Knorr's further conclusion that "a coercive element is present in many aid relationships",[32] there are some difficulties involved in classifying aid as a form of economic coercion. It is true, of course, that governments do in general give aid as a means of promoting foreign policy objectives, but this does not make all aid coercive. Given the great need which many countries have today for aid there is a justifiable reluctance to stigmatize aid by identifying it as part of a coercive process.

2. Reasons for Aid: Political Motivations of the Donors

a) Aid and the National Interest

Why is it that states are sometimes willing to aid other states financially? Knorr states categorically that "[i]nternational aid transactions are always motivated by government interests on both sides."[33] It is generally accepted that governments try to promote their own interests (as they perceive them), thus the statement seems indisputable. In the words of Raymond Mikesell "[f]oreign aid has become an instrument of foreign policy and this instrument is being employed not only in the cold war between the larger Western powers and the Soviet bloc but is used by individual members of the Western bloc for promoting their special foreign policy interests".[34]

But to say that aid serves the interest of the donor is not necessarily to imply that the better interests of the recipient are not served as well. Baldwin states that "[f]oreign aid is very

31 KNORR, *op. cit.*, at p. 176.
32 *loc. cit.*
33 KNORR, *op. cit.*, at p. 172.
34 MIKESELL, R.F., *The Economics of Foreign Aid*, Chicago, Aldine Publishing Co., 1968, at p.254.

much like an ordinary commercial exchange transaction in that one party uses economic resources to get another party to change his behavior."[35] This, however, is an extreme and unnecessarily cynical view. While the purchase of influence is certainly one of the dominant goals of foreign aid, it is not the only possible motivation for donor states. Frequently, aid may be given in order to support a weak government or regime[36] which shares certain political or ideological perspectives with the donor.

Apart from the political matters mentioned above, the donors of aid may sometimes be motivated by national economic or commercial interests. Aid flows can allow the recipients to purchase more in international trade. Particularly when the aid given is tied to procurement in the donor country, it can help create foreign markets for goods produced by that country. Additional aid by a donor state can benefit certain of its industries which may have surplus capacity, particularly when the aid is tied to the products of that industry,[37] thus farmers in both the United States and the European Economic Community have favored aid which expands their markets. Economists have sometimes expressed doubts as to whether a donor country as a whole can really expect to profit economically from aid even when it is tied in this way.[38] Nevertheless, the commercial argument is often used to elicit popular support for foreign aid.

b) Aid for the Promotion of Development

It has frequently been observed that there are two competing conceptions of what the main objective of foreign aid should

35 BALDWIN, D.A., *Economic Statecraft*, Princeton N.J., Princeton University Press, (1985), at p. 292.

36 See, KNORR, *op. cit.* at pp. 190–192, where he describes numerous cases where supporting a foreign government rather than influencing it was the exclusive or predominant objective of the donor state.

37 See, LITTLE, I.M.D. and CLIFFORD, J.M., *International Aid*, London, George Allen and Unwin, 1965, at p. 82.

38 One economist, (MIKESELL, *op. cit.* at p. 11) notes that:
"If there are any national economic benefits accruing to aid donors (other than from export credits), they are largely indirect, highly tenuous, and of such a long-term nature that their discounted value will almost surely be exceeded by present costs."

be.[39] In 1964 Edward Mason contrasted "those who regard aid as a relatively disinterested attempt to assist the poor countries of the world towards economic development" and "those who consider that the only possible justification of aid is its contribution, if any, to the security" of the donor.[40] More recently, a former official of the US Agency for International Development has written of the "debate between those who want bilateral economic assistance to be a short-run policy instrument and those who want it to enhance a global process of development."[41]

No analysis of the many important issues of development theory, such as what truly constitutes "development", will be attempted in this study, but it must be acknowledged that donor states are, at certain times and to some extent motivated by a desire to promote development. There are a number of ways in which the development of poorer countries is assumed to serve the interests of the richer donor states, essentially by contributing to world peace, stability,[42] and prosperity, thus it is not solely out of altruism that they may wish to promote this objective. The objectives of donor states will often be mixed.

When considering the factors which motivate the donors of

39 Hans Morgenthau developed a distinction between six policies which go by the name of foreign aid. These are humanitarian foreign aid, subsistence foreign aid, military foreign aid, bribery, prestige foreign aid, and foreign aid for development. While some of these, such as military foreign aid, are not international *financial* aid, Morgenthau's typology and analysis help to underline the diversity of ways in which a donor can attempt to use foreign aid as a policy instrument. See, MORGENTHAU, H., "A Political Theory of Foreign Aid", *American Political Science Review*, Vol. 61, (1962), pp. 301–309.

40 MASON, E. S., *Foreign Aid and Foreign Policy*, New York, Harper and Row, 1964, at p. 8.

41 WASSERMAN, G., "The Foreign Aid Dilemma", *The Washington Quarterly*, Vol. 6, No. 1, (1983), at p. 96.

42 In a 1961 address to the National Conference on International Economic and Social Development, (*The New York Times*, June 17, 1961, at p. 2) President John F. Kennedy of the United States linked worldwide economic development to his country's struggle against communism:

" . . . the so-called wars of liberation Mr. Krushchev has described cannot be stopped by a B-38 Squadron. They cannot be deterred – these internal movements cannot be deterred – by military guarantees . . .

"I therefore urge those who want to do something for the United States, for this cause, to channel their energies behind *the new foreign-aid program to help prevent the social injustice and economic chaos upon which subversion and revolt feed*; to encourage reform and development, to stabilize new nations and encourage weak governments, train and equip the local forces upon whom the chief burden of resisting local communist subversion rests" (emphasis added)

international financial aid, the question arises as to whether the objectives of the donor, and the use of aid to meet those objectives, should be considered to be "coercive". To the extent that a country gives aid to promote development rather than to buy influence, it would not appear to be pursuing an impermissible coercive objective

It does not follow, however, that aid given for the purpose of promoting development will be totally "stringless". Although the idea of aid without strings attached is appealing to the recipients of aid, it is doubtful whether donor states would be willing to give very much aid without conditions of some type being imposed.[43] Conditions intended to insure that the aid given has a positive developmental effect may be imposed by even the most politically disinterested donors.[44] It is a particular type of conditional element, the linkage of aid to foreign policy objectives, which is generally identified with the coercive use of aid.

c) The Political and Coercive Use of Aid

Whatever the original objective of an aid program may be, there is always the potential that it might at some point be used as an instrument of coercion.[45] Aid can be used as such an instrument in either a positive or a negative way. Positive coercion

43 Mason, (*Foreign Aid and Foreign Policy, op. cit.*,at p. 41), observes in this regard:

" . . . The demand in many underdeveloped countries is for 'massive aid without strings.' But aid is never supplied without conditions of some sort. The only questions worth discussing are what kind of conditions, imposed by whom, and under what circumstances."

Similarly, Baldwin, (in *Economic Statecraft, op. cit.*, at p. 299), speaking of what is sometimes referred to as "stringless aid" says that:

"The concept of aid without strings implies both that aid would be distributed randomly and that aid would continue to be allocated regardless of the behavior of the recipient states. This is useful since the sooner the preposterous requirements of stringless aid are understood, the sooner one can get on with examining the important problems of the number and kind of strings on aid that are desirable from various points of view."

44 Morgenthau notes that "to give foreign aid for economic development without stipulating conditions that maximize the chances for success will surely maximize the chances for failure. On the other hand, to give foreign aid 'with strings' arouses xenophobic suspicions and nationalistic resentments", MORGENTHAU, "A Political Theory of Foreign Aid", *op. cit.*, at p. 306.

45 See, HOLSTI, K.J., *International Politics: A Framework for Analysis*, Englewood Cliffs, N.J., Prentice-Hall, 1983, at p. 233.

can be attempted by promising aid, or more aid to the target state if it meets certain conditions. One could argue that such promises of aid are not truly coercive since the target state is not strictly speaking compelled to accept the conditions of the aid. Nonetheless, the need of that state for aid may be compelling.

While positive coercion involves an "actual or promised reward" negative coercion involves an "actual or threatened punishment".[46] The threats and/or punishments of negative coercion may seem more coercive than do the promises and rewards of positive coercion. It is also likely that in the target state "a negative effort generally will be received with a much more unyielding attitude than a promised reward."[47]

Klaus Knorr develops a number of analytical distinctions regarding the objectives of donor states in extending foreign aid. In his view, a coercive element in such aid may be identified most clearly in cases where there is a threat to cut off aid unless certain conditions are met, but he notes that "when a new aid offer is used as a positive sanction, that is, when the prospective recipient is told that he will get aid provided he satisfies certain stipulated conditions . . ." this may be considered to be coercive "whenever the prospective recipient finds the conditions onerous."[48] There are some problems with this view of what constitutes "coercion". Even benign conditions, such as guarantees that the aid will be used on a high development priority, might be considered to be coercive according to this test. Furthermore, the standard he describes is hopelessly vague. To say that coercion is present when the conditions attached to aid are "onerous" would already be quite vague, but under Knorr's formulation the question is a thoroughly subjective one as well, since it depends on whether the "prospective recipient finds the conditions onerous".[49]

Regardless of whether aid is coercive, it is viewed by many

46 See WEINTRAUB *op. cit.* p. 21, and BALDWIN, D. A., "The Power of Positive Sanctions", *World Politics*, Vol. 28, (1971), pp. 19–38.

47 WEINTRAUB, *op. cit.* p. 21.3.

48 KNORR, K., *The Power of Nations*, New York, Basic Books, (1975), at p. 174.

49 Knorr acknowledges this subjectivity when he says later that " . . . any coercive level is also a variable in terms of the peculiar value sensitivity of the recipient . . . there is a substantial subjective element in the experience of recipients." KNORR, *op. cit.*, at p. 176.

as highly political. In discussing the political nature of foreign aid Hans Morgenthau states that:

> "The problem of foreign aid is insolvable if it is considered as a self-sufficient technical enterprise of a primarily economic nature. It is solvable only if it is considered an integral part of the political policies of the giving country – which must be devised in view of the political conditions, and for its effects upon the political situation, in the receiving country. In this respect, a policy of foreign aid is no different from diplomatic or military policy or propaganda. They are all weapons in the political armory of nations.
>
> "As military policy is too important a matter to be left ultimately to the generals, so is foreign aid too important a matter to be left in the end to the economists . . . the formulation and over-all execution of foreign aid policy is a political function. It is the province of the political expert."[50]

Morgenthau is correct in emphasizing that foreign aid is a tool of the donor state's foreign policy, but there is considerable doubt about the effectiveness of aid as a means of purchasing influence and/or coercing recipient states.[51] Nonetheless, donor states do attempt to use foreign aid as a political "weapon". Multilateral aid is often seen as a means of circumventing this problem.

3. MULTILATERAL AID AS A LEGAL-INSTITUTIONAL REMEDY FOR CERTAIN POLITICAL PROBLEMS OF BILATERAL AID

Multilateral aid is aid which is distributed through a legal-institutional structure which involves more than one donor state. What are the advantages of creating and using such a multilateral structure? The economist Raymond Mikesell has noted that "[t]he arguments favoring multilateral over bilateral aid, or vice

50 MORGENTHAU, "A Political Theory of Foreign Aid", *op. cit.*, at p. 309.

51 KNORR, (*op. cit.* at p. 205), concludes that "[o]n the whole, the power to give foreign aid ordinarily has uncertain effectiveness and decidedly low utility when used for the purposes of coercing other states or of establishing a position of unequal influence over them."

versa, are perhaps more political and administrative in nature than economic."[52]

Partly because bilateral aid programs can be easily used by the donor state for either positive or negative coercion, the developing countries, as the potential targets of the aid weapon, have generally favored increasing multilateralization of aid. Multilateral aid institutions, such as the multilateral development banks (MDBs), are viewed as being less likely to place political conditions upon the aid they dispense.

a) Multilateral Aid as More Devoted to Development and as Relatively Less Politicized than Bilateral Aid

As was mentioned above, there is ongoing debate within donor countries about whether aid is given mainly to promote the development of the recipient or to serve the foreign policy goals of the donor. One of the most frequently heard arguments for multilateral aid is based on the assumption that it is more development oriented and less subject to political manipulation than bilateral aid,[53] an assumption that seems for the most part to be justified.

The terms and conditions of multilateral financial aid are generally determined pursuant to a treaty or other international agreement which gives an international body (often composed of national representatives) the authority over the use of the funds contributed. Because of the involvement of other donor countries, once funds are contributed to a multilateral aid agency, such as the World Bank, it will be more difficult for any one donor country to use that aid for political purposes unrelated to development.

Since multilateral aid is less closely linked with the national interest of the donor states than is bilateral aid it is generally in the interests of recipient states to receive more of the former as opposed to the latter.[54] From the point of view of the donor states, however, this can hardly be seen as an advantage. When

52 MIKESELL, *op. cit.*, at p. 254.

53 FRIEDMANN, et al, *International Financial Aid, op. cit.*, at p. 430, speak of "the belief that multilateral aid is more concerned with the objectives of economic development than the bilateral sources, which are under constant pressure to implement the more varied objectives of a national government."

54 But FRIEDMANN, et al. (*op. cit.* at p. 432) note that politically linked bilateral aid will be in the interest of certain politically favored recipients.

they contribute funds to a multilateral aid agency the donor countries are in effect relinquishing much of their control over how those funds will be used. (Just how much of that control they surrender in practice will, of course, vary.) These donors must themselves recognize that there are some advantages to multilateral aid, otherwise they would not bother to fund these institutions.

Multilateral aid is based on the common interest of the donors and recipients in promoting development, but this does not mean that it is given unconditionally. Because multilateral aid is less subject to use for political purposes, it may be a more effective instrument for bringing influence to bear on the economic policies of the recipients. Even this aid is not entirely "stringless", because as Holsti points out, "donors – including multilateral agencies – always insist that their goods and funds be used in a manner consistent with their own purposes."[55] Multilateral agencies devoted to development will attempt to apply some type of "genuine development criteria"[56] in order to promote the efficient use of their aid funds. In theory, the motivations of multilateral agencies are supposed to be beyond suspicion, therefore there should be no charges of intervention, and stricter technical conditions for aid can be laid down by these agencies than by a single country.[57] Former World Bank President Eugene Black, made this point in his farewell address to the Bank's Board of Governors:

> "An international organization will make aid available with the sole purpose of helping the country receiving that aid . . . Because they are known to have no ulterior motive, *they can exert more influence over the use of a loan than is possible for a bilateral lender*: they can insist that the projects for which they lend are established on a sound basis, and – most important – they can make their lending

55 HOLSTI, *op. cit.*, at p. 237.

56 FRIEDMANN, et al. *op. cit.* at p. 431, in discussing the advantages of multilateral aid over bilateral aid note that "[m]ultilateral agencies are also better able to bring their influence to bear toward more efficient use of aid by recipient countries and to apply *genuine development criteria* to their financing assistance" (emphasis added).

57 See, FEIS, H. *Foreign Aid and Foreign Policy*, London, Macmillan & Co. Ltd., 1964, at p. 215.

conditional on commensurate efforts being made by the recipient country itself."[58] (emphasis added)

Multilateral aid, like bilateral aid can be used to influence the recipient country, but in theory the difference lies in the interests served. Instead of being used to serve the narrow national interests of one donor state, the purpose of multilateral aid is to serve the broader "common interests" which inspire the creation of multilateral aid mechanisms. At the most general level there is the common interest in promoting economic development; but within a global agency such as the World Bank there can be considerable disagreement about the specifics. The ideological cleavages which divide international political bodies correspond to ideological cleavages on development policy, and these have been evident in UNCTAD negotiations since that organization was created in 1964.

The World Bank was established in 1945, at a time when most of today's developing countries were still under colonial rule. As the pre-eminent world economic powers of that era the US and the UK designed the Bank to promote a model of economic development consistent with their free market ideology, and the Bank's Charter reflects this.

In this context one can, for example, refer to Article I of the World Bank's Articles of Agreement which lists the agreed purposes of that organization. In addition to assisting and encouraging development, the Bank is to "promote foreign investment", and to "promote the long-range balanced growth of international trade".[59] Is it therefore intended that the Bank's loans should be used as an incentive to encourage countries to adopt pro-investment and pro international trade policies? As will be discussed later in the context of the case studies, the Bank has taken its role in promoting investment very seriously. In practice this has meant that potential borrowers who have nationalized foreign investments without making arrangements for suitable compensation have generally been denied access to the Bank's resources.

One could argue on this basis that even though the Bank is a multilateral aid agency, aid from that institution is at times

58 Eugene Black's farewell address to the IBRD Board of Governors, September 1962, *Summary Proceedings – 1962 Annual Meetings of the Boards of Governors, IBRD and IDA, IBRD*, Washington, D.C., 1962, at pp. 13–14.

59 IBRD Articles of Agreement, Article I(ii) and (iii).

used as an instrument of positive coercion, and that it is in fact official Bank policy to withhold that aid when to do so will promote the agreed purposes of the Bank.

b) The Role of Multilateral Agencies in the Coordination of International Financial Aid

In addition to providing financing and technical assistance the World Bank also plays an important role in the coordination of aid flows to specific developing countries. Coordination is necessary in order to maximize the effectiveness of aid flows from different sources. Ideally, the development efforts of different donors should reinforce each other and not work at cross purposes.[60] The coordination of aid to increase its efficiency and effectiveness must be considered to be in the interest of the donors as well as the recipients,[61] and is perhaps the most important reason for cooperating in multilateral aid programs.

Since 1958 the World Bank has taken the lead in organizing a number of country coordinating groups (both consortia and consultative groups) which help donors to coordinate their aid to a specific recipient country.[62] The exact form of these groups

60 See, KAPLAN, J. J., *International Aid Coordination: Needs and Machinery*, Washington, West Publishing Co., 1978, at pp. 3-4.

61 In 1967 the US Congress enacted a legislative declaration recognizing, and in effect cataloguing certain advantages of multilateral aid; (The Foreign Assistance Act of 1961, Section 209(a); Public Law ("PL") 87-195, approved September 4, 1961, as Amended by The Foreign Assistance Act of 1967, PL 90-137, approved November 14, 1967, and by The Foreign Assistance Act of 1971, PL 92-226, approved February 7, 1971; Codified at 22 U.S.C. Sec. 2169.):

"The Congress recognizes that the planning and administration of development assistance by, or under the sponsorship of the United Nations, multilateral lending institutions, and other multilateral organizations may contribute to the efficiency and effectiveness of that assistance through participation of other donors in the development effort, improved coordination of policies and programs, pooling of knowledge, avoidance of duplication of facilities and manpower, and greater encouragement of self-help performance."

62 Country coordinating arrangements have been undertaken by the IDB, the Development Assistance Committee (DAC) of the OECD and by the IMF as well as by the World Bank. See, FRIEDMANN, *et al. op. cit.* at pp. 433–437, and KAPLAN, *International Aid Coordination, op. cit.*, at pp. 34–37.

has varied,[63] but today their primary function is to help donors to understand the needs, policies, and priorities of a recipient's development program so that individual donors can more effectively target their assistance to the country involved.[64]

The role of the MDBs in coordination is increasingly important today because of the magnitude of the international debt crisis. This role can best be fulfilled only if the Bank and the other MDBs maintain a reputation as non-political technical organizations, and this is the image which they have always attempted to project. In later chapters this study will explore the extent to which the United States government has nonetheless injected political (i.e., other than economic) considerations into the Bank through the use, or threatened use, of its voting power in that organization.[65] The politicization of the Bank in this way could eventually impair its ability to fulfill this important coordinating role.

c) The Role of Multilateral Development Institutions in Mobilizing Private Capital for Development

The legal and financial structure of the IBRD (and other MDBs which make "hard loans" for development) is such that most of the capital which it makes available to developing countries is actually drawn from private sector capital markets. Since the capital subscriptions of the member countries guarantee that the Bank will pay its debts, it has a very good credit rating, and because of this rating it can borrow funds at a favorable rate of interest. It is then able to re-lend these same funds to developing countries on better terms than those borrowers could hope to obtain on their own.

IBRD members have paid in only 10% of the value of their subscriptions to the Bank's capital stock, yet because of the

63 The first of these groups was the India consortium organized by the Bank in 1958. In their earlier form these *consortia* had two main functions; the review and endorsement of the country's development plan, and fund-raising through the pledging of additional assistance by donors. The reluctance of donors to commit themselves to specific quantities of additional aid eventually became a major problem with many of these consortia. The Bank then began to organize *consultative groups* which, unlike the consortia, do not involve the pledging of specific amounts. See, KAPLAN, *International Aid Coordination, op. cit.*, at pp. 34–37.

64 KAPLAN, *International Aid Coordination, op. cit.*, at p. 35.

65 See Chapters VI, VII and VIII, *infra*.

Bank's ability to mobilize private capital it is able to make hard loans whose outstanding value is equal to the entire amount of the pledged capital. Bilateral aid programs do not normally mobilize private capital in this way, and the proven ability to do so may be seen as a major advantage of multilateral aid (or at least MDB aid) from the point of view of both the donors and the recipients.

d) Other Possible Advantages of Multilateral Aid

A number of other possible advantages of multilateral aid have been cited in the past,[66] and many are variations on one of the themes discussed above. We have seen, for example, that foreign aid transactions are often used to promote the interests, (especially the security interests), of the donor state. Largely as a result of this, bilateral aid tends to be concentrated upon a relatively small number of recipient countries. One possible advantage from the point of view of the recipients is that multilateral aid can help to fill the gaps by providing aid to countries which are less attractive to bilateral donors. In a similar vein it has also been noted that the poorest countries which need the most aid are bad financial risks, and that the multilateralization of aid can allow the risk of loans to these countries to be "internationalized." This could be an advantage for both donors and recipients.[67]

Another possible advantage for recipients is that the international aid agencies sometimes encourage donors to give more aid by setting international targets and standards for aid-giving.[68] Foreign aid tends to have little popular support in the donor countries, and thus this type of encouragement could make at least a marginal difference in the internal debate on foreign aid funding.

From the point of view of conservative donors another poss-

66 For an extended discussion of these issues see, BETZ, J., "Functions of the Multilateralization of Development Assistance", *Law and State*, Vol. 18, (1978) at pp. 40–71. See also The Foreign Assistance Act of 1961, Section 209(a), *op. cit.*, (Codified at 22 U.S.C. Sec. 2169) in which the US Congress, by legislative declaration recognizes certain advantages of multilateral aid.

67 BETZ, *op. cit.*, at pp. 48–56.

68 Negotiation of IDA replenishment agreements involves establishing targets of this type, and the country consortia organized by the World Bank in the 1950s and 1960s were partially based on pledging by donors to meet overall aid targets for a particular recipient country.

ible advantage is that permitting recipients to participate in the decision-making of the aid agencies, (even if it is under a weighted voting system which disfavors them), may decrease their sense of "alienation" in the development dialogue. This could reduce friction between the donors and the recipients,[69] and encourage greater self-help performance on the part of the latter.

e) The Possibility of Politicization of Multilateral Aid

While it is fairly easy to identify the advantages which multilateral aid has for aid recipients, there are also certain disadvantages from the point of view of the donors. There are various unilateral steps which donor states can always take in an effort to insure that the funds which they disburse for bilateral aid will promote their national interests, but the situation with regard to multilateral aid is quite different. The disbursement and use of multilateral aid funds is not so closely linked with the interests of any particular donor. Donors may not always find it easy to accept limits upon their control of the funds they have contributed to multilateral aid schemes. Occasionally the government of a donor country may be tempted to subvert the agreed multilateral decision-making procedure in order to advance its interests. This will often take the form of an attempt to prevent lending to a target country which that donor currently disfavors.

A donor may have valid reasons for opposing multilateral loans to a particular country or for a particular project, that is to say it may have reasons considered valid in terms of the agreed purposes and terms of reference of the multilateral agency involved. It is only when loans are blocked for reasons unrelated to those purposes that multilateral aid becomes effectively politicized.

As a practical matter, donor states will always have the option of refusing to provide any further funds to a particular multilateral agency. This gives major donors such as the US a type of influence which it may be difficult to appreciate fully. Two of the case studies which follow later in this study will explore the use of this influence. The Chile case study will deal with some

69 See, BETZ, *op. cit.*, at pp. 60–63.

of the subtle ways in which a major donor may prevent loans which it strongly opposes for political or other reasons. The so-called "Case Study on Restrictions" (concerning threats by Congress to subject US contributions to the Bank to unacceptable restrictions) demonstrates some of the not so subtle ways in which a donor can accomplish this same purpose.

4

AID AS COERCION: SOME GENERAL LEGAL ISSUES

This chapter examines the question of whether under general international law there is any legal restriction upon the right of states to use their economic power coercively against other states, particularly through the use of the "aid weapon". Particular rules established by the World Bank's constitutive treaty, and other restrictions which may be specifically applicable to the use of World Bank voting power will be discussed in Chapters V, VI and VII.

The classical system of international law which is sometimes referred to as "the international law of coexistence" consists chiefly of principles and rules requiring the different territorial states to respect each other's national sovereignty.[1] The international law of state responsibility has long provided that states may bear economic responsibility for their acts. While the economic acts of a state may engage its responsibility, these acts have not been the traditional focus of international law.[2]

The colonial rivalries of the 17th–20th centuries saw repeated

1 Wolfgang Freidmann suggested that a new "international law of cooperation" was developing with a much broader scope than the traditional "international law of coexistence." See, FRIEDMANN, W., *The Changing Structure of International Law,* London, Stevens and Sons Ltd., 1964, p. 68. This Chapter discusses the legal issues primarily in terms of the international law of coexistence, but the possible relevance of the international law of cooperation will be discussed in Chapter V, *infra*.

2 See, FUKATSU, E., "Coercion and the Theory of Sanctions in International Law", in MACDONALD, R. St. J., and JOHNSTON, D.H., (eds.), *The Structure and Process of International Law: Essays in Legal Philosophy Doctrine and Theory,* The Hague, Martinus Nijhoff, 1983, at p.1193.

Whatever the traditional view, the Draft Articles on State Responsibility prepared by the International Law Commission confirm that in modern international law international responsibility results from the breach of any international obligation by a state regardless of the subject matter of the

use of economic weapons such as trade boycotts and capital embargoes, often but not always used as just another tool in interstate war. The legality of using economic weapons does not seem to have been directly questioned.[3] The use of economic methods of coercion was accepted as falling within the legitimate prerogatives of a sovereign state at a time when even the use of armed force was not considered to be prohibited.[4] Emer de Vattel described the state of late 18th century legal doctrine on the right to condition trade relations in the following terms:

> "Puis donc qu'une Nation ne peut avoir naturellement aucun droit de vendre ses Marchandises à une autre, qui ne veut pas les acheter; qu'elle n'a qu'un droit imparfait d'acheter des autres ce dont elle a besoin . . . il est évident qu'il dépend de la volonté de chaque Nation, d'exercer le Commerce avec une autre , ou de ne pas l'exercer. Et si elle veut le permettre à quelqu'une, il dépend d'elle encore de le permettre sous toutes les conditions qu'elle trouvera à-propos. Car en lui permettant le Commerce, elle lui accorde un droit; et chaqu'un est libre d'attacher telle con-

---

obligation breached. See the Yearbook of the International Law Commission, 1976, Vol. II, Part 2, Report of the International Law Commission to the General Assembly on the Work of its twenty-eighth Session, New York, UN, 1977, pp. 96, where the Commentary to Draft Article 19 on State Responsibility notes that:
" . . . In specific cases, the exact content of an obligation imposed on a State by international law is often discussed in order to determine whether, in the particular instance concerned, there has been a breach of the obligation; it has never been contended, however, that only breaches of international obligations relating to a given field, or requiring the State to behave in some particular way, entail State responsibility."

3 A historical look at the law of economic coercion suggests that before the 20th century international legal scholars made little attempt to define legal limits to the use of economic weapons except for their recognition that customary laws of neutrality forbade belligerent states from impairing the right of neutral states to continue trading without undue interference. See NEFF, S. C., "The Law of Economic Coercion: Lessons from the Past and Indications of the Future", *Columbia Journal of Transnational Law*, Vol. 20, No. 3 (1981), at pp. 413–427.

4 "From the perspective of international law . . . international economic relations formed 'a sort of no man's land in which every side was free to do what it pleases' ", PETERSMANN, E.U., "International Economic Theory and International Economic Law: On the Tasks of a Legal Theory of International Economic Order", in MACDONALD, R. St. J., and JOHNSTON, D.H., (eds.), *The Structure and Process of International Law: Essays in Legal Philosophy Doctrine and Theory*, The Hague, Martinus Nijhoff, 1983, at pp. 231–232 (quoting FISCHER-WILLIAMS).

ditions qu'il lui plait à un droit qu'il accorde volontairement."[5]

Thus in the mid 18th century it was considered to be a sovereign right of every state to subject its trade with other states to whatever conditions it might see fit to impose. According to Vattel, states had a right to use the so called "trade weapon." At that time, of course, the right to declare and wage war was also considered to be a prerogative of every sovereign state, but this is no longer true today. The new rule finds its formal expression in the prohibition on the use of force contained in the United Nations Charter. Might that prohibition also be applicable to the use of "economic force"?

A. THE CHARTER PROHIBITION ON THE USE OF FORCE

Article 2, paragraph 4 of the UN Charter expresses a general prohibition on the use of force in the following language:

> "All Members shall refrain in their international relations from the threat or use of force against the territorial integrity or political independence of any State, or in any manner inconsistent with the purposes of the United Nations."

In deciding whether this prohibition applies to the use of economic coercion, the basic issue is whether the word "force" as used in this article should be limited to "armed force." There is a great deal of literature examining this issue, and in the past the consensus has generally been that Article 2(4) prohibits only the use of armed force.[6] The arguments for so limiting it are many.

First of all, the ordinary meaning of the term "force" simply

5 VATTEL, E. de, *Le droit des gens ou principes de la loi naturelle*, Vol. I, Washington, Carnegie Institution, 1916 (reproduction of the edition of 1758), at p. 86, (Book I, Chap. VIII, Sec. 92).

6 The argument that the prohibition on the use of force applies only to the use of armed force has been considerably weakened by the decision of the ICJ in the case brought by Nicaragua against the US over aid to Nicaragua's Contra rebels. The opinion very clearly asserts that there may be illegal uses of force other than a full blown armed attack. See discussion of this case, *infra*. Military and Paramilitary Activities in and Against Nicaragua, Judgment, 27 June 1986, *ICJ Reports*, (1986), p. 14, at p. 101, 104.

does not include economic pressures. To speak of using "economic force" is to stretch a familiar concept well beyond its generally accepted meaning. What is more, the records of the United Nations Conference on International Organizations in 1945 show that a Brazilian proposal that Article 2(4) be extended to cover "the threat or use of economic measures" as well as of force was voted down by a vote of 26–2.[7]

It has been suggested that the reasons for that vote may be unclear, since some of the delegates might have considered it to be unnecessary to state the obvious (i.e., that the use of economic measures was limited along with the use of military force).[8] The fact remains that the amendment was rejected and that, as Bowett says, "taking the words in their plain, common sense meaning, it is clear that . . . they will not apply to economic or political pressure, but only to physical armed force."[9] It has also been argued that since the right to self-defense under Article 51 of the Charter is limited to situations where there has been a previous armed attack, and considering that this right is a specific exception to the article 2(4) prohibition, symmetry and consistency in the Charter would seem to require that both articles be seen as referring only to "armed force".[10]

There are, of course, some arguments in favor of a broader application of this article. It has sometimes been suggested that the use of the words "armed force" in Article 51 is proof that if the framers of the Charter had intended to say "armed force" in Article 2(4) they would have done so. But since the Charter recognizes the potential power of the economic weapon, and places the collective use of this sanction in the hands of the Security Council in Article 41,[11] shouldn't the Charter be inter-

7 *United Nations Conference on International Organization Documents*, (U.N.C.I.O. Documents) Vol. 6, pp. 331, 334–335, Doc. 784, I/1/27 (1945).

8 See, "Use of nonviolent coercion: A Study in Legality under Article 2(4) of the Charter of the United Nations", *University of Pennsylvania Law Review*, Vol. 122, (1974), at pp. 994–995.

9 BOWETT, D. *Self-Defense in International Law*, Manchester, Manchester University Press, (1958), at p. 148.

10 Otherwise, the argument goes, "[a] target state could be the victim of an illegal use of force and yet find itself unable legally to exercise its natural right of self-defence." "Use of nonviolent coercion", *op. cit.* p. 995.

11 The economic weapon corresponds to the "measures not involving the use of force" mentioned in Article 41 of the Charter. The French text uses the term *"contrainte non-armée"* for these measures.

preted so as to prohibit threats and actions by states which involve the misuse of this same type of weapon?

Most of the arguments for a more expansive reading of Article 2(4) (or for broader application of a non-intervention principle under the Charter for that matter) are based on a teleological approach to the interpretation of the Charter. The Charter's primary purpose is to maintain international peace and security. The use of economic coercion could not only threaten the political independence of the target state, it could also constitute a threat to the peace.[12] Thus some commentators have suggested that if the expressed purposes and principles of the Charter are considered, a broad interpretation of Article 2(4) seems appropriate.[13]

It has become a commonplace to observe that economic interdependence is increasing in the world today, and the use by states of economic power as a means of exercising influence over other states does appear to be quite prevalent.[14] If, as many suspect, economic coercion has taken on a greater importance now than it had when the Charter was drafted, the teleological/-constitutional argument justifies a dynamic interpretation designed to fit the new situation.[15]

In the recent case brought by Nicaragua against the United States the International Court of Justice discussed the prohibition on the use of force as it exists in customary international

12 It is beyond dispute that if economic measures taken by a state were to constitute a threat to peace then the Security Council could legally act to remedy the situation under Chapter VII of the Charter. This supports, to some extent, the argument that economic measures can in some cases be considered to be a use of "force". But even if both the use of force and the use of economic coercion might constitute potential threats to the peace, this does not mean that the two (force and economic coercion) should be equated.

13 See, for example, PAUST, J. J., "International Law and Economic Coercion: 'Force', the Oil Weapon and Effects Upon Prices", *Yale Studies in World Public Order*, Vol. 3, No. 1 (1976), at pp. 214–218.

14 See, FUKATSU, E., "Coercion and the Theory of Sanctions in International Law", *op. cit.*, at p.1194.

15 In the words of Inis L. Claude, Jr., (*Swords into Plowshares: The Problems and Progress of International Organization*, 4th edition, New York, Random House (1971), at pp. 167–168):

"Sound constitutional interpretation, in international organization as in national government, balances insistence upon the legally formulated consensus of the past, awareness of the political configuration in the present, and consciousness of the community's requirements and demands for the future."

law today.[16] In the judgment on the merits the Court recognized that an illegal use of force need not take the extreme form of an armed attack but could take "other less grave forms",[17] but there is nothing in the decision to suggest that purely economic activities could constitute an illegal use of force when not connected (as in the Nicaragua case) with the use of military or paramilitary force.

Could one condemn economic coercion as a form of "economic aggression"? Both the 1970 "Declaration on Principles of International Law Concerning Friendly Relations and Cooperation Among States in Accordance with the Charter of the United Nations"[18] and the 1974 "Definition of Aggression"[19] are relevant in this regard. Since these resolutions of the UNGA apply the term "aggression" only to situations where armed force is used, they support the conclusion that economic coercion, though it may or may not be permissible, is at least not an act of aggression.[20]

Considering economic coercion to be an illegal use of force and/or act of aggression would have some rather troubling implications. Target states which were victims of economic coercion might then claim the right to initiate the use of force

16 Because of the multilateral treaty reservation which limited the extent to which the US had accepted the compulsory jurisdiction of the Court, the ICJ was limited to applying "principles of customary and general international law" to the case rather than the more familiar treaty law of the UN Charter. In practice, however, the Court identified no specific differences between the customary law principle and the principle embodied in article 2(4) of the Charter. *ICJ Reports*, 1986, pp. 97–104.

17 *Ibid.*, at p. 101 the Court notes that "it will be necessary to distinguish the most grave forms of the use of force (those constituting an armed attack) from other less grave forms".

18 UNGA Resolution 2625(XXV) of 24 October 1970, UN GAOR, Vol. 25, Supplement 28, at pp. 121, 123, UN Document A/8028 (1971). See the discussion of this resolution *infra.*, this same Chapter.

19 UNGA Resolution 3314 (XXIX), of 14 December 1974, 29 UN GAOR, Vol. 29, Supp. 31, at p. 142, UN Doc A/9631 (1975).

20 See also the "Declaration on the Prohibition of Military, Political, or Economic Coercion in the Conclusion of Treaties", adopted by the UN Conference on the Law of Treaties, UN Conference on the Law of Treaties Official Records, First and Second Sessions, 26 March–24 May 1968, and 9 April–22 May 1969, Documents of the Conference (UN Document A/CONF. 39/26), p. 285. This Declaration, which forms part of the Final Act of the Conference on the Law of Treaties, "Solemnly condemns the threat or use of pressure in any form, whether military, political, or economic, by any State in order to coerce another State to perform any act relating to the conclusion of a treaty in violation of the principles of the sovereign equality of states and freedom of consent" (Paragraph 1).

in self defense.[21] This would lower the threshold of violence in international relations, and the net effect would be to weaken the effect of the prohibition found in Article 2(4) of the Charter.

However reprehensible it may be, the use of economic coercion does not constitute a threat or use of force. The judgment in the Nicaragua case supports this conclusion, and as we shall see below, that judgment also raises the question of whether the principle of non-intervention might prohibit economic coercion.

B. THE PRINCIPLE OF NON-INTERVENTION

Another possibility is that economic coercion might be considered illegal as a violation of the principle of non-intervention.[22] There has long been a great deal of confusion about this principle. Wolfgang Friedmann considered it to be "one of the least precise parts of international law,"[23] and Talleyrand is said to have considered the term "non-intervention" to be meaningless.[24]

In spite of this confusion, non-intervention is one of the basic principles upon which the modern nation-state system is founded, and indeed it is an essential corollary of the idea of state sovereignty.[25] While it may be useful to keep in mind

21 Both customary international law and Article 51 of the UN Charter recognize the right of states to individual and collective self-defense, but this right applies only in cases of "armed attack". The ICJ has expressed its view that the concept of "armed attack" does not apply to every illegal use of force by states. *Ibid.*, p. 104.

22 VATTEL, who is one of the first jurists known to have referred to this principle observed (*Le Droit Des Gens, op. cit.*), at p. 38, (Book I, Chapter II, section 37)):

"Enfin toutes ces choses n'intéressant que la Nation, aucune Puissance Etrangère n'est en droit de s'en mêler, ni ne droit y intervenir autrement que par ses bons offices, à moins qu'elle n'en soit requise, ou que des raisons particulières ne l'y appellent. Si quelqu'une s'ingère dans les affaires domestiques d'une autre, si elle entreprend de la contraindre dans ses délibérations, elle lui fait injure."

23 FRIEDMANN, W., *The Changing Structure of International Law*, London, Stevens and Sons Ltd., 1964, at p. 304.

24 Talleyrand supposedly described "non-intervention" as "a metaphysical term, which means about the same as intervention." Quoted in GUELKE, A., "Force Intervention and International Conflict", in NORTHEDGE, (ed.), *The Use of Force in International Relations*, at p. 101.

25 BROWNLIE, (*Principles of Public International Law*, Oxford, Clarendon Press, 1979, at p. 291) observes that "The corollary of the independence and equality of states is the duty on the part of states to refrain from intervention in the internal or external affairs of other states."

that the respect of state sovereignty is the rationale behind the principle, the principle itself remains quite vague. Derek Bowett points out that "[m]uch depends upon what a State assumes its sovereign rights to be."[26] This is especially true when one attempts to apply the principle of non-intervention to economic coercion, since sovereign rights have not traditionally been well defined in their relation to economic activity

Hans Kelsen refers to a "duty of nonintervention" which is sometimes seen as correlative to a "right of political independence." He describes that duty as "the duty to refrain from dictatorial or forcible interference in the affairs of another state," but notes that "no clear agreement exists in the customary law on the scope of the duty of nonintervention."[27]

1. Different Conceptions of Intervention

Perhaps the greatest source of confusion concerning the scope of the principle of non-intervention, arises from disagreement about the types of behavior which may constitute "intervention".[28] The term intervention has often been applied to non-violent conduct such as statements of support for an opposition group or criticizing the human rights situation in another country. The situation with regard to human rights criticisms belongs in a special category. Today, few would dispute the conclusion that the human rights failures of a state may legitimately be criticized by other states.[29] As far as other types of

26 BOWETT, "Economic Coercion and Reprisals by States" *Virginia Journal of International Law*, Vol. 13, No. 1, (1972), at p. 3.

27 KELSEN, H., *Principles of International Law*, 2nd edition, revised and edited by Robert W. Tucker, New York, Holt, Rinehart and Winston, 1966, at p. 74.

28 CALVO, C., (*Le droit international théorique et practique*, 4th ed., Vol. I, Paris, Guillaumin et Cie., 1887, Book III, Sec. 139, at p. 278), after reviewing the literature on intervention one hundred years ago, acknowledged the confusion on the issue when he noted that "La conclusion qui ressort . . . c'est qu'il exist autant d'opinions différentes qu'il y a d'auteurs."

29 Today, the following conclusion (from HIGGINS, R., "Intervention and International Law", in BULL, H. (ed.), *Intervention in World Politics, op. cit.* at p. 34) seems inevitable:

> " . . . Human Rights have shifted from being a matter traditionally of solely domestic concern into a matter of legitimate international concern. We thus now have a situation where other parties are entitled to raise complaints in all appropriate forums without any charge of intervention being reasonably raised against them."

non-violent intervention are concerned, it can be difficult to identify the point or threshold at which normally innocuous conduct such as speech and public statements may come to constitute prohibited intervention in the internal affairs of another state.

It is sometimes assumed that only the threat or use of force can constitute intervention. According to this view, the Charter's prohibition on the use of force could be considered as a restatement of the principle of non-intervention.[30] Kelsen comes very close to accepting this view, but he is also keenly aware that this would render the "duty" of non-intervention an inadequate counterpart to the "right" sometimes said to be involved.[31]

Opposed to this narrow concept of intervention is a much broader concept, based to a large extent on theories of the "absolute sovereignty" of states such as those enunciated by Calvo in the late 19th century.[32] According to this view any outside influence which could arguably be said to interfere with the autonomy of a state is considered to constitute intervention. Calvo himself deplored the tendency of some publi-

30 BROWNLIE, (*Principles, op. cit.* at p. 291) sees the duty of non-intervention as "a master principle which draws together many particular rules on the legal competence and responsibility of states." He then notes that "One aspect of the duty concerns the illegality of the use or threat of force." Of course the identification of this as one aspect of that principle or duty does not in any way preclude the possibility that another aspect might be applicable to economic coercion.

31 KELSEN, *op. cit.* at p. 75, admits that:
"There is, of course, the further consideration that a state's independence may be impaired by the behavior of another state, although the latter does not employ force or even the threat of force. To the extent that intervention is held to encompass only those acts of interference in the affairs of another state that take an imperative and dictatorial form and involve the use or threat of force, the duty of nonintervention becomes irrelevant in dealing with behavior that may nevertheless effectively jeopardize political independence.

" . . . A state's political independence may even be endangered through the economic pressures to which it is subjected by another state, though these measures of economic coercion may not themselves be expressly forbidden by international law."

32 CALVO, *op. cit.* at page 264 (Book III, Sec. 107) affirmed the view that:
"Les Etats possèdent, en vertu de la loi même de leur organization et de leur souverainté, une sphère d'action propre, exclusive et particulière à chacun d'eux . . . La souverainté absolue implique forcément une complète indépendence . . . "

cists to restrict the term to uses of violent force.[33] Others, particularly in Latin America, have agreed with him on this point.[34] The term "intervention" is increasingly used (especially by the leaders of developing countries) to refer to non-military behavior as well as whenever it may interfere with the independence of a state.[35] A broad notion of intervention is called for in view of increasing global interdependence (particularly in economic matters) and to the opportunities which this has created for the use of subtle and sophisticated means of interference which do not necessarily involve the use of armed force.[36] While it is quite possible that the term intervention has gained a political meaning (and a utility in political debate) which goes well beyond its actual legal significance, the narrow concept of intervention is already obsolete. While there is a definite lack of agreement concerning the meaning and content of intervention in international law, it is both inevitable and desirable that eventually the scope of the legal concept

33 CALVO, (*op. cit.*, at p. 267) distinguishes between four different types of intervention, and observes that:

"Certains publicistes ne donnent le nom d'intervention qu'à ce dernier cas, [l'intervention armée] en objectant que si l'entremise de la part d'un Etat dans les affaires d'un autre n'est pas violente, mais pacifique et purement bornée à des conseils, elle se résout en une interposition amicale, ou en bons offices, ou encore en médiation ce qui n'est plus l'intervention. C'est, selon nous, prendre le résultat pour le fait lui-même. La forme sous laquelle a lieu l'intervention n'en altère pas le charactère."

34 One relatively modern study of intervention in the Americas, (THOMAS, A.V.W. and THOMAS, A.J. Jr., *Non-Intervention: The Law and its Import in the Americas*, Dallas, Southern Methodist University Press, 1956, at p. 69), after reviewing the Latin American literature on the subject, reaches the following conclusion about non-military intervention:

". . . the type of compulsion used by the interfering state is of little importance. The important point to be considered is whether constraint or threat thereof was used, whether by armed force or by diplomacy, whether concealed or open, whether direct or indirect. Therefore, interference to be intervention must constitute compulsion or threat thereof. And 'threat' is to be understood to mean that there is a direct or indirect request by one state that another do or refrain from doing something upon pain of compulsion."

35 As David BALDWIN wrote in 1969, ("Foreign Aid, Intervention and Influence", *World Politics*, Vol. 21, (1969) at p. 426) "Reasonable and responsible leaders from developing nations have applied the label of 'intervention' to almost every conceivable form of influence during the last twenty years. Only a very broad definition of intervention will allow us to discuss the matter in a way that is relevant to the concerns of these nations."

36 See, OPPERMANN, T., "Intervention", *Encyclopedia of Public International Law*, (hereinafter cited as "*EPIL*") Vol. 3, Max Planck Institute, Amsterdam, Elsevier Science Publishers B.V., (1982), at pp. 234, 236.

should come to reflect the changes in the international situation.[37]

Higgins points out that the idea of non-military intervention is linked to the notion of jurisdiction in international law, and that it suggests interference with the domestic jurisdiction of a state.[38] It is also true, however, that intervention can consist of interference in either the internal or external affairs of another state.[39] The following language from the ICJ judgment in the Nicaragua case supports this last point, and also leaves little doubt that prohibited intervention need not involve the use of force.

> " . . . A prohibited intervention must accordingly be one bearing on matters in which each state is permitted, by the principle of state sovereignty, to decide freely. One of these is the choice of a political, economic, social, and cultural system, and the formulation of foreign policy. Intervention is wrongful when it uses methods of coercion with regard to such choices, which must remain free ones. The element of coercion, which defines, and indeed forms the very essence of, prohibited intervention, is particularly obvious in the case of an intervention which uses force . . ."[40]

Of course it is impossible, as a practical matter, to prohibit every intervention however minor. Thus Virally accepts the idea that there are many non-military forms of intervention, but he then finds it necessary to distinguish between legal intervention and

37 OPPERMANN, (*op. cit.* at p. 236), concludes that "In general the problem of definition of the act of intervention can and must be solved by recognizing the new balance between sovereignty on the one hand and the increasing importance of cooperation, interdependence and internationalization on the other."

38 See, HIGGINS, R., "Intervention and International Law", in BULL, H. (ed.), *Intervention in World Politics*, Oxford, Clarendon Press, (1984), at pp. 30–33.

39 THOMAS and THOMAS, (*Non-Intervention, op. cit.* at pp. 69–70), argue that: " . . . External independence – that is, the power of a state to determine the relations it desires to maintain with other states without interference – is a fundamental rule of independence. No valid distinction can be made between intervention in internal and external affairs."

40 *ICJ Reports*, (1986) p. 108.

illegal intervention.[41] This broad approach to the concept of intervention still brings us back to the fundamental question of the scope of the principle of non-intervention.

2. Non-Intervention and the UN Charter

The United Nations Charter does not refer to the principle of non-intervention as such, but it does mention a number of related principles. These include the principles of equal rights and self-determination of peoples[42] and of sovereign equality,[43] the prohibition on the threat or use of force against the territorial integrity or the political independence of any state[44] (discussed above), and the qualified prohibition on intervention, by the United Nations, in matters which are essentially within the domestic jurisdiction of any state.[45] On the basis of the above, it has often been suggested that the principle of non-intervention is implicit in the Charter.[46] This may well be true, but confusion regarding the meaning and scope of that principle remains.

Certain resolutions of the UN General Assembly have related

41 See, VIRALLY, M., "Panorama du droit international contemporain", (cours général), *Recueil des Cours*, Vol. 183, (1983,V), at pp. 108, 112, and also at p. 114 where he summarizes his conclusions on this point in the following terms:
"Il apparaît, finalement, comme il a été dit plus haut, que l'appréciation du caractère licite ou illicite d'une intervention dépend d'un examen in concreto de toutes les circonstances entourant cette intervention et de ses caractères propres, beaucoup plus que de l'application de formules générales. Cet examen doit prendre en compte à la fois l'objet de l'intervention, les moyens mis en oeuvre et sa finalité. C'est seulement au terme d'une telle analyse qu'il est possible de décider si l'intervention en cause porte atteinte à la souveraineté d'un autre Etat de façon contraire au droit international."

42 UN Charter Article 1, Section 2.

43 UN Charter Article 2, Section 1.

44 UN Charter Article 2, Section 4.

45 UN Charter Article 2, Section 7.

46 See, for example, the discussion in Goodrich, L.M.; Hambro, E.; and Simmons, A.P., *Charter of the United Nations: Commentary and Documents*, 3rd and revised edition, New York, Columbia University Press, 1969, at pp. 37–40, and the various statements of national representatives to the UN cited in FONTEYNE, J.P.L., "Forcible Self-Help by States to Protect Human Rights: Recent Views from the United Nations", in R.B. LILLICH, (ed.), *Humanitarian Intervention and the United Nations*, Charlottesville, University Press of Virginia, 1973, at p. 205. SCHRÖDER, M., ("Principle of Non-Intervention", *EPIL, op. cit.* Vol. 7, (1984), at p. 359), considers the proposition that the Charter implicitly prohibits intervention by states to be both "doubtful and controversial".

the use of economic methods of coercion to the principle of non-intervention in an effort to clarify the existing state of international law on this subject. They provide evidence of a growing international consensus that the use of economic methods of coercion can violate the principle of non-intervention.

Although resolutions of the General Assembly are not in themselves binding under international law, they may claim a certain authoritativeness as an expression of the expectations and opinions of the international community,[47] particularly when those resolutions purport to interpret the principles enshrined in the Charter itself.[48] In the recent Nicaragua case judgment the ICJ attached considerable importance to the UNGA resolutions discussed below as an expression of an *opinio juris* concerning the binding nature of certain rules as customary international law.[49]

It is important to note that those General Assembly resolutions which address the issue of economic coercion condemn it not as an illegal use of force but as a violation of the principle of non-intervention. For example, the 1966 Declaration on the Inadmissibility of Intervention in the Domestic Affairs of States and the Protection of Their Independence and Sovereignty states that:

> "1. No state has the right to intervene, directly or indirectly, for any reason whatever, in the internal or external affairs of another state. Consequently, armed intervention and all other forms of interference or attempted threats against the personality of the State or against its political, economic and cultural element are condemned.

47 See LILLICH, R. B., "Economic Coercion and the 'New International Economic Order': A Second Look at some First Impressions", *Virginia Journal of International Law*, Vol. 16, No. 2 (1976), at p. 237.

48 See, *Les résolutions dans la formation du droit international du développment*, Geneva, Institut Universitaire de Hautes Etudes Internationales, 1971, (Etudes et Travaux de l'IUHEI No. 13) for discussions of this entire range of issues. See also, BROWNLIE, *Principles, op. cit.*, at pp. 695–696.

49 In that case the ICJ noted that:
" . . . The effect of consent to the text of such resolutions cannot be understood as merely that of a "reiteration or elucidation" of the treaty commitment undertaken in the Charter. On the contrary, it may be understood as an acceptance of the validity of the rule or set of rules declared by the resolution by themselves." (*ICJ Reports*, (1986), at p. 100. See also p. 107.)

> "2. No state may use or encourage the use of economic political or any other type of measures to coerce another State in order to obtain from it the subordination of the exercise of its sovereign rights or to secure from it advantages of any kind
>
> . . .
>
> "6. All states shall respect the right of self-determination and independence of peoples and nations, to be freely exercised without any foreign pressure . . ."[50]

Baldwin complains that the wording of UNGA resolutions on economic coercion goes too far. According to him such broad interpretations if taken literally would:

> "make compliance by powerful countries like the United States virtually impossible since almost any action of the United States could be viewed as interference or pressure. An increase in American interest rates, for example, may reverberate throughout the international economic system, thus 'interfering' with the 'economic elements' in other states and exerting pressure on them."[51]

In fact, the terms of those declarations do not truly lend themselves to this conclusion. What Baldwin seems to be suggesting is that there is a possible clash between the sovereign rights of states to control and use their economies and economic power as they must;[52] and the supposed right of states as outlined under the this declaration, to be free from outside pressure. Strictly speaking, there can be no conflict between two rights,[53] thus a more careful effort to define these rights (and

50 UNGA Resolution 2131(XX) of 21 December 1965, UN GAOR, Vol. 20, Supplement 14 at p. 11, UN Document A/6014 (1966).

51 BALDWIN, *Economic Statecraft, op. cit.*, at p. 343.

52 As THOMAS and THOMAS, *op. cit.* at p. 409 note the obvious on this point: "International law, for the most part, acknowledges that each state has a right to decide what economic policy it will follow in its dealings with other states, for the choice of a foreign economic policy which a government feels will best benefit its national economy is a matter ordinarily within the domestic jurisdiction of a state."

53 But see the discussion of the principle of abuse of rights, *infra*.

their limits) is needed so that the jurisdictional line can be drawn between them.[54]

3. Intentional Conduct as a Necessary Element in "Economic Intervention"

It should be understood that intervention, at least when it is effected by exclusively economic means, requires a deliberate act taken for the purpose of interfering with or threatening another state. In other words economic intervention can exist only where there is an "interventionist objective". This element of economic coercion analysis is indispensable to a proper understanding of this phenomenon.[55]

It is interesting to note that paragraph 6 of the Intervention Declaration (quoted above) speaks of certain rights of states "to be freely exercised without any foreign pressure." This language suggests that states have a "right" to be free from foreign pressure, but surely it cannot be intended to imply that states live in a vacuum. All states feel pressure from time to time due to the simple fact that they exist and act within the context of a larger international system (which includes other states), and it would be unreasonable to assert that states have a right to be free from even this background pressure.

Logically, and as a matter of legal theory, there would have to be a "duty" or "obligation" corresponding to the "right" mentioned in paragraph 6. That same paragraph does affirm that states are to "respect" the right it sets out, but the significance of this duty is subject to question since the extent of the "right" involved remains unclear. Paragraph 2 of that same Declaration attempts to articulate the obligation in the form of

54 PETERSMANN, ("International Economic Theory and International Economic Law: On the Tasks of a Legal Theory of International Economic Order", *op. cit.*, at p. 253), notes that "The legal protection of the autonomy of the international economic actors requires the mutual delimitation and avoidance of conflicting exercises of sovereign rights of states and of the economic freedoms of their nationals."

55 VIRALLY, (*op. cit.*, at p. 113), believes that considerations of the objective sought are an essential element of any legal evaluation of intervention:
"La finalité, habituellement, a peu d'importance sur la qualification d'une action juridique. Il en va un peu différemment en matière d'intervention, puisque celle-ci comporte une finalité dans sa définition même : elle a toujours pour objective de modifier le cours d'une affaire intéressant au premier chef un ou plusieurs Etats étrangers."

a prohibition. This section would prohibit the use of various measures "to coerce another state in order to obtain from it the subordination of the exercise of its sovereign rights or to secure from it advantages of any kind."[56] This language clearly applies only to deliberate or intentional acts done by one state to another.

Another more recent expression of both the putative right and the duty which would correspond to it can be found in the 1970 Declaration on Principles of International Law Concerning Friendly Relations and Cooperation Among States in Accordance with the Charter of the United Nations.[57] Like the Declaration on Intervention, it is supposed to be declaratory of principles of international law under the Charter. It contains language virtually identical to paragraphs 1 and 2 of the latter declaration (as quoted above). It also states that:

> "By virtue of the principle of equal rights and self-determination of peoples enshrined in the Charter, all peoples have the right freely to determine, without external interference, their political status and to pursue their economic, social and cultural development, and every State has the duty to respect this right in accordance with the provisions of the Charter."[58]

The true extent of both the right and the duty outlined in this paragraph depends upon the meaning of the term "external interference". It must be conceded that this term could be applied to any external factors which might impede the freedom of choice and action of a state, and not only to deliberate actions by other states. Nevertheless, freedom from external inter-

56 At the beginning of Chapter III, *supra* it was suggested that the semantic line between "pressure" and "coercion" should correspond to the normative threshold of illegality. When discussing international economic coercion it seems logical to draw the semantic and normative lines at the same place. The Intervention Declaration does not recognize any conceptual distinction between "coercion" and "pressure". While it refers to a "right" of states to be free from pressure, this is paired with an "obligation" not to coerce. Although this use of language may be imprecise, it is more or less consistent with the common usage of these terms. It is sufficient to note here that since the Intervention Declaration is concerned with the rights of states under international law, it would arguably have been more appropriate to refer only to "coercion".

57 UNGA Resolution 2625(XXV) of 24 October 1970, UN GAOR, Vol. 25, Supplement 28, at pp. 121, 123, UN Document A/8028 (1971).

58 *loc. cit.*

ference cannot be taken to imply freedom from external reality. Thus the only reasonable interpretation will limit this declaration to intentional conduct or "deliberate" interference.[59]

In 1974 the UNGA passed the Charter of Economic Rights and Duties of States in an attempt to affirm and strengthen certain principles which were intended to form the basis of a New International Economic Order.[60] Article 32 of that document incorporates language on economic coercion which had already appeared in the 1966 Intervention Declaration.

> "Article 32. No State may use or encourage the use of economic, political or any other type of measures to coerce another State *in order to* obtain from it the subordination of the exercise of its sovereign rights." (emphasis added)

Once again, this language seems to proscribe only deliberate conduct. In effect it defines what we might refer to as a tainted interventionist objective.

What all of this suggests is that when we attempt to distinguish simple conflicts of economic interest from the economic coercion which may constitute intervention, one likely element of the latter is the element of intent, or more specifically of a coercive objective. The difficulty lies in defining that class of objectives which it might be illegal to pursue by economic means, and in identifying the other necessary element or elements which we might expect to characterize illegal economic intervention.[61] What if the objective of the sending state were to gain complete control over the target state's government and to usurp all of its prerogatives and authority? If it succeeded in this objective by economic means it would be ludicrous to deny that intervention had occurred. Unfortunately the principle is much more difficult to apply in real-life situations where the objectives of men and governments are rarely so clear.

59 In an interdependent world states should not throw their weight around totally oblivious to the consequences for other states, and principles of international law (such as the obligation of good neighborliness) do proscribe some conduct which causes harm to other states even where there is no intent to intervene. Even when proscribed though, acts not deliberately aimed at causing interference would not constitute intervention unless the use of force was involved.

60 UNGA Resolution 3281 (XXIX) of 12 December 1974, UN GAOR, Vol. 29, Supplement 31, at p. 50, UN Document A/9631.

61 The necessity for a certain constraining effect, in addition to a coercive purpose or objective will be discussed below.

Derek Bowett has drawn an analogy between international economic coercion and the English law tort of "economic conspiracy", a necessary element of which "is that the defendant's predominant purpose or motive be to cause injury to the plaintiff rather than to advance or protect his own economic interests."[62] Applying a variation of this same principle we could define international economic measures as illegal only if they were taken for a predominantly political objective. Bowett suggests that "once a State is allowed to coerce in the furtherance of its political goals, there is little point in even attempting legally to restrict economic coercion."[63]

But Ibrahim Shihata has argued that international law does not, and indeed should not, condemn all economic measures taken by one state with the intent to influence the political policies of another state or group of states. He maintains that "the prohibition on the use of economic coercion should be realistically limited to the use by states of economic measures for achieving illegitimate purposes."[64] This seems entirely reasonable, but it still leaves open the question of which purposes should be considered illegitimate. What criteria of legitimacy are to be applied, and who will have the authority to define the legitimate uses of this weapon?[65]

Shihata's solution is to limit the prohibition "to measures involving the subordination of sovereign rights of other states, and not merely seeking some advantage from them."[66] Interestingly enough this is the same standard articulated in Article 32 of the Charter of Economic Rights and Duties of States (quoted above). While this approach would answer some objections to the effect that earlier UNGA declarations on the subject are excessively broad, the standard still suffers from the problems of vagueness we have discussed above. As always, disagreement remains about the exact extent of the "sovereign rights" of states.

62 BOWETT, D. W., "International Law and Economic Coercion", *Virginia Journal of International Law*, Vol. 16, (1975–1976), at p. 249.

63 *loc. cit.*

64 SHIHATA, I. F. I., "Destination Embargo of Arab Oil: Its Legality under International Law", *American Journal of International Law*, Vol. 68, No. 4 (1974), at p. 619.

65 The possible role of the UNGA in justifying use of the economic weapon is discussed later in this chapter.

66 SHIHATA, *op. cit.* at p. 617.

One of Shihata's most important points is that a militarily weak state might find economic measures to be the only effective countermeasures it can take when its rights are being violated.[67] As will be discussed below, states may have recourse to economic measures whenever countermeasures are justified under international law. The use of economic measures of self-defense or of reprisal, for example, can be legal even though their use might under normal circumstances be seen as a deliberate and illegal act of intervention.[68]

4. The OAS Charter and Non-Intervention

Before drawing any final conclusions concerning the applicability of the non-intervention principle to economic measures, the Charter of the Organization of American States (OAS) should be considered. The US, which refused to support the language prohibiting economic coercion in the 1974 Charter of Economic Rights and Duties of States, has nonetheless accepted binding treaty language to the same effect as a member of the OAS.[69] The OAS Charter incorporates very specific language affirming the illegality of economic intervention. This reflects the very broad conception of state sovereignty which is generally held by Latin American jurists. The relevant Articles read as follows:

> "Article 18
> No state or group of states has the right to intervene, directly or indirectly, for any reason whatever, in the internal or external affairs of any other state. The foregoing principle prohibits not only armed force but also any other form of interference or attempted threat against the personality of the state or against its political economic and cultural elements.

67 See *Ibid.*, pp. 591–627.

68 See the discussion of measures of self-defense and of economic reprisals, *infra* this same chapter.

69 In the UNGA's Second Committee an article by article vote was taken on the Charter of Economic Rights and Duties of States. The vote on Article 32 (quoted above) was 119 for, none against, with 11 countries abstaining (including the US and a number of other Western states). See *I.L.M.* Vol. 14, (1975), at p. 265. The US was also among those countries which were opposed to including economic measures in the UNGA's Definition of Aggression, *op. cit.* As has been mentioned above, that resolution does not include economic measures within the Definition of Aggression.

> "Article 19
> No state may use or encourage the use of coercive measures of an economic or political character in order to force the sovereign will of another state and obtain from it advantages of any kind."[70]

This appears to be a definite and unequivocal[71] prohibition of any deliberate coercive use of economic measures against another state. As between states which are parties to the OAS Charter (including, of course, the US) there should be little doubt about the illegality of economic coercion or about its characterization as intervention.

5. A Proposed Standard of Non-Intervention Applicable to the Use of Economic Coercion

States frequently engage in economic activity which they know is likely to have an adverse effect upon other states, but given the prevalence of this practice it would make little sense to classify all such behavior as illegal. It is therefore necessary to identify those elements which delimit the definition of illegal economic intervention. An earlier section of this Chapter established that an illegitimate interventionist objective is one of those elements which must be present, but it is not the only such element. There must also be a certain effect upon the target of the intervention

To understand why this is so consider the following attempt to apply both the "use of force analysis" and "non-intervention analysis" to a hypothetical case of economic coercion. Suppose that State A tries to coerce State B through economic means in order to obtain some type of political concessions from it, but State A's economic power turns out to be so inadequate that

70 Charter of the Organization of American States, done at Bogota, 30 April 1948, *U.N.T.S.*, Vol. 119, (1952), pp. 3–97; Protocol of Amendment done at Buenos Aires, 27 February 1967, *U.N.T.S.*, Vol. 721, (1970), pp. 266–389. These two articles originally appeared as articles 15 and 16 of the OAS Charter. While these articles were not changed when the OAS Charter was revised in 1970, they were renumbered as articles 18 and 19.

71 At least one exception must nonetheless be implied. There can be little doubt that UN authorized collective measures are intended to be exempt from the general prohibition expressed here. See the discussion of authorization by a competent international body as a justification for the application of economic measures of coercion, *infra*.

nothing is felt by the target state. Were this to be seen as a use of "economic force" then the fact that the action was ineffective might not prevent it from being illegal. An ineffective use of force is as illegal as an effective use of force if directed against the territorial integrity or political independence of another state.[72] If it is seen as attempted intervention, the conclusion will be different.

There are some types of actions which can, under certain circumstances, constitute illegal intervention, but which are considered to do so only when some type of threshold of effect has been crossed.[73] In this hypothetical example, where the effect of the attempted coercion is zero, it is clear that threshold has not been crossed.

It could, of course, be argued that economic intervention is illegal regardless of whether it is effective, i.e. that "attempted intervention" is illegal under international law. States are under a legal obligation not to intervene in each others affairs through economic or other means, but does a wholly ineffective attempt at economic intervention constitute a breach of that legal obligation and therefore an internationally wrongful act?

Consider the consequences of imposing legal responsibility upon a state for such an attempt. To do so might encourage

72 If, for example, (paralleling the example above), one state tries to coerce another through the use of armed force, and launches a bombing raid on the territory of the other, this constitutes an illegal use of force even if those bombs fall harmlessly onto an unpopulated desert.

73 That threshold has been described in various ways. OPPERMANN, (*op. cit.*, at p. 235), notes that:
"Even if domestic affairs are touched in a given situation, the measure of the acting state can only be qualified as illegal interference if a certain degree of coercion is employed. Mere discussion and even propaganda are not unlawful if they do not result in very direct pressure on the victim."
"SCHRÖDER, *op. cit.* at p. 360 speaking of the principle of non-intervention, quotes from Article 32 of the Charter of Economic Rights and Duties of States in describing a rather vague threshold:
" . . . The principle can be invoked only if 'the subordination of the exercise of sovereign rights' has occurred. In other words, interference in the economic field must be coercive or 'dictatorial'."
THOMAS and THOMAS, (*op. cit.*, at p. 274), clearly disagree, and maintain that no actual effect is needed for what they refer to as "intervention by propaganda":
" . . . Thus if the end in view of foreign propaganda indicates a clear and present danger to the local form of government, *independent of the probability that success will be achieved in* that end, and independent of the nature of the symbols used, the foreign government sponsoring such propaganda has committed an international delict." (emphasis added)

states to level charges of illegal economic intervention in polemical exchanges with their adversaries even when no true problem had been encountered. This would not serve any positive purpose. Where the actual effect is absent or *de minimis,* the concept of illegal economic intervention does not apply.

If properly applied, the principle of non-intervention is quite suitable for legally regulating the use of economic coercion. Characterizing some forms of economic coercion as illegal intervention would not open the door to a military response thereby creating more problems than it would solve, nor would it prevent states from managing their internal economic policies to their own benefit. Only when an interventionist, and illegally coercive motive is present should there be any question of illegality, and even then, this bad motive alone does not constitute an illegal intervention. Illegal economic intervention should be found only where there is a sufficiently noxious and dictatorial combination of intent by the sender state to coerce, together with an effect truly threatening to the independence or freedom of action of the target state. The standard which is proposed here[74] can be justified as appropriate in light of present day circumstances,[75] and it is also consistent with the international consensus reflected in the UNGA resolutions discussed above.

74 FUKATSU, E., "Coercion and the Theory of Sanctions in International Law", *op. cit.,* at p.1194, suggests that three criteria be applied to distinguish permissible from impermissible economic conduct by states *in imposing sanctions.* Two of these, purpose or intent, and outcome or consequences, correspond to the standard set out in this study. His third criterion, which concerns the degree and extent of conduct, is more applicable to the specific situation he discusses (economic measures of law enforcement) than to the general issue which is being discussed here of what legal limits there may be upon economic intervention.

75 Noting the need for redefining concepts in a changing international environment Harold Lasswell (LASSWELL, H.D., *Politics: Who Gets What, When, How,* New York, Meridian Books, 1958, (Twelfth printing 1972), at pp. 7–8), once wrote that:
"Concepts for the study of influence must be changed or invented when influence is sought by novel means or under changed conditions. In epochs of rapid development, there is a need to reassess the relevance of intellectual effort."

C. FACTORS WHICH MAY JUSTIFY THE USE OF ECONOMIC METHODS OF COERCION

Although the use of economic methods of coercion can sometimes violate the principle of non-intervention, certain special circumstances can nonetheless justify the use of such methods. Those which concern only unilateral action can be distinguished from those which involve collective decision-making and/or multilateral action. The two types of justifying circumstances will therefore be discussed separately below.

1. Multilateral Authorization and/or Collective Action

Whatever the legal restrictions upon the use of unilateral economic coercion, it is clear that collective economic measures of a coercive nature can legally be imposed by the United Nations. The economic sanctions which were applied against the Rhodesian regime after the Unilateral Declaration of Independence were specifically authorized by the UN Security Council according to the terms of the Charter, and therefore could not be characterized as illegal. The same goes for the economic sanctions imposed against Iraq after its invasion of Kuwait. UN member states, as parties to the Charter, can be considered to have consented to collective economic intervention by the UN, whenever that intervention takes the form of measures decided upon according to Article 41 of the Charter. It is less clear, however, whether a General Assembly resolution could legally authorize otherwise unlawful acts of economic coercion.[76]

Since the UNSC does have the right to intervene under articles 41 and 42, it can be argued that under the Charter it is not intervention as such that is proscribed, but only unilateral intervention. Following this line of reasoning some have concluded that any intervention which has been authorized or legitimized by either the UNSC or the UNGA is permissible.[77]

It is generally accepted today that "in the case of a breach of

76 SEIDL-HOHENVELDERN, ("The United Nations and Economic Coercion", *Revue Belge de Droit International*, Vol. 18, (1984–1985 – 1), at p. 13), concludes that "The legality of any exercise of economic coercion should be beyond any doubt only if the measures concerned were ordered in so many words by the Security Council pursuant to Art. 41 of the U.N. Charter."

77 See, CHIMNI, B.S., "Towards a Third World Approach to Non-Intervention: Through the Labyrinth of Western Doctrine", *Indian Journal of International Law*, Vol. 20, No. 2, (1980), at p. 263.

the peace or act of aggression," and when certain other conditions have been met, (including the inability of the UNSC to act due to use of the veto), the UNGA can, pursuant to the Uniting for Peace formula, recommend that collective measures be taken and that these measures may include the use of armed force when necessary.[78] The UNGA has in fact used this formula to recommend the use of armed force in the past, and such uses of force have not been seen as a violation of the Charter. Article 2(4) of the Charter sets out a general prohibition upon the threat or use of force by states acting outside of the organization, but this does not necessarily prohibit the use of collective measures by the UN even if they are authorized by the UNGA instead of by the Security Council.[79]

Nonetheless, there are very definite grounds for questioning the UNGA's authority to authorize such measures. The International Court of Justice, in its Advisory Opinion in the *Certain Expenses* case has expressed the view that "it is the Security Council which exclusively, may order coercive action".[80]

The question of the UNGA's authority to validate collective economic intervention should be viewed in the context of the expanding jurisdiction of the UNGA. The role of the UNGA has grown not only because of the paralysis of the UNSC caused by the veto, but also because of a fundamental change which has occurred in the membership of the UN. This change resulted from the process of decolonization; a process which the UNGA itself did much to accelerate through the use of

78 This formula applies only when (1) The Security Council has failed to exercise its primary responsibility for the maintenance of international peace and security, (2) This failure is due to the lack of unanimity of the permanent members of the Security Council, (3) there appears to be a breach of the peace, or act of aggression, and (4) the Security Council has already attempted to deal with the issue. See, REICHER, H., "The Uniting for Peace Resolution on the Thirtieth Anniversary of its Passage", *Columbia Journal of Transnational Law*, Vol. 20, No. 1, (1981), at pp. 9–16; and the "Uniting for Peace Resolution", Resolution 377A (V), 3 November 1950, UN GAOR, 5th Session, Supplement No. 20, UN Doc. A/1775, paragraph 1.

79 See, REICHER, H., *op. cit.*, at p. 44.

80 It did so in the context of an examination of the respective functions of the General Assembly and the Security Council under the UN Charter. The Court noted that while the Security Council has *primary* responsibility for the maintenance of international peace and security, that responsibility is not exclusive, and therefore the General Assembly is entitled to recommend measures short of enforcement action. See, International Court of Justice, Advisory Opinion on Certain Expenses of the United Nations, 20 July, 1962, *ICJ Reports*, at p. 163.

declarations and other resolutions. The newly independent states of the developing world, who are the newest members of the UN, rely upon the UNGA to reflect their special concerns in a way that the UNSC does not.

While it is true that the Charter does not explicitly grant to the UNGA the power to authorize coercive economic measures, it does empower that organ to make recommendations on matters relating to the maintenance of international peace and security.[81] Were such a recommendation to call for economic measures to be taken against a target state that recommendation would be legally significant, especially if passed by an overwhelming majority. Perhaps a distinction should be made between the measures "authorized" by the UNSC and those "collectively legitimized" by the UNGA.[82] Although this legitimization may be more moral than legal, it does have a legal aspect.[83] Many states have imposed economic sanctions against South Africa in protest against that country's apartheid policies, and few recognize the present South African government's claim that these sanctions constitute illegal economic intervention. One argument for the legality of these sanctions is based on UNGA resolutions[84] which request both states and international organizations to withhold assistance to the government of South Africa until it renounces policies of racial discrimination.

We must also consider whether regional organizations (such as the Organization of American States) and other types of international organizations (such as the Organization of Arab Petroleum Exporting States) might be competent to authorize economic measures of coercion by their members. Once again, the question is relevant only to situations where the economic measures being applied would otherwise be illegal. If not, then there is, legally speaking, no need for the authorization of any international agency.

81 Charter of the United Nations, Article 11.

82 See CLAUDE, I.L. Jr., "Collective legitimization as a Political Function of the United Nations", *International Organization*, Vol. 20, (1966), at pp. 367–379.

83 See, *Ibid.*, *loc. cit.*, and SCHERMERS, H. G., *International Institutional Law*, Alphen aan den Rijn, The Netherlands, Sijthoff & Noordhoff, (1980), at p. 607.

84 Cf. "Implementation of the Declaration on the Granting of Independence to Colonial Peoples and Territories", Resolution 2105 (XX) of 20 December 1965, UN GAOR 20th Session, Supplement No. 14, UN Document A/6014. This resolution is discussed in another context in Chapter VI, *infra*.

Article 53 of the Charter states that:

> "The Security Council shall when appropriate, utilize such regional arrangements or agencies for enforcement action under its authority. But no enforcement action shall be taken under regional arrangements or by regional agencies without the authorization of the Security Council . . ."

This language makes it clear that even where action by a regional organization is involved, the authorization of the UNSC is needed for any "enforcement action." The question remains as to whether collective economic measures constitute enforcement action. Surely, such measures are, or at least can be, "coercive", and according to the equally authoritative French text, which uses the term "*action coercitive*" in place of "enforcement action", any coercive measures require the authorization of the UNSC. Even setting aside the French text, the records of the San Francisco Conference strongly suggest that the term "enforcement action" refers to any measures that the UNSC can take under Articles 41 and 42, and this includes economic sanctions.[85] And, as we have seen above, the International Court of Justice has expressed the view that "it is the Security Council which exclusively, may order coercive action".[86]

On the basis of these various factors Bowett and others have concluded that "sanctions, whether military or economic, can be taken only by the Security Council or by a regional organization, pursuant to Security Council authorization".[87] In their view, only the UNSC can authorize collective economic measures which would otherwise be illegal, unless those measures can be independently justified as an allowed exception such as self-defense.[88] But given the expanding role of the UNGA, as discussed above, this seems to be an unnecessarily restrictive conclusion. In appropriate circumstances a clear mandate from the UNGA should be sufficient to legitimize the collective use of economic measures.[89]

85 U.N.C.I.O. Documents, *op. cit.*, at pp. 507–508.
86 International Court of Justice, Advisory Opinion on Certain Expenses of the United Nations, *op. cit.* at p. 163.
87 BOWETT, "Reprisals", *op. cit.*, at p. 7; BEIRLAEN, op. cit., at p. 73.
88 See the discussion of self-defense, *infra*, this Chapter.
89 One UNGA resolution (referred to above) based its call for economic measures against the government of South Africa upon a determination that the

2. Unilateral Action

a) Self Defense

It should also be possible to justify either unilateral or multilateral economic measures when they are taken in self-defense. Article 51 of the Charter guarantees members of the UN the right of self-defense, whether individual or collective, against armed attack. This right includes the right to use force in self-defense and is thus an express limitation upon the prohibition on the use of force found in Article 2(4) of the Charter.[90] If armed measures of self-defense are sometimes justified, clearly economic measures of self-defense can be justified as well.[91] There are, of course, a number of conditions which must be met before this right can be exercised even in cases of armed attack. In order to be legally justified, the use of force in self-defense must be reasonable and proportionate to what is needed to meet the threat, and acts may be justified as necessary for self-defense only while the danger is still present.[92] Furthermore, when a third state exercises the right of collective self-defense, the state for whose benefit the right is invoked must declare itself to be the victim of an armed attack and must request the assistance of the third state claiming this right.[93]

The use of economic measures is not legally equivalent to the use of force and therefore one could argue that the conditions governing their use in self defense should not be as strict as those governing the use of force in self defense. But if the use of these measures is to be justified according to the traditional

---

continuation of the policy of apartheid threatened international peace and security and also constituted a "crime against humanity." See, "Implementation of the Declaration on the Granting of Independence to Colonial Peoples and Territories", Resolution 2105 (XX) of 20 December 1965, UN GAOR 20th Session, Supplement No. 14, UN Document A/6014.

90 KELSEN, *op. cit.* at p. 61.

91 SHIHATA, argues that the Arab oil-exporting states had exhausted all other remedies in their attempt to regain Arab lands seized by Israel in the 1967 war. See SHIHATA, I. F. I., *op. cit.*, pp. 591–627.

92 KELSEN, for example, (*op. cit.* at p. 80) notes that "the danger that gives rise to the right of self-defense must be immediate and of such a nature as to leave no reasonable possibility for recourse to alternative means of protection." He goes on to discuss the requirement of proportionality as well.

93 International Court of Justice, Military and Paramilitary Activities in and Against Nicaragua, *ICJ Reports*, (1986), at pp. 104–105.

right of self-defense then the traditional conditions attached to that right must be met.

b) Economic Reprisals

Although the imposition by one state of certain types of economic measures against another state may sometimes constitute illegal intervention, it might be possible to justify such measures as a form of reprisal even when the immediate danger is past. Reprisals have been defined as "acts which, although normally illegal, are exceptionally permitted as reaction of one state against a violation of its rights by another state."[94] Reprisals are justified only if three conditions have been met.[95] It is generally agreed that there must have been prior wrong conduct by the target state against the state exercising the reprisals, other remedies must have been exhausted, and the actions in reprisal must be proportionate to the original wrong.[96]

Because economic reprisals do not involve the use of force they are less likely to lead to an escalation of violence than are armed reprisals. For the same reason, economic reprisals are in general less likely to be disproportionate.

c) Economic Retorsion

To speak of economic countermeasures as retorsion is, in effect, to suggest that there is no rule of international law which prohibits their use. Such measures could be classified as a form of retorsion only if they were not in themselves illegal. Retorsion can be defined as "an unfriendly, uncourteous or unfair act in reply to another unfriendly uncourteous or unfair act."[97] Insofar as measures are not illegal, they need no legal justification, but

94 KELSEN, *op. cit.* at p. 21.

95 See, BOWETT, *Reprisals op. cit.* at p. 9–10.

96 Certain other conditions have sometimes been mentioned. BEIRLAEN, A., "Economic Coercion and Justifying Circumstances", *Revue Belge de Droit International*, Vol. 18, (1984–1985 – 1), at pp. 62, 70, and 71, also affirms that reprisals must not consist of acts prohibited by *jus in bello*; that they should come to an end as soon as reparation of the unlawful act has occurred (this may be implicit in the requirement of proportionality); that reprisals should only be taken by competent state organs; and that while nationals of the delinquent state may be the objects of reprisals, reprisals are not permitted against a state for actions undertaken by its national subjects.

97 BEIRLAEN, *op. cit.* at p. 63.

they may sometimes be justified on a more political level as retorsion.

d) Humanitarian Intervention

Even if economic measures can constitute illegal intervention, they might under certain circumstances be considered to be justifiable as humanitarian intervention. There is considerable controversy about the status of humanitarian intervention in international law. While there is 19th century authority for the doctrine, some believe that international law does not presently permit humanitarian intervention, that it is inconsistent with the UN Charter, and that in any case the doctrine is undesirable because it would be subject to wide abuse.[98] Others insist that humanitarian intervention is presently authorized by international law, at least in cases where the UN fails to act.[99]

There is also uncertainty about the scope of the doctrine. Sometimes it is said to justify only action to protect or rescue nationals of the intervening power, as a sort of extended application of the right to self-defense.[100] Another view is that it may apply whenever there is an "immediate and extensive threat to fundamental human rights, particularly a threat of widespread loss of human life".[101]

As the above comments indicate, at present there is no real consensus concerning this doctrine and whether it constitutes

98 See, BROWNLIE, I., "Thoughts on Kind-Hearted Gunmen", in LILLICH, R.B. (ed.), *Humanitarian Intervention and the United Nations*, Charlottesville, University Press of Virginia, 1973, at pp. 139–148.

99 See REISMAN, M., (with the collaboration of M. S. MCDOUGAL), "Humanitarian Intervention to Protect the Ibos", in LILLICH, R.B. (ed.), *Humanitarian Intervention and the United Nations, op. cit.*, pp. 167–195.

100 AKEHURST, M., ("Humanitarian Intervention", in BULL, H. (ed.), *Intervention and World Politics, op. cit.* at pp. 102, 106–107), concludes that the right to self-defense under Article 51 of the Charter does not provide any justification or basis for humanitarian intervention. BOWETT, D., (*Self-Defense in International Law, op. cit.* at pp. 184–193, and 91–94), has argued that this type of intervention can be justified as a form of self-defense.

101 MOORE, J.N., "The Control of Foreign Intervention in Internal Conflict", *Virginia Journal of International Law*, Vol. 9, (1969), at p. 264.

part of positive international law.[102] Nonetheless it is sometimes invoked to justify intervention by one state on the territory of another.[103] One contemporary example of a unilateral attempt to use economic intervention to serve humanitarian purposes is the US policy of disfavoring development aid flows to governments held responsible for systematic violations of human rights.[104] Multilaterally authorized actions have been discussed above, and these too can involve the use of economic measures for a humanitarian purpose.

In spite of the many questions about humanitarian intervention, it should be easier to justify "economic intervention" under this doctrine than armed intervention. The risks of intervention are not the same when no use of military force is involved.

D. CONCLUSIONS

1. The Legality of Using Economic Coercion under General International Law

As the UNGA resolutions discussed above indicate, there does appear to be an emerging international consensus that economic coercion does, or at least can, constitute illegal intervention. Can one conclude on the basis of the UN Charter and various interpretative resolutions of the General Assembly that "economic intervention" is illegal under general international law?

It must be recalled that the consensus on the illegality of

102 Many diverging views on that doctrine were expressed at a two day conference on March 11–12, 1972 at the University of Virginia. The conference proceedings have been published as LILLICH, R.B. (ed), *Humanitarian Intervention and the United Nations, op. cit.* For a summary of the views expressed see one of the essays in that volume entitled "Humanitarian Intervention: The View from Charlottesville", by T.J. FARER. For a survey of statements on humanitarian intervention by national delegates to the UN, which indicates widespread rejection of that doctrine by most states, see FONTEYNE, *op. cit.*, at pp. 205–218.

103 Cf. for example the 1960 Belgian intervention in the Congo, the 1965 US intervention in the Dominican Republic, the 1976 Israeli raid on Entebbe airport in Uganda, and the US invasion of Grenada in 1983.

104 For example the "Harkin Amendment" which generally prohibits US foreign assistance from being sent to countries which are found to be systematic and gross violators of human rights. Foreign Assistance Act of 1961, PL 87-195, Sec. 116, 22 USC 2151 note (Supp. II 1978) (added by International Development and Food Assistance Act of 1975), PL 94-161, Sec. 310, 89 Stat. 849 as subsequently amended.

economic coercion is not total, and the practice of states (both those participating in that consensus and those outside of it) suggests that they often do not consider such conduct to be illegal. Sometimes those very states which have condemned the use of economic coercion on one day may soon thereafter seem all to anxious to practice it themselves. Furthermore, the language of UNGA resolutions concerning economic coercion is too broad. Only if that language is read narrowly so as to include only intentionally coercive conduct does it begin to resemble a workable normative standard.

States condemn economic coercion in the abstract, but are in practice hesitant to dispense with what they may see as their "sovereign right" to use it as a foreign policy tool in support of favored values. Developing countries, sensing their own vulnerability to economic measures, oppose economic coercion, but support the idea of permanent sovereignty over natural resources and by implication the right of commodity producing countries to withhold their resources from the international marketplace.

For the most part the major industrialized Western countries consider it inconceivable that international law could limit their right to give or withhold bilateral aid subject to whatever conditions they may wish to impose. Yet when a different form of economic coercion affected their oil supplies during the Arab oil embargo many of these same countries complained bitterly. The two situations can in no way be equated, but taken together they help to demonstrate the difficulties in attempting to generalize about a supposed international consensus on the illegality of measures of economic coercion.

It does seem that in some cases the use of economic coercion can constitute illegal intervention under customary international law; particularly where there is a deliberate and truly threatening attempt to subordinate the sovereign rights of the target. In many cases, however, the evidence of coercive intent may be only circumstantial or inconclusive. Even in cases where there is no doubt about the interventionistic intent of the sender state, the effect upon the target may be insubstantial, raising questions about whether any effective intervention has occurred. In other cases, one of the justifications discussed above may be applicable. Because of these limitations only in a rather limited number of cases will it be possible to identify specific measures of economic coercion as clearly illegal.[105]

2. The Legality of Using the "Aid Weapon"

It is, as we have seen, quite difficult to identify and apply workable standards concerning the definition of illegal economic coercion. Attempting to apply such standards to the use of the "aid weapon" is especially problematic. Unless one is willing to consider the actual *quid pro quo*[106] behind international aid agreements to be illegal intervention, it is hard to escape the conclusion that any conditions placed upon bilateral aid by the donor are voluntarily consented to by the recipient.

Thomas and Thomas, two authors who generally favor a very broad view of intervention, admit that even where the conditions of aid touch on the internal or external affairs of the recipient, the effect may only constitute interference and not illegal intervention.[107] They nonetheless conclude that under

105 Writing in 1971, Wolfgang Friedmann described the state of the law on intervention and economic coercion as of that time as follows, (FRIEDMANN, W., "Intervention and International Law", at p. 55 in *Intervention in International Politics*, edited by JACQUET, L. G. M., pp. 40–68. The Hague, Netherlands Institute of International Affairs, 1971):
"In the present state of international law, it would seem that only physical coercion, lack of legal or political freedom of decision-making, and perhaps exceptional situations where an economic emergency, such as a national famine or disease, would be exploited by the donor for the imposition of oppressive conditions, could be characterized as illegal forms of economic intervention."
SEIDL-HOHENVELDERN, (*op. cit.*, at p. 14), also favors a sparing application of the non-intervention principle to economic coercion. He suggests that:
" . . . any attempt to restrict the sue (sic) of economic force beyond the most serious cases of intervention would be counterproductive. Larger states often consider even the prohibition on the use of armed force hardly compatible with their interests . . . . If stronger states . . . [were to be] . . . deprived even of their means of economic retaliation, or to see their use submitted to severe restrictions, I would be afraid that they would then brush aside as unrealistic any rule attempting to restrict their freedom of action and would resort even to armed force in defence of their rights. *The relative freedom in the recourse to the use of economic force thus acts as a safety valve.*" (emphasis added)

106 See the next footnote, *infra*. for comments by Thomas and Thomas on the significance of the *quid pro quo* inducement which motivates recipient states to accept the conditions often attached to international financial aid.

107 THOMAS and THOMAS, (*op. cit.*, at p. 96), stress this distinction:
"This difference between intervention and interference must be kept clearly in mind. *Some interference in the affairs of states is created of necessity by treaties*

certain circumstances the cutting off of aid would constitute legally proscribed intervention, with the motive of the aid cutoff being the criteria of distinction.[108]

While it is certainly appropriate to take probable motives into consideration in the analysis of non-violent intervention, in the case of economic intervention it would be absurd to hold a state responsible for its bad intentions alone. An improper motive is a necessary but not a sufficient condition of illegal economic intervention, and any standard which judges such intervention illegal solely on the basis of such a motive is clearly unworkable. For this reason, the standard of economic intervention proposed in this chapter would require that there be a certain degree of harmful effect in addition to the interventionist intent.

Applying this standard to the use of bilateral aid as an instrument of pressure raises certain special difficulties. Although an argument can easily be made, applying the criteria discussed above, to the effect that some types of aid cutoffs should be considered to be illegal intervention, it is not appropriate to

---

whereby states bind themselves to take certain measures having to do with their internal or external affairs. For example, by the Marshall Plan the United States made funds available to certain European states, but upon condition that the states receiving the funds should co-operate with other participating nations to make efficient and practical use of their individual resources, to promote industrial and agricultural production within their borders, to stabilize their currencies, to balance their budgets as soon as possible, etc. Here there was interference, but the states were free to accept or reject this financial aid as they saw fit. *No pressure was brought to force them to accept the conditions other than the inducement, the quid pro quo, and since coercive pressure was not present there was no intervention*. The offer to enter into a treaty must always contain certain persuasive or inducing elements for the benefit of the parties. When, because of these inducements, a state agrees to perform or restrain from performing an act, it has not abandoned its sovereign rights by coercion, but rather has exercised its sovereign right to conclude treaties – so long, let it be emphasized, as the other state does not threaten to take other action of a hurtful nature in case the treaty is not entered into." (emphasis added)

108 They suggest, (*Ibid*. at p. 411), that:
" . . . A nation may refuse to grant public loans to another state; [or use other methods of public finance affecting other states] . . . None of these activities is intervention under general international law *if it is engaged in for strictly national purposes* such as increasing governmental revenues, or maintaining a government's solvency. But if the activity is undertaken as a measure of economic compulsion or pressure in order to dictate the policy of another state, there is an invasion of the protected sphere of interests of that state and it becomes intervention." (emphasis added)
Note that what they describe as "strictly national purposes" might better be described as "strictly national *economic* purposes".

apply a motive and effect test, such as the one discussed above, to the use of the aid weapon. For now, the distribution of bilateral aid remains a voluntary and discretionary activity on behalf of the donor state, and it would be unwise to attempt to extend the principle of non-intervention into this realm. To do so might have the unintended and undesirable effect of discouraging further flows of aid from the donor countries.

The situation is different, however, when aid is given through the multilateral structure of an international organization such as the World Bank. The next chapter examines some of the principles of international institutional law which make it inappropriate for a donor state to make unilateral use of the World Bank's multilateral aid programs as an instrument of economic coercion.

5

INTERNATIONAL INSTITUTIONAL LAW AND POSSIBLE BASES FOR RESTRICTING THE USES OF VOTING POWER WITHIN THE BANK

A. THE FEASIBILITY OF SUCH RESTRICTIONS

1. Definition of International Institutional Law

The term "international institutional law" can be applied to certain aspects of what is more commonly referred to as "the law of international organizations." H.G. Schermers, notes that "International institutional law is regarded . . . as embracing, not only the structure of international organizations, but also the rules concerning their operation."[1] He also points out that the law of international organizations is somewhat broader since it may refer to rules of law formulated by those organizations as well as to the more purely institutional matters mentioned above.[2]

The proliferation of international agencies, especially since the end of the Second World War, has inevitably entailed the development of concepts, both legal and political, which apply to their structure and organization. It is, of course, the legal aspect which is our focus here. Given the institutional differences between the various international organizations, it may be wondered whether there are sufficient common elements to form a more or less unified body of international institutional

1 SCHERMERS, H.G., *International Institutional Law*, Alphen aan de Rijn, The Netherlands, Sijthoff & Noordhoff International Publishers B.V., (1980), at p. 2.
2 *loc. cit.*

law.[3] In fact, to speak of international institutional law is not at all to deny the great diversity among IGO structures. The point is that there are a number of common institutional features shared by many if not all of these organizations. This is because certain problems, such as those involving membership, decision-making and voting, relations between different organs, and relations between organs and members, are common to most IGOs.[4] Furthermore, the international system in which these different organizations must operate is the same. The solutions worked out by one organization will tend to influence future developments within others, especially those with similar functions and with substantially identical membership. Member states will tend to expect, and thus to create, a certain degree of "parallel development" within different organizations.[5]

It is appropriate to ask whether international institutional law should be considered as a category of law separate from public international law in general. One cannot pretend that all of the concepts of international institutional law are new ones. This law draws on concepts of municipal constitutional law, of public international law and of corporate or company law to name but a few. In addition, certain new rules, principles and procedures have been developed by the different agencies.

2. The Idea of Restrictions Upon the Use of Voting Power

The introduction to this study (Chapter 1) briefly reviewed the distribution of voting power within the World Bank, and noted that certain industrialized states, especially the US, have legally been granted the lion's share of the voting power in the Bank. The issue which remains to be discussed is one which is very

3 Reuter acknowledges that the political significance of the phenomenon of international organization is somewhat ambiguous, and that the significance ("portée") of any general theory of international organization remains limited; nonetheless, he outlines just such a general theory. See REUTER, P. *Institutions internationales*, Paris, Presses Universitaires de France, (1967), at p. 204, and p. 205 where he observes that:
"sur un plan juridique, il y a certain problèmes et certain notions qui sont communs à toutes les organizations ou à de larges groupes d'organizations; d'autre part, sur un plan de science politique, seule une vue d'ensemble de la matière permet d'en dégager les traits essentiels."

4 Cf. for example BOWETT, D., *The Law of International Institutions*, 3rd edition, London, Stevens & Sons, (1975), Part Four of which (pp. 299–373) is entirely devoted to "Common Institutional Problems".

5 SCHERMERS, *op. cit.* at p. 1.

seldom raised, i.e. what legal restrictions, if any, apply to the use of that voting power? Voting in an international organization is essentially a means of aggregating the wills of the member states so as to arrive at a decision reflecting the collective choice of those states. The question of what is required for a binding decision is distinct from that of how voting power may legally be used. It is the latter issue which concerns us here.

It is appropriate at this point to consider whether the idea that there might be "restrictions" on the use of voting power is consistent with the very notion of voting and voting power. One aspect of this is the abstract and philosophical question of what is the *nature* of voting.

The purpose of voting in an international organization is to permit the expression of a state's will, and that will in itself is hardly amenable to legal control. But voting is also an act which has legal consequences, (through the collective decision ultimately reached), upon the rights and/or duties of other states. Thus it is not contradictory to speak of restrictions upon the use of voting power under international law. The International Court of Justice has implicitly endorsed this viewpoint.[6]

Considering this issue on the practical level, it must be acknowledged that states are devoted to promoting their own particular national interests. This being the case, it is to be expected that some states will attempt to use their voting power in international organizations to serve these same interests. This does not, of course, mean that legal considerations should be considered irrelevant to the issue of how that voting power is used. What it does suggest, however, is that if states are to respect rules concerning the proper use of this type of voting power then those rules must be perceived by states as serving their interests in some way.[7]

6 See, International Court of Justice, Advisory Opinion on Conditions of Admission of a State to Membership in the United Nations, 28 May 1948, *ICJ Reports* (1947–1948), pp. 4–40. This advisory opinion is discussed further *infra*.

7 GOLD, J., in *The Rule of Law in the International Monetary Fund*, Washington, IMF Pamphlet Series, No. 32, 1980, at p. 11, makes a similar point when he states:
"The effectiveness of the legal norms of the Fund depends on the extent to which they are respected by members, and respect for them depends on the extent to which members are convinced that the norms promote their interests."

A number of arguments can be made to the effect that rules governing the use by member states of their voting power can serve the national interest of those states. The basic argument is that without such rules, an international organization might find it difficult to accomplish its purposes, and in general all member states can be presumed to support those purposes. But while support for these purposes represents the common interest upon which the organization is founded, there may well be narrow national interests to which individual members give priority. In deciding how to use its voice and vote in an IGO, a member state may focus upon particular national interests which are not necessarily shared and which it may be tempted to pursue even at the expense of the organization and its purposes as a whole.

The difficulty in precisely defining the purposes of an IGO has been discussed earlier, and it is worth noting at this point that member states may favor an interpretation of the rules, (including the rules relating to the use of voting power), which allows them to take those actions which they deem necessary and in their national interest.

It has sometimes been suggested that international law cannot resolve disputes which are "political," i.e. those which involve matters states see as vital or even very important for their interests. This doctrine is sometimes formulated as *de maximis non curat praetor*. After reviewing that doctrine Hersch Lauterpacht concluded that it was "contrary to accepted notions of the purpose of law" and "not in accordance with existing international law".[8] This doctrine of political disputes, if too broadly applied, would reduce international law to irrelevance, but it is also advisable to keep in mind the limitations of a totally legalistic approach to issues such as this.

There is nothing unusual, from the legal point of view, about the idea of restricting the use of voting power. Under principles of American corporate law, for example, a controlling shareholder may at times be penalized for damages he has caused by voting within a corporation for policies by which he benefited at the expense of the other shareholders. The dominant or controlling shareholder is considered to be in a "fiduciary relationship" with respect to the corporation and its other stock-

8 See, LAUTERPACHT, H., *The Function of Law in the International Community*, Oxford, Clarendon Press, (1933), at p. 183.

holders.[9] While it would be unwise to insist upon an analogy between an IGO and a private corporation, the above example does serve to illustrate that legal limits upon voting have sometimes been recognized.

3. ICJ Advisory Opinion on Conditions of Admission of a State to Membership in the United Nations

The issue of what conditions could properly be required of a state seeking admission to the UN was the subject of an advisory opinion of the International Court of Justice in 1947.[10] Article 4 of the UN Charter reads as follows:

> "1. Membership in the United Nations is open to all other peace-loving states which accept the obligations contained in the present Charter and, in the judgment of the Organization, are able and willing to carry out these obligations.
>
> "2. The admission of any such state to membership in the United Nations will be effected by a decision of the General Assembly upon the recommendation of the Security Council."

Early in the history of the UN both the USSR and the US, as permanent members of the Security Council, followed a policy of opposing, through the veto or "hidden veto,"[11] many states which applied for admission to the UN. The US, with the support of other states, "vetoed" states it believed to be supporters

9 Cf. *Zahn v. Transamerica Corporation*, 162 F.2nd 36, (United States Circuit Court of Appeals, Third Circuit, 1947), and *Southern Pacific Co. v. Bogert*, 250 U.S. 483, 39 S.Ct. 533, 63 L. Ed. 1099 (1919). In the latter case the US Supreme Court stated (at 250 U.S. pp. 487–488):
"The rule of corporation law and of equity invoked is well settled and has been often applied. The majority has the right to control; but when it does so it occupies a fiduciary relation toward the minority, as much so as the corporation itself or its officers and directors."

10 Advisory opinion on Conditions of Admission of a State to Membership in the United Nations, *ICJ Reports* (1947-1948), p. 57.

11 Technically, a veto only occurs when the negative vote of one or more permanent members of the Council nullifies the affirmative votes of other members which would otherwise have been a sufficient to constitute a majority. Since in the early days of the UN the US could rally the support of a majority of the states on the Security Council to support its positions, its negative votes did not go on record as official vetoes. This process of defeating Security Council decisions without a formal veto is sometimes referred to as the use of a "hidden veto".

of the USSR, while the USSR vetoed states it believed supported the US. This effectively closed the door to UN membership for many countries until a pragmatic "package deal" solution allowing supporters of both sides to be admitted together was reached in 1955.[12] The policy of the superpowers before the deal was made was obviously and overtly political, and was also clearly unrelated to the purposes of the Charter and to the criteria for membership stated in its Article 4. The ICJ was requested by the UN General Assembly to give an advisory opinion on the question of whether a state was entitled to make its consent to admission of new members dependent upon conditions other than those stated in Article 4 of the Charter.

The ICJ's advisory opinion in that case eventually concludes:

> "that a Member of the United Nations which is called upon, in virtue of Article 4 of the Charter, to pronounce itself by its vote, either in the Security Council or in the General Assembly, on the admission of a state to membership in the United Nations, *is not juridically entitled to make its consent to the admission dependent on conditions not expressly provided by paragraph 1 of the said Article*." (emphasis added)[13]

What is perhaps most striking about this language of the Court is the implication that when a UN member state is called upon to express its will in a vote on this particular question of membership it is "not juridically entitled" to vote in any way it sees fit and for whatever reasons. Voting then does not necessarily imply the totally free and unrestricted expression of a member government's will

The Court tempered the impact of its ruling in two different ways. First of all it held that the exhaustive character of the conditions of admission set out in Article 4(1) of the UN Charter did not exclude the discretionary evaluation of elements of fact with a view to answering the question of whether those conditions had been met.

> "It does not, however, follow from the exhaustive character of paragraph 1 of Article 4 that an appreciation is

12 See Claude, *op. cit.*, at pp. 89–92.
13 Advisory Opinion on Conditions of Admission, at p. 65.

> precluded of such circumstances of fact as would enable the existence of the requisite conditions to be verified
>
> "*Article 4 does not forbid the taking into account of any factor which it is possible reasonably and in good faith to connect with the conditions laid down in that Article.* The taking into account of such factors is implied in the very wide and very elastic nature of the prescribed conditions; no relevant political factor – that is to say, none connected with the conditions of admission – is excluded."[14] (emphasis added)

Furthermore, in preliminary remarks at the beginning of this opinion the ICJ limited the ultimate impact of its decision with the following comment.

> "Although the members are bound to conform to the requirements of Article 4 in giving their votes, the General Assembly can hardly be supposed to have intended to ask the Court's opinion as to *the reasons which, in the mind of a Member, may prompt its vote. Such reasons, which enter into a mental process, are obviously subject to no control*. Nor does the request concern a member's freedom of expressing its opinion. Since it concerns a condition or conditions on which a member 'makes its consent dependent', the question can only relate to the statements made by a member concerning the vote it proposes to give."[15] (emphasis added)

Thus the opinion only concerns cases where a member has explicitly stated that its vote will be cast pursuant to inappropriate criteria. Where no such statement has been made the Court cannot inquire into the state of mind of UN members casting their votes. This limitation made it much more difficult to challenge the legality of votes cast within the UN. Nonetheless, another legal challenge of sorts would soon be forthcoming, and once again the UN General Assembly would request an advisory opinion from the ICJ.

14 *Ibid.*, at p. 63.
15 *Ibid.*, at p. 60.

4. ICJ Advisory Opinion on the Competence of the General Assembly for the Admission of a State to the United Nations

The 1948 advisory opinion provided strong support for the argument that the admission of certain states to membership in the UN had been prevented by illegal voting in the Security Council. The logical question then arose as to how this state of affairs could be remedied, and one possible course of action considered by the UN General Assembly at the time, was to attempt to admit new members without the recommendation of the Security Council.

In 1949 the General Assembly requested a further advisory opinion on the following question:

> "Can the admission of a State to membership in the United Nations, pursuant to Article 4, paragraph 2, of the Charter, be effected by a decision of the General Assembly when the Security Council has made no recommendation for admission by reason of the candidate failing to obtain the requisite majority or of the negative vote of a permanent Member upon a resolution so to recommend?"[16]

Basing its opinion upon the clear terms of Article 4, paragraph 2, the Court expressed its view that under the UN Charter the General Assembly could not admit new members without a favorable recommendation to that effect by the Security Council.[17] Afterwards, the General Assembly abided by the Court's findings and made no attempt to admit new members except upon the recommendation of the Security Council. As is mentioned above, a number of candidates for membership were admitted *en bloc* in 1955, and the issue of conditions of membership, and of the proper grounds for refusing membership, has only infrequently been raised since then.[18]

It is true, of course, that the opinion in the Competence case does not deal with issues such as those raised in the Conditions case (i.e. the reasons why a member state votes for or against

16 The request for an advisory opinion was included in UNGA Resolution 296 (IV)J of November 22, 1949.

17 Advisory Opinion on the Competence of the General Assembly for the Admission of a State to the United Nations, *ICJ Reports* (1950), pp. 4–10.

18 See, HERNDL, K., "Admission of a State to Membership in the United Nations (Advisory Opinions)", *Encyclopedia of Public International Law*, Vol. 2, 1981, at p. 4.

a candidate for membership).[19] The question of whether an improperly motivated vote could or should be disallowed rather than being counted was never explicitly presented to the Court. Nevertheless, these two cases, when considered together with the subsequent practice of the UN on admissions, demonstrate that even if there is a situation involving the overt misuse of voting power within an IGO, the effect of the vote may be allowed to stand, and there may be no effective remedy against the improper conduct. Thus the matter of remedies and of how to compensate for the improper use of voting power is a separate issue. The policy discussion in Chapter VIII touches upon the need to look beyond purely legal solutions to this problem.

Since the ICJ has affirmed that international law can at least in principle impose restrictions upon the use of voting power within an IGO, we can now turn to the task of identifying those restrictions applicable to the use of voting power within the World Bank. The possible sources of rules restricting the use of that voting power include the Bank's Articles of Agreement, applicable customary international law, and applicable general principles of law. Each of these will be considered in turn below.

B. INTERGOVERNMENTAL ORGANIZATIONS AND CONSTITUTIONAL CONCEPTS

1. The Nature of the Constitutive Treaty of an IGO

As we have seen, international institutional law may be defined as that law dealing with the structure and functions of international organizations.[20] In many ways, this law resembles the constitutional law of a state. A number of legal scholars have stressed the constitutional nature of this law, and more specifi-

19 See the Advisory Opinion on Competence of the General Assembly etc., at p. 7, where the Court takes note of the narrow question raised by the request for an advisory opinion.

"It is not the object of the Request to determine how the Security Council should apply the rules governing its voting procedure in regard to admissions or, in particular, that the Court should examine whether the negative vote of a permanent member is effective to defeat a recommendation which has obtained seven or more votes. The question, as it is formulated, assumes in such a case, the non-existence of a recommendation.

"The Court is, therefore, called upon to determine solely whether the General Assembly can make a decision to admit a State when the Security Council has transmitted no recommendation to it."

20 See SCHERMERS, *op. cit.* pp. 2–4.

cally, of the constitutive treaties of IGOs. It can easily be observed that the Bank's Charter is a treaty, and that it creates rights and obligations for member states in international law. Beyond this obvious point, however, there are a number of reasons for imparting to that treaty a special importance superior to that of many other treaties.

A distinction is sometimes made between treaties which are like contracts (*traités contrats*) and multilateral treaties which are in a sense "law-making" (*traités lois*) because they create a set of rules intended to govern the future conduct of the parties.[21] What is the importance of the distinction between these two types of treaties? It has often been suggested that law-making treaties should be interpreted differently from other treaties.[22] McNair identified three ways in which they might be interpreted differently, stating that *travaux préparatoires* should not be used in the interpretation of these treaties; that it is only when such a treaty is involved that one party to a treaty can claim that it does not necessarily recognize the other parties as states or governments; and that perhaps the doctrine of *rebus sic stantibus* should not be applied to them in the same way.[23]

Some scholars have expressed doubt about the analytical utility of this twofold distinction.[24] It is interesting to note that the Vienna Convention on the Law of Treaties says nothing about these two types of treaties and makes no distinction between them, although it does include certain special rules applicable only to multilateral treaties,[25] as well as a general statement to the effect that that convention does apply to any treaty which is the constituent instrument of an international organization.[26]

Treaties of a constitutional nature should be recognized as a special sub-category of multilateral treaty. Constitutive treaties such as the UN Charter and the Charter of the World Bank do

21 See ROUSSEAU, C., *Droit international public*, huitième éd., (Précis Dalloz), Paris, Dalloz, (1976), at pp. 24-25, and also McNAIR, A.D. (Lord McNair), *The Law of Treaties*, Oxford, Clarendon Press, 1961, and his discussion of "The Functions and Differing Legal Character of Treaties" at pp. 739–754.

22 RIDEAU, J. *Juridictions internationales et contrôle et respect des traités constitutifs des organizations internationales*, Paris, Librarie Générale de Droit et de Jurisprudence, (1969), at p. 4.

23 MCNAIR, *op. cit.*, at pp. 744–749.

24 BROWNLIE, *op. cit.*, at p. 631.

25 The Vienna Convention on the Law of Treaties, Articles 40, 41, 58 and Article 60 paragraph 2.

26 *Ibid.*, Article 5.

have a constitutional character. This was recognized by the individual opinion of Judge Alvarez in the Admissions case. That opinion refers to the UN Charter as "the constitution of the United Nations" and as "the constitutional Charter".[27] In one notable passage Judge Alvarez asserts that:

> "The preparatory work on the constitution of the United Nations Organization is of but little value. Moreover, the fact should be stressed that *an institution, once established, acquires a life of its own, independent of the elements which have given birth to it,* and it must develop, not in accordance with the views of those who created it, but in accordance with the requirements of international life."[28] (emphasis added)

He clearly believes that an international institution such as the UN should be independent and dynamic enough to transcend the original intention of the states which founded it should this be warranted by the international situation. He presumably considered this characteristic to be exclusive to treaties constituting international institutions. Judge Alvarez's opinion makes no secret of his desire to see the court become involved in the progressive development of international law,[29] and in many ways it goes well beyond generally accepted doctrines.[30] Nonetheless, the argument that constitutive treaties should be interpreted in a somewhat special manner is difficult to dismiss.

Scelle, Berlia, and Rideau have all endorsed the idea that these treaties should be considered as having a distinct consti-

27 Admissions case, at pp. 68, 70.
28 *Ibid.*, p. 68.
29 See *Ibid.*, p. 67.
30 See for example *Ibid.*, p. 70 where Judge Alvarez concludes that "the Constitutional Charter cannot be interpreted according to strictly legal criterion; another and broader criterion must be employed and room left, if need be, for political considerations." See also p. 69 of the same opinion where he states that "the traditionally juridical and individualistic conception of law is being progressively superseded" by an international law which is not only juridical but also "political, economic, social and psychological". He refers to this new law as the "law of social interdependence", and it bears more than a passing resemblance to the late Wolfgang Freidmann's "international law of cooperation".

tutional nature,[31] but a certain amount of resistance to this notion remains. Rideau stresses the danger of *"étatomorphisme"* in international constitutional law, by which he refers to any tendency to ascribe to an international organization the legal attributes of a state. The principles of constitutional law developed and applied in internal law cannot all be applied internationally given the fundamental differences between a state and an intergovernmental organization.[32] But if entirely new constitutional doctrines must be developed for international organizations, why bother to apply constitutional notions to them at all?[33]

Essentially, this type of analysis is worthwhile because there are certain basic elements common to constitutions of all kinds. There are also certain fundamental notions, both legal and political which are generally applicable, although sometimes (as with IGOs) in an adapted form. Thus international constitutional doctrines will be neither entirely new nor entirely the same as those applying to states.

It is fairly easy to identify some of the basic elements of a constitution. First of all, a constitution normally defines the purposes and the mandate of the legal entity being created. Second, a constitution outlines rules concerning membership in that entity. Thirdly, it will define the different operative organs and their powers and functions, the relationship between those organs and the relation between the constituent members of the entity and the whole.[34]

Identifying the fundamental notions applicable to constitutions is a more difficult task, but if it can be done it should provide us with a clearer idea of how "constitutional" treaties might be interpreted and applied differently from other treaties.

31 SCELLE, G., "Droit constitutionel international", in *Mélanges R. Carré de Malberg*, Paris, Sirey, 1933, pp. 501–515; BERLIA, G., "Admission d'un état aux Nations Unies", *R.G.D.I.P.*,Vol. 53, (1949), at p. 501 ; RIDEAU, *op. cit.*, at p. 5.

32 RIDEAU, *op. cit.*, at p. 6.

33 The Soviet view, as expressed by Tunkin, is that "[T]he attempt to ascribe certain features of state constitutions to the charters of international organizations has no justification, since international organizations are qualitatively different from states." TUNKIN, G.I., *Theory of International Law*, London, George Allen & Unwin, 1974, at p. 326.

34 See RIDEAU, *op. cit.*, at p. 7, and JENKS, C.W., "Some Constitutional Problems of International Organizations", *British Yearbook of International Law*, 1945, at pp. 16–28.

While an exhaustive review of these notions would go beyond the scope of this study, at least two basic notions associated with constitutions can be identified which are directly relevant to the subjects at hand.

2. The Constitution as an Evolving, Dynamic Instrument

Judge Alvarez, in the passage from the ICJ Admissions case quoted earlier, advanced the view that constitutional treaties like the UN Charter take on a dynamic life of their own which may (properly in his view) take them beyond the intention of the states framing the treaty. Jenks agrees, and stresses the need for flexibility and adaptability of international institutions.[35] Constitutive acts, whether national or international, are often said to have this character. One well known formulation of this idea can be found in *Missouri* v. *Holland*, a decision of the US Supreme Court rendered in 1920. In that opinion Justice Holmes made the following observation concerning the interpretation of the US Constitution.

> " . . . when we are dealing with words that also are a constituent act, like the Constitution of the United States, we must realize that they have called into life a being the development of which could not have been forseen completely by the most gifted of its begetters."[36]

Inis Claude Jr., in his discussion of the constitutional problems of the UN, also focuses on the need for constitutions to develop and evolve in response to new realities. He does not hesitate to make a careful use of the analogy between the US Constitution and the UN Charter, and he concludes that "even though the problem of constitutional relationships starts as a problem of interpretation, it ends as a problem of development."[37] He continues by noting that:

> "Sound constitutional interpretation, in international organization as in national government, balances insist-

35 See JENKS, *op. cit.*, at p. 16, where he quotes *Missouri v. Holland* (see the next footnote, *infra*) in support of his observation that a successful constitutive instrument takes on a dynamic life of its own which goes beyond what its drafters originally intended.

36 Quoted from *Missouri v. Holland*, 252 U.S. 416 (1920).

37 CLAUDE, *op. cit.*, at p. 167.

ence upon the legally formulated consensus of the past, awareness of the political configuration of the present, and consciousness of the community's requirements and demands for the future. This is not an easy stunt to perform in the United States, and it is immensely more difficult in the United Nations."[38]

To some of those who reject the application of constitutional concepts to IGOs, it is the claim of "flexibility" which is the most objectionable part of that approach. The noted Soviet jurist Tunkin, for example, says the following about constitutional theory:

> "The basic idea of this theory, which is oriented toward American and English constitutional practice, is that the charters of international organizations are 'flexible' documents from whose provisions one may digress in practice, and this digression will not be a violation, but a modification of these charters . . .
>
> "There is no doubt whatever that the constitutional theory is worked out and propagandized strenuously in the West because it is aimed at justifying the numerous violations of the charters of general international organizations, and above all of the United Nations, which did and do occur under the pressure of the imperialist powers. Herein is the political significance of this theory."[39]

This viewpoint reflects both Soviet ideology and Soviet resentment of the methods by which the UN circumvented the Soviet veto during the Korean crisis. More generally, it reflects the dogmatic theory of state sovereignty which the Soviet Union has subscribed to in the past. Recent comments by Soviet leader Mikhail Gorbachev suggest that this Soviet attitude, like many others, is rapidly changing.

3. The Constitution as a Source of Superior Norms

Another even more fundamental aspect of any constitution is the notion that it should be at the top of the hierarchy of laws,

38 Loc.cit.
39 TUNKIN, *op. cit.*, at pp. 322–323.

at least within the legal order which it creates.[40] Thus in theory the organs of an IGO are not legally free to act contrary to the terms of that organization's constitutive instrument, notwithstanding any limited law-making power which those organs may possess.

While the constitution of an IGO may be considered to be at the top of the legal hierarchy of the IGO itself, as a practical matter the member states may not always consider the norms of such an "international constitution" to be superior to their own internal constitutional norms. The Supreme Court of the United States, for example, has long taken the position that as a matter of the internal law of the US, a federal statute which is inconsistent with a treaty renders the treaty null to the extent of the conflict.[41] Some further implications of this doctrine will be considered later, in the discussion of US national legislation concerning voting in the Bank.

Other less relevant aspects of constitutive treaties which are frequently mentioned in the literature include the special regime which may apply to them as far as reservations are concerned.[42]

C. THE WORLD BANK'S ARTICLES OF AGREEMENT, THE LEX SPECIALIS, AND THE USE OF VOTING POWER WITHIN THE BANK

These Articles, the Bank's constitutive instrument, are a logical place to look for principles governing the use of voting power within the Bank. Article V deals with the organization and management of the Bank and it is in the various sections of that Article that we find the formula for allotting votes to members (section 3) and the procedures for the casting of those votes by the Board of Governors and the EDs (sections 2 and 4 respect-

40 See RIDEAU, *op. cit.*, at p. 33.

41 See, for example, the US Supreme Court case of *Reid v. Covert*, 354 U.S. 1, 77 S.Ct. 1222, 1 L.Ed.2nd 1148 (1957).

42 With regard to reservations, it is only logical that a special rule should apply to constitutive treaties, either ruling out reservations altogether or at least restricting them. Otherwise a situation could occur where unanticipated differences between the rights and duties of different members might lead to serious confusion. This concern is reflected in Article 20, paragraph 3 of the Vienna Convention on the Law of Treaties which provides that "When a treaty is a constituent instrument of an international organization and unless it otherwise provides, a reservation requires the acceptance of the competent organ of that organization."

ively). Nothing in this Article, however, expresses a limitation upon the exercise of voting rights by members.

1. Article IV Section 10 of the Bank's Charter, the so called "Political Activity Prohibition"

Article IV section 10 of the Bank's Agreement expresses an important principle which is quite relevant to any analysis of possible politicized decision-making within the Bank. This section, entitled "Political activity prohibited" reads as follows:

> "The Bank and its officers shall not interfere in the political affairs of any member; nor shall they be influenced in their decisions by the political character of the member or members concerned. *Only economic considerations shall be relevant to their decisions*, and these considerations shall be weighed impartially in order to achieve the purposes stated in Article I."[43] (emphasis added)

a) The Purpose of Article IV(10)

There are at least two fundamentally different views of the purpose and end of these provisions. On the one hand, the purpose of this language could be to protect member states from intervention or interference by the Bank in their *internal affairs*. If so, it could be seen as similar to Article 2(7) of the UN Charter. According to another view, this section may be seen as a prohibition on the politicization of the Bank, and as the constitutional embodiment of the *functionalist* principle within the Bank's Charter.

i) Article IV(10) and "Internal Affairs" or "Domestic Jurisdiction"

The constitutive treaty or "constitution" of an IGO will sometimes include language which is intended to underline the fact that the member states retain sovereign power and exclusive authority over certain matters even as they accept the obli-

43 The IDA Articles of Agreement, Art. V, section 6 is identical to this except that at the end it refers to "the purposes stated in this Agreement" instead of to "the purposes stated in Article I." The following discussion applies equally to both.

gations of membership in an international body. Article 15(8) of the Covenant of the League of Nations and Article 2(7) of the UN Charter are good examples. The problem is that the matters concerning which states reserve exclusive jurisdiction are often vaguely defined.

Article 2(7) of the UN Charter states (in part) that "Nothing in the present Charter shall authorize the United Nations to intervene in matters which are essentially within the domestic jurisdiction of a state . . . ". The Covenant of the League of Nations had contained similar language. It referred (in Article 15(8)) to matters "solely within the domestic jurisdiction". An extended analysis of these two phrases would be beyond the scope of this study, but it is in any case fairly clear that both reflect the desire of states to protect and retain their sovereignty. The question is whether this is also the real purpose, and perhaps the only purpose, of the Bank's Article IV(10). Under any conceivable interpretation of this section, it would provide some protection for the states against interference by the Bank in internal and sovereign affairs, even if that protection is only incidental.

But though it does to some extent protect member states from interference by the Bank in their internal affairs, this is not necessarily the only purpose of the so-called prohibition on political activity. A closer look at Article IV(10) reveals that there are really two distinct parts of that section. The first part, consists of prohibitions which are limitations upon the activities and decision-making discretion of the Bank and its officers. Thus they are not to "interfere in the political affairs of any member", nor are they to "be influenced in their decisions by the political character of the member or members concerned." Because of the emphasis which this language places on the affairs and character of *members* of the Bank, it is logical to conclude that it is intended to protect the rights and the independence of those members.

The first sentence in Article IV(10) of the Bank's Charter can therefore be seen as having a function similar to that of Article 2(7) of the UN Charter.

ii) Article IV(10) and the Theory of "Functionalism"

It is the second sentence of Article IV(10), along with the second clause of the first sentence,[44] which sets out a positive definition of how the Bank, its organs, and its officers, are to exercise their discretion in decision-making. If the only purpose of this section is to protect member states from interference in their domestic affairs, then why is the second part of this section needed?

One plausible explanation is that this part of section 10 (especially when viewed in connection with the first part), reflects an agreement that the Bank should operate in accordance with functionalist theory, in the sense that all decisions made within the Bank should be based on technical considerations and not on politics. Both the General Counsel of the Bank, and the Bank's EDs have endorsed the view that section 10 "is no more than a reflection of the technical and functional character of the Bank as it is established under its articles of agreement."[45]

The positive injunction that "only economic considerations shall be relevant" to Bank decisions is very much reminiscent of the ICJ advisory opinion on conditions of Admission where the court concluded that UN members were not "juridically entitled" to make their affirmative votes concerning the admission of new states dependent on conditions other than those expressed in Article 4, paragraph 1 of the UN Charter. In effect, the ICJ opinion says that "only the conditions enumerated in the UN Charter shall be relevant."[46] The Bank's Charter says something very similar.

44 The second clause of that Article's first sentence mandates that the Bank and its officers shall not "be influenced in their decisions by the political character of the member or members concerned." This clause serves a dual purpose, providing some protection for the internal affairs of states while also setting out a "functionalist" definition of how the Bank is supposed to reach its decisions.

45 From a letter dated 5 May, 1967 from the IBRD General Counsel to the UN Secretariat, cited in *United Nations Juridical Yearbook*, 1967, at p. 121. This letter, and associated legal memoranda of the IBRD General Counsel and of the Legal Counsel of the United Nations, are examined further in the section on the organizational practice of the Bank, *infra*.

46 That opinion also notes that the article interpreted "does not forbid the taking into account of any factor which it is possible reasonably and in good faith to connect with the conditions laid down in that Article." Admission Case, *ICJ Reports*, 1947–1948 at p. 63.

Thus, according to the "functionalist" interpretation of Article IV(10), that section partakes more in the rationale of Article 4(1) of the UN Charter than in that of Article 2(7) of that same document.

b) The Applicability of Article IV(10) to the Bank's Executive Directors

Does the prohibition of this section bind the Governors and EDs who exercise voting power in the Bank on behalf of member countries? By its terms the prohibition applies to the "bank and its officers", thus the meaning of the term "officers" is crucial. Governors and EDs are almost certainly not "officers" within the meaning of this section. Throughout the Bank's Charter the term is used to refer to those who (along with the "staff") are appointed and organized by the President, subject to the general control of the EDs.[47]

i) The Status of the EDs as an Organ of the Bank

A basic question is whether a prohibition which applies to the "Bank" must apply to Governors and EDs of the Bank as organs of that institution. Since only the "Bank and its officers" are mentioned in this section, the principle *expressio unius est exclusio alterius* could arguably be applied to support the conclusion that the unmentioned Governors and EDs are not bound.[48]

But there is evidence to suggest that the drafters of this article (including representatives of the USSR) intended it to protect the member countries from political interference by the Bank.[49] It can only have this effect if the EDs (who run the Bank) are

47 See Art. V, sections 5(b), (c) and (d) of the Bank's Articles.

48 It should be noted that even if Article IV section 10 did not apply to the EDs, the principle of non-intervention would make it illegal for them to interfere in the political affairs of borrowers. See the discussion of this principle in chapter IV, *supra*.

49 One participant in the Bretton Woods negotiations concludes, with reference to Article IV, section 10, that "these phases were probably intended principally as reassurances to the USSR." BITTERMAN, H. J., "Negotiation of the Articles of Agreement of the International Bank for Reconstruction and Development," *The International Lawyer*, Vol. 5, no. 1, (1971) at p. 79.

so bound, as logically they must be.[50] It is worth noting that in the past, senior members of the Bank staff have supported a broad interpretation of this prohibition which would specifically apply it to all the Bank's organs including the Board of Governors and the EDs.

Between 1964 and 1968 the UN General Assembly adopted a number of resolutions requesting the Bank (along with other specialized agencies) to deny technical, academic and other assistance to South Africa and Portugal because of their policies of apartheid and colonialism respectively.[51] The General Counsel of the Bank appeared before the Fourth Committee of the General Assembly on 28 November 1966 to explain why the Bank had continued to make loans for projects in Portugal and South Africa in spite of these resolutions. He asserted that Article IV, section 10 of the Bank's Charter made compliance with those resolutions impossible, since those resolutions would require that the Bank and its officers consider political matters even if unrelated to economic factors. In making his point he stated:

> "I draw your attention to the fact that the provision is addressed to the Bank and its officers. The 'officers' are the President and the other senior members of the staff. *The words 'the Bank' refer to the institution as such and to its organs, the Board of Governors and the Executive Directors.*"[52]

50 Under Article V, section 2 of the Bank's Articles of Agreement "all the powers of the Bank" are "vested in the Board of Governors" who then delegate certain of these powers to the EDs. Is it not logical then to assume that any restriction upon "the Bank" must apply to the bodies in which its powers are vested? YOKOTA, (*op. cit.*, page 62) considers this logical argument to be compelling. Any restriction upon the Bank as a whole must also restrict the parts, i.e. the Bank's organs.

51 See for example, "The Policies of Apartheid of the Government of the Republic of South Africa", Resolution 2054A(XX), 15 December 1965, UN GAOR 20th Session, Supplement No. 14, UN Document A/6014.

The dispute between the UN and the Bank concerning the interpretation of the Bank's Articles of Agreement and the nature of the Bank's relationship with the UN is discussed *infra*, as a case study.

52 Statement of the IBRD General Counsel (Mr Broches) to the Fourth Committee of the UN General Assembly on 28 November 1966 as distributed to the Executive Directors of the Bank on 1 December 1966. Reproduced in *International Legal Materials*, Vol. VI (1967), pp. 150–153, quoted language at p. 152. (emphasis added).

In a 1987 legal opinion the Bank's Legal Department reached the same conclusion.

> "The Board of Executive Directors, as an organ of the Bank, is subject to the provision of Article IV, Section 10 of the Bank's Articles of Agreement and is therefore prohibited from interfering in the political affairs of any member or from being influenced in its decisions by the political character of the member concerned. Only economic considerations, which are weighed impartially, are relevant to the Board's decisions.[53]

ii) The Role of the US Appointed ED as a Political Representative

When discussing the constitutional limits upon the use of voting power in the World Bank, a preliminary question arises concerning exactly whose voting power it is. Is it the members who have voting power, or does it actually belong to the Governors and Executive Directors that they have appointed and elected? According to the Bank's Charter, it is the members who have the voting power,[54] but it is the Governors and/or the EDs who are actually entitled to cast the votes of those members.[55] Thus the Governors and EDs are the representatives of the members for the purpose of voting and decision-making,[56] although the

53 "Prohibition of Political Activities Under the IBRD Articles of Agreement and its Relevance to the Work of the Executive Directors", legal opinion by Ibrahim F.I. Shihata, Vice President and General Counsel of the World Bank, section M87-1409, at p. 8 (December 23, 1987), (unpublished). Quoted in SHIHATA, I.F.I., "The World Bank and Human Rights: An Analysis of the Legal Issues and the Record of Achievements", *Denver Journal of International Law and Policy*, Vol. 17, No. 1, (1988), at p. 46.

54 Article V, Sec. 3(a) of the Bank's Articles of Agreement which states that; "Each *member* shall have two hundred and fifty votes plus one additional vote for each share of stock held." (emphasis added)

55 Cf. *Ibid.*, Article V, Sec. 4(g):
"Each appointed *director shall be entitled to cast* the number of votes allotted under section 3 of this Article to the member appointing him. Each elected *director shall be entitled to cast* the number of votes which counted toward his election . . . " (emphasis added).

56 The conclusion that the EDs are representatives is further supported by the language of Article V Sec. 4(h) which reads as follows:
"The Board of Governors shall adopt regulations under which a member not entitled to appoint a director under (b) above may send a representative

situation of the Governors is somewhat different from that of the EDs.[57]

Interestingly enough, except for the fact that he is paid by the Bank (and not by the US government), US internal law allows the US appointed ED to be treated very much like a typical civil servant in the employ of the US government. On the basis of the time spent as the US ED, a US citizen may be "eligible . . . for all employee benefits afforded employees in the civil service of the United States."[58]

Article IV section 10 of the Bank's Charter also applies to the EDs by virtue of the treaty obligations it creates for the Bank's members. When a member acts through an IGO and in its capacity as a member, it is fully bound by the constitutional rules which are applicable to the organization as a whole. The EDs, as "representatives" of member states, must legally be bound to the same extent as the state or states they represent.

Representatives to IGOs have what might be referred to as a political responsibility to defend the national interests of the governments they represent, but they also have responsibilities as members of an international organ.[59] It is to be expected that

---

to attend any meeting of the Executive Directors when a request made by, or a matter particularly affecting, that member is under consideration."

This section reflects the clear and quite logical assumption that an ED appointed by a Bank member acts, at least in part, as a representative of the interests and the point of view of that member within Bank councils.

57 Article V, Sec. 2(a) of the Bank's Charter states that each Governor serves "subject to the pleasure of the member appointing him", while no such statement is made regarding the EDs. This does suggest that the EDs are intended to have a somewhat more independent status than the Governors, but it may simply reflect the fact that each Governor is appointed by one member, while most of the EDs are elected by several governments.

58 According to the applicable federal statute, whether the US ED is to be eligible for these benefits or not is a matter left the discretion of the Secretary of the Treasury. If he or she is to be eligible for the benefits concerned (which may include health, life and disability insurance as well as participation in a retirement fund), the ED must pay contributions to the benefit funds involved. Any such payments are to be channeled through the US Department of the Treasury. The US EDs in the IMF, the IBRD, the IDB, the ADB, the AfDB and the AfDF may all be accorded these benefits. Public Law 97-35, Title XIII Sec. 1342(d) of August 13, 1981, 95 Stat. 743; as amended by PL 98-473, Title I, Sec. 101(1), of October 12, 1984, 98 Stat. 1885, codified at 22 USC Sec. 276c-2.

59 See, JENKS, *op. cit.*, at pp. 28–29 where he suggests that:
"If a constitutional foundation can be laid for the gradual acceptance of the conception that the responsibility of persons discharging such duties to their individual constituencies – the individual nations – is paralleled by a

at times reconciling both aspects of this double role will be difficult. Constitutional guidelines, such as those in Article IV Section 10 of the Bank's Charter, are highly relevant to this task.[60]

The analogy with the UN Charter provides further confirmation of the above points. The Advisory Opinion on Conditions of Admission suggests that the General Assembly, the Security Council, and individual UN member states are all equally limited in their legal powers by the clear terms of Article 4 of the UN Charter. That opinion states at one point that:

> "The political character of an organ cannot release it from the observance of the treaty provisions established by the Charter when they constitute limitations on its powers or criteria for its judgment. To ascertain whether an organ has freedom of choice for its decisions, reference must be made to the terms of its constitution. In this case, the limits of this freedom are fixed by Article 4."[61]

The reasoning of the Advisory Opinion on Conditions of Admission supports the view that the Bank's political activity prohibition must be binding upon the Bank's EDs collectively as an organ. By logical extension, that same prohibition must also be binding upon the individual EDs constituting that

---

responsibility as members of an international organ with a collective international responsibility, a sound basis will be available for long-term institutional development."

60 With regard to the double role of the Bank's EDs, a legal opinion prepared in 1987 by the General Counsel of the World Bank concluded that an ED could legally vote on the instructions of the member or members who appointed or elected him, but not if this implied acting contrary to the EDs obligations to the Bank. The relevant passage of that opinion (quoted in SHIHATA, I.F.I., "The World Bank and Human Rights", *op. cit.*, at p. 46) reads as follows:
"2. An Executive Director as an official of the Bank who is appointed or elected by a member or members of the Bank and whose votes depend on the voting strength of the member or members who appointed or elected him, owes his duty both to the Bank and to his "constituency". He may express the views of such a "constituency" and vote on its instructions, but he may not split his votes. However, he is not to act simply as an ambassador of the government or governments which appointed or elected him and is expected to exercise his individual judgment in the interest of the Bank and its members as a whole. Members of the Bank are under an obligation not to influence the Bank's President and staff in the discharge of their duties, and the Executive Directors are under a duty not to act as the instrumentality of members to exert such prohibited influence."

61 Admission Case, *ICJ Reports*, 1947–1948 at p. 64.

organ.[62] In sum, there is every reason to conclude that juridically speaking, the decision-making discretion of the Bank's EDs is limited by the terms of Article IV, section 10 of the Bank's Charter.

2. Other Articles of Possible Relevance

a) The Bank's Article I and the Analogy with the IMF

It is interesting to note that the IMF's charter does not contain any language similar to Article IV(10) of the Bank's articles.[63] In practice though, the Fund has taken the position that it is prohibited from making decisions based upon political considerations. Sir Joseph Gold, former General Counsel of the Fund and now a senior consultant there, maintains that this prohibition results from the last sentence of Article I of the Fund's Articles of Agreement.[64] That Article lists the purposes of the Fund and states that "[T]he Fund shall be guided in all its policies and decisions by the purposes set forth in this Article."

Virtually identical language appears in Article I of the Bank's charter. After listing the Bank's purposes that Article states that "[T]he Bank shall be guided in all its decisions by the purposes set forth above."

Sir Joseph states categorically in a recent article, that:

> "Domestic policies are 'social' or 'political' if they do not fall within the scope of the purposes of the Fund as set forth in Article I, and the Fund may not base its decisions on political considerations of this character."[65]

Not content with merely stating that political considerations should be excluded, in a separate publication Sir Joseph Gold raises the question of what should be done if politically motivated votes are cast within the IMF.

> "Suppose that an Executive Director, whether or not

62 See YOKOTA, *op. cit.* p. 62, for a separate argument to the same effect.

63 YOKOTA (*op. cit.* p. 45) suggests that "For the Americans who [at Bretton Woods] held a view that economics cannot be separated from politics, it was perhaps easier to accept a non-political Bank than a non-political Fund."

64 See GOLD, J. "Political Considerations are Prohibited by Articles of Agreement when the Fund Considers Requests for Use of Resources", *IMF Survey*, Vol. 12, No. 10, 23 May 1983, p. 146.

65 loc. cit.

> acting under what he regards as instructions, takes a position in the Executive Board on the basis of considerations that are inconsistent with the Articles. (The Executive Board would decide any question of consistency if it were raised and a decision became necessary.) What would be the legal effect of this position in the determination by the Chairman of the Executive Board of the sense of the meeting, or of the vote of the Executive Director if voting were to take place? Is his position or his vote to be ignored?"[66]

He does not venture to answer this question. But if the Fund's Article I applies to the voting decisions of its EDs as well as to the decisions of the Fund staff, should not the Bank's Article I (and Article IV(10)) be given similar effect? A recent legal opinion by the General Counsel of the World Bank supports the view that it should.[67]

b) Article V, Section 8

The Southern Africa case study in the next chapter illustrates how resolutions of the United Nations were once invoked in support of calls for a politically motivated cutoff of Bank lending to certain targeted countries.[68] Could political decisions by the Bank be reconciled with the Bank's Charter if taken pursuant to UN resolutions? Can the legality of a given use of voting power within the Bank be determined by the relationship of the Bank to the UN? In the context of these questions Article

66 GOLD, J., *The Rule of Law in the International Monetary Fund, op. cit.*, pp. 63–64.

67 Ibrahim Shihata, Vice President and General Counsel of the World Bank, has recognized that "there is no legal sanction available to challenge a vote by an Executive Director that was motivated by political considerations", but in a recent legal opinion he concluded that "The Chairman of the Board is entitled to rule out of order a political debate or statement which does not have a clear relevance to the economic considerations related to the subject matter under discussion." SHIHATA, I.F.I., "The World Bank and Human Rights: An Analysis of the Legal Issues and the Record of Achievements", *op. cit.*, at p. 46 and ff.

68 The countries involved, South Africa and Portugal, were singled out for their policies of *apartheid* and of colonial domination, respectively. See Chapter VI, *infra*, for details.

V, section 8 of the Bank's Charter must be examined.[69] The relevant provision of Article V of the Bank's Charter reads as follows:

> "Section 8. *Relationship to other international organizations*
> "(a) The Bank, within the terms of this Agreement, shall cooperate with any general international organization and with public international organizations having specialized responsibilities in related fields. Any arrangements for such cooperation which would involve a modification of any provision of this Agreement may be effected only after amendment of this Agreement under Article VIII.
> "(b) In making decisions on loans or guarantees relating to matters directly within the competence of any international organization of the types specified in the preceding paragraph and participated in primarily by members of the Bank, the Bank shall give consideration to the views and recommendations of such organization."

Could this article justify the making of Bank decisions according to political criteria even though Article IV(10) states that only economic considerations are to be relevant? Upon reflection, it does not seem that it could. First of all this section states in no uncertain terms that the cooperation with other organizations authorized by this section must fall "within the terms of this agreement", and that "only after amendment to this agreement" could any arrangements for such cooperation modify any provision of the agreement. It would thus be futile to seek in this section (or in any arrangement with another international organization pursuant to this section) any modification of fundamental rules found elsewhere in the Bank's Charter.

At first glance, the language of the second paragraph of this article appears to suggest that decisions by the Bank on loan applications should reflect the views and recommendations of certain other international organizations, but in fact, there is very little substance to (even) this paragraph. Although the words "the Bank shall" imply an obligation for the Bank, that obligation is not at all concrete. It is simply an "obligation" to "give consideration to the views and recommendations" of the

69 The relationship agreement which the Bank has entered into with the UN is also relevant to this issue. This agreement is also discussed in Chapter VI.

organization involved. Those views may be considered and then rejected, and thus they in no way truly limit the decision-making discretion of the Bank or its organs. Furthermore, the Bank need only give this limited consideration to an organization's views if and when a particular loan decision relates "to matters directly within the competence" of the organization involved, and if that organization is "participated in primarily by members of the Bank". In the final analysis, this section can do nothing to restrict the use of voting power within the Bank.[70]

c) The Negotiating History of the Bank

One institutional issue raised by this study concerns the scope of the discretion enjoyed by the Bank's EDs and the extent to which their decision-making is subject to the political control of the governments which appoint or elect them. It is worthwhile briefly to consider the negotiating history of the Bank to see what insights it may provide concerning the original intent of the Bank's founders on this issue.[71]

An examination of that history reveals that the two most important delegations at Bretton Woods, those of the US and of the UK, were in complete disagreement about the way in which the EDs were to exercise control over the Bank. According to Mason and Asher:

> "The UK delegation, led by Lord Keynes, strongly supported the view that executive directors should, like members of the staff, consider themselves to be international civil servants with an allegiance only to the Bank. This was totally unacceptable to the United States, which was putting up most of the money and wanted its representative on the Board of Directors to be subject to close governmental control."[72]

70 The agreement with the UN which the Bank entered into pursuant to Article V, section 8, will be considered *infra.* in Chapter VI.

71 The negotiating history is of interest in this case in spite of the observation made earlier to the effect that it may be inappropriate to refer to the *travaux préparatoires* of "constitutional" treaties as an aid to interpreting them. See the discussion of the nature of constitutive treaties of IGOs, *infra,* this same chapter.

72 MASON and ASHER, *The World Bank Since Bretton Woods,* Washington, The Brookings Institution, (1973), p. 30.

Referring to that dispute Richard Gardner has aptly noted that:

> "The political and economic circumstances of the [post World War II] transition period made it virtually inevitable that the American viewpoint should finally prevail."[73] (bracketed clarification added)

But the Articles of Agreement signed at Bretton Woods did not clearly resolve the issue, and it was primarily in the subsequent practice of member states, beginning with the first meeting of the Governors of the Bank and the Fund held in Savannah, Georgia in March of 1946, that the American viewpoint did prevail.[74] Since that first 1946 meeting the US appointed EDs of the Bank have, on the whole, functioned as national representatives[75] and not as the dispassionate international civil servants which functionalist theory might have them be. The Case Studies in Chapter VI will explore in greater detail the custom and practice of the Bank relative to the political activity prohibition of Article IV, Section 10.

D. GENERAL PRINCIPLES OF INTERNATIONAL LAW

1. The Doctrine of Abuse of Rights

There is something rather disturbing about the term abuse of rights as well as the concept. The concept of right seems absolute in the sense that anything done which is within the scope of a true right should be considered to be legal.[76] Illegality, and responsibility for illegal acts, (whether in municipal or international law), should in theory result only from conduct which exceeds the rights of the actor.[77] The underlying issue is the

73 GARDNER, R. *Sterling Dollar Diplomacy in Current Perspective*, New York, Columbia University Press, 1980, at p. 267.

74 See MASON and ASHER, *op. cit.* p. 31, and pp 36–52.

75 Most of the Bank's EDs are elected by Governors from a number of different countries and so cannot really be considered to be national representatives. The five major contributors to the Bank do appoint their own directors and these appointed directors hold over 43% of the total voting power.

76 Indeed, the doctrine of abuse of rights is in derogation of the well known legal maxim *neminem laedit qui suo jure utitur*, ("He who stands on his own rights injures no one").

77 See ILUYOMADE, B.O., "The Scope and Content of a Complaint of Abuse of Right in International Law", *Harvard International Law Journal*, Vol. 16, No. 1, (1975), at p. 48, where he quotes from M. PLAINIOL, (*Treatise on the Civil Law*, 11th Edition) on the subject of what he refers to as the "linguistic dispute" on this point.

scope of the rights concerned, because prohibiting abuse is just a way of narrowing the scope of the rights which can legally be exercised.

Before the theory of abuse of rights can be applied to inter-state relations the following elements must be present: 1) The "abusing" state must have a right to act as it does, and be acting within its apparent rights. 2) That state must exercise its right so as either to impede the enjoyment by other states of their own rights, or must exercise it in order to accomplish some other improper purpose. 3) Injury must result to another state or states due to the exercise of this right in this way.[78] If indeed the abuse of a right is prohibited by international law, then this principle must be considered to take precedence over more specific rules which establish particular rights.[79]

This principle is recognized, in one form or another, by the municipal law of many states in the world,[80] but there is considerable disagreement about whether the legal concept of abuse of rights actually exists in international law.[81] The doctrine has been referred to in passing by international tribunals,[82]

78 See, PAUL, V., "The Abuse of Rights and Bona Fides in International Law", *Österreichische Zeitschrift fur Öffentliches Recht und Völkerrecht*, Vol. 28, (1977), at p. 113.

79 KISS, A.C., "Abuse of Rights", *E.P.I.L.*, Vol. 7, (1984), at p. 4.

80 Fawcett reviews related principles of law recognized by the legal systems of a number of Western countries before concluding that détournement de pouvoir should be recognized as a general principle of law. See, FAWCETT, *op. cit.* at p. 313. Iluyomade, after a more detailed and broadly based review, comes to the same conclusion. ILUYOMADE, *op. cit.* at p. 61.

81 See OPPENHEIM, L., *International Law*, Vol. I, Peace, eighth edition, ed. by H. Lauterpacht, London, Longman Group Ltd. (1974), at pp. 345–347 concluding that it is; SCHWARZENBERGER, G. and BROWN, E. D., *A Manual of International Law*, 6th ed. London, Professional Books Ltd. (1976) at pp. 84–85, suggesting that it is not; and BROWNLIE, I., *Principles of Public International Law*, 3rd ed., Oxford, Clarendon Press (1979) at pp. 443–445, also skeptical.

82 See the case concerning Certain German Interests in Polish Upper Silesia (1926), P.C.I.J., Series A., No. 7, where the Permanent Court of International Justice (at pp. 30, 37–38) considered at some length the issue of whether there had been an abuse of rights by Germany in selling certain property in lands which it knew were soon to be ceded to Poland under the Treaty of Versailles. The Court examined the arguments and evidence of both sides before concluding that in this case there had been no "misuse" of right by Germany. See also the case concerning Free Zones of Upper Savoy and the District of Gex, (1932) P.C.I.J., Series A, No. 24, p. 12 and Series A/B, No. 46, where (at p. 167) the Court again referred to the possibility of an abuse of rights but noted that such an abuse cannot be presumed by the Court.

but no decision has ever been based on this principle.[83]

There are certain problems with the doctrine of abuse of rights which cause many judges and scholars to eschew it. First of all there is the fact, already referred to above, that it challenges the absolute concept of right. In addition, some legal scholars have argued that the principle of abuse of rights adds nothing new to international jurisprudence which is not already covered by other existing notions such as good faith.[84]

One major cause for concern is that generally it is the motive for the acts in question (the objective) which must be examined in order to determine whether an abuse of rights has occurred. Given the difficulty in applying such a test it is not surprising that some consider the doctrine to be dangerous and destabilizing.[85]

In 1953 Fitzmaurice described attitudes toward the doctrine of abuse of rights in the following terms:

> "Certainly this principle is beginning to gain currency in international law and, if used with circumspection, can play a useful part as a means of regulating situations that cannot be dealt with by the application of the ordinary rules (*ex hypothesi* this is so, since the 'offending' State is acting within its strict legal rights)."[86]

Even today, there is still no general consensus on the status of this principle in international law, but many scholars who have recently examined the issue have concluded that the concept is useful and in the future should be applicable in appropriate circumstances.[87] This doctrine can appropriately be applied to the abuse by a member state of its voting rights in the World Bank.

83 Some more recent references to the principle may be found in individual or dissenting opinions for the International Court of Justice written by the following Judges: Judge Alvarez (individual opinion) in the Corfu Channel Case (Merits), *ICJ Reports* (1949), at pp. 47–48, and (dissenting opinion) in the case on Competence of the General Assembly for the Admission of a State to the United Nations, ICJ Reports (1950), at p. 20; Judge Read in the Nottebohm Case, *ICJ Reports* (1955), at p. 37; and Judge Ammoun (separate opinion) in the Barcelona Traction Case, *ICJ Reports* (1970), at p. 324.

84 See KISS, *op. cit.* at pp. 2-3.

85 BROWNLIE, *op. cit.* at p. 445.

86 FITZMAURICE, G. *Law and the Procedure of the International Court of Justice, B.Y.I.L.*, Vol. 30, (1953), at p. 53.

87 See ILUYOMADE, *op. cit.*, at p. 92; and PAUL, op. cit., at pp. 128–130.

2. Détournement de Pouvoir

The concept of *détournement de pouvoir* is more generally accepted than is the doctrine of abuse of rights.[88] A *détournement* occurs when an organ which has been granted discretionary powers exercises them for a purpose other than the proper end for which they were established.[89] That discretion is supposed to be used "according to the rules of reason and justice",[90] which is much the same thing as saying that it is to be used in good faith.[91]

This doctrine is applicable to actions by the organs of international organizations,[92] and applies in this context to many of the same types of situations which we have earlier identified with their politicization.[93] If the World Bank's EDs were to deny loans on the basis of political criteria unrelated to the Bank's agreed purposes, this would amount to an illegal *détournement de pouvoir*.

88 See, KISS, *op. cit.*, at pp. 1, 3–4.

89 FAWCETT, J.E.S., ("Détournement de Pouvoir by International Organizations", *B.Y.I.L.*, Vol. 33, (1957), at p. 311), offers the following definition: "A détournement de pouvoir may be said to occur where the grantee of a discretionary power exercises that power in the course of public administration, not in breach of any legislative prohibition, but for a purpose other than that contemplated in the grant."

90 FAWCETT, "Détournement", *op. cit.*, quoting Lord Halsbury's opinion in *Stoop v. Wakefield*, (1891), A.C. 173, at 179.

91 See the discussion of Good Faith later in this chapter.

92 FAWCETT, ("Détournement", *op. cit.*, at pp. 313–314) identifies three conditions which must be satisfied before an international organization can be held capable of *détournement de pouvoir*. It must have a corporate legal personality, it must take decisions by some kind of majority vote (rather than by common consent of all members), and it must have direct administrative responsibilities (rather than merely the power to make recommendations or proposals). The World Bank satisfies all of these conditions.

93 FAWCETT, (*op. cit.* at p. 315), identifies as "typical" of *détournement de pouvoir* the following situations which are also for the most part characteristic of politicization:
" . . . actions or decisions by any organ which, though formally consistent with the provisions of the founding instrument of the organization, are designed (i) to accord unequal treatment to a particular member by diminishing its rights, or reducing or increasing its burdens as compared with other members of the organization, or (ii) to alter generally relations of the members established in the founding instrument."

3. Good Faith and Related Doctrines

Good faith is widely recognized as a general principle of law and of international law.[94] Article 2(2) of the United Nations Charter enshrines the principle that all member states "shall fulfill in good faith the obligations assumed by them in accordance with the present Charter", while the Vienna Convention on the Law of Treaties refers to a duty of good faith in both the performance and interpretation of treaties (Articles 26 and 31(1) respectively). In spite of this general recognition, the exact role of good faith in international law is far from clear.

Elisabeth Zoller, author of the most exhaustive recent study of the principle, concludes that it is merely an ethical principle although it is sometimes invoked in the legal analysis of situations better understood in terms of more concrete and precise principles such as *pacta sunt servanda*.[95] In commenting on Zoller's study Michel Virally acknowledges that the principle "has only marginal value as an autonomous source of rights and duties",[96] but he nonetheless concludes that it is a fundamental principle of international law. He sees it as the foundation of *pacta sunt servanda* and as an essential catalyst for the functioning of the international legal system.[97]

It is only logical to require that member states act in good faith so as not deliberately to defeat the object and purpose of the organizations of which they have agreed to become members. Article 18 of the Vienna Convention of the Law of Treaties goes even beyond that; it recognizes that a state has an obligation not to defeat the object and purpose of a treaty prior to its entry into force if it has signed or otherwise expressed its consent to be bound by the treaty. At the very least member states which have accepted the terms of a constitutive treaty which is in force, should be held to the same standard of obli-

94 As Virally puts it, "It is commonly understood by international lawyers that a requirement of good faith in various contexts is a well-established principle of international law and even one of the most fundamental ones." VIRALLY, M., "Review Essay: Good Faith in Public International Law", *American Journal of International Law*, Vol. 77, No. 1, (1983), at p. 130.

95 See ZOLLER, E., *La Bonne Foi en Droit International Public*, Paris, Editions A. Pedone, 1977.

96 VIRALLY, *op. cit.*, at pp. 133.

97 Ibid., at pp. 132–134.

gation as long as they remain parties to the treaty and members of the organization.[98]

When applied to the activities of World Bank member states the principle of good faith implies for those members a duty to comply with their obligations under the Bank's Charter (as does the basic rule *pacta sunt servanda*). It also implies a duty of member states to interpret their obligations under that Charter in good faith.[99] Zoller may be correct in stating that good faith obligations of this type are essentially ethical and not legal. The subjective element is crucial, and thus it is difficult to imagine how violations of a good faith standard of this type (as opposed to simple violations of *pacta sunt servanda*) could be proven in most cases. To say that there is an obligation of Bank members to act in good faith to promote or at least so as not to defeat the purposes of the Bank does not preclude good faith disagreements about the details of what those purposes may be, the Bank's Charter notwithstanding.

Ultimately, both the principle of good faith and the rule *pacta sunt servanda* lead to the same simple conclusion. The Bank's members are parties to its Charter and are bound to respect it; including Article IV(10) which defines the criteria for decision-making by the Bank and its organs (most notably the EDs). In exercising their control over the EDs members are obliged to see that they function according to the rule of that Article.

E. CUSTOMARY LAW, INCLUDING THE ORGANIZATIONAL PRACTICE OF THE BANK, AS WELL AS THE PRACTICE OF MEMBER STATES CONCERNING THE BANK

The focus of this study is upon the practice of the US government as a member of the Bank. As was noted briefly in the last section, that practice suggests that some policymakers in

98 The member states of an international organization will always be free to withdraw from membership and its obligations according to the terms of the constitutive treaty. Thus the obligation which is referred to here is not necessarily an obligation in perpetuity for the member states, but will persist only for so long as they remain members and parties to the constitutive treaty.

99 These two duties which can be considered to be part of customary international law, are now codified in Articles 26 and 31(1) of the Vienna Convention of the Law of Treaties.

Washington, are of the opinion that an ED of the Bank may properly be subjected to political control by the government which has appointed him, even to the extent of requiring him to vote according to political criteria which are inconsistent with the constitutional functioning of the Bank's Executive Board. While there is considerable evidence of this practice, there is reason to doubt whether it has been accepted as law, and thus has modified the constitutional rules of the Bank. Even today, the original disagreement between the UK and the US concerning the allegiance of the EDs has never been satisfactorily resolved as a question of law. In practice, the US has continuously exercised direct control of its ED, and it might seem futile to challenge its right to do so after over 40 years. The important question which this situation raises, is whether the Bank's Charter has been amended through the inconsistent practice of its members.

Any investigation of the customary law applicable to the Bank must include an examination of both the state practice of Bank members concerning the Bank, and of the organizational practice of the Bank itself. Practice can aid both in the interpretation of a treaty (in this case the Bank's Charter), and in identifying any new customary rules which may have been formed.

The ICJ has recognized that the collective conduct of members in the interpretation of the UN Charter has an important legal effect,[100] and the practice of Bank members is equally relevant to the interpretation of the Bank's Charter. It is even arguable that the continued toleration of violations of a constitutive treaty could lead to a tacit revision of that treaty,[101] which increases the potential importance of state practice in the development of the international institutional law of any intergovernmental organization.

There must, however, be some limit to the extent to which such a modification by practice is possible, or at least a limit to the manner in which it can be accomplished. The whole idea of a legal order would be undermined if today's violations could always simply be recast as part of tomorrow's emerging law.

100 See for example, the International Court of Justice, Advisory Opinion on the Legal Consequences for States of the Continued Presence of South Africa in Namibia (South West Africa) Notwithstanding Security Council Resolution 276 (1970), 21 June 1971, *ICJ Reports* (1971), at p. 22.

101 See, SCHERMERS, *op. cit.* at p. 88.

The legal maxim *ex injuria jus non oritur* reflects this concern, but some scholars, including Kelsen, have questioned whether that maxim should be applied to the activities of an international organization such as the UN.[102]

The debate about whether law can originate in illegal actions assumes that the illegality of the actions in question is established. In practice, there is often disagreement within the international community, about the interpretation of the law. As a result, the illegality of an action under international law is often not established beyond a reasonable doubt.

Morgenstern has observed that:

> " . . . care is usually taken to bring *actions within a possible interpretation of the law,* which *may thus gradually alter its original character,* without violent breach of continuity . . . In any community, new or altered situations raise questions as to the law applicable. In the organized international community . . . such questions may arise more frequently and cut more deeply. But their solution, as in other communities, usually involves *a choice of possible rules or interpretations* rather than a flouting of the law. The choice will be *influenced by political factors,* as indeed it often is in other communities . . . "[103] (emphasis added)

According to this view law could originate in acts of questionable legality, so long as those acts could be considered legal under some possible and reasonably plausible interpretation of the applicable rule of law.

There have always been doubts as to whether it is actually illegal to "politicize" the decision-making process of the World Bank. Under such circumstances, can law perhaps develop as a result of the arguably illegal act of politicization? Indeed, it may well be that it is only through the accommodation of such "political factors" as those mentioned by Morgenstern that the law of an international institution such as the Bank can hope to remain relevant and acceptable to its members. The import-

102 Cf. the points made in the introduction to KELSEN, H., *Recent Trends in the Law of the United Nations*, (1951).

103 MORGENSTERN, F. "Legality in International Organizations", *B.Y.I.L.*, Vol. 48, (1976–1977), at pp. 255–256.

ance of these factors is confirmed by the case studies on politics and Bank decision-making in Chapter VI.

6

CASE STUDIES

A. BACKGROUND

1. The Negotiation of the Relationship Agreement Between the Bank and the UN

Articles 57 and 63 of the UN Charter provide for the specialized agencies defined in Article 57 to be brought into relationship with the UN. Under the terms of the latter article, agreements defining the terms of the relationship are to be negotiated by the Economic and Social Council (ECOSOC) with the agencies concerned, subject to the approval of the UNGA.

As we have seen, Article V, Section 8(a) of the Bank's Charter also anticipates a cooperative relationship between the Bank and the UN, but this section makes it clear that arrangements for this cooperation cannot modify the provisions of the Bank's Charter without a formal amendment. In spite of this built-in limitation upon the legal effect of any agreement between the Bank and the UN, or perhaps because of it, the actual negotiation of such an agreement was not an easy matter.

On February 16, 1946, at its very first session, the ECOSOC established a Committee of the Council on Negotiations with the Specialized Agencies ("Negotiating Committee"), and directed this committee to begin negotiations with the Bank (as well as other specialized agencies) as soon as possible. A letter from the President of ECOSOC requesting the establishment of liaison with the Bank was received by the Bank during the inaugural meeting of the Bank and the IMF at Savannah, Georgia in March of 1946.[1]

1 See MASON and ASHER, *op. cit.*, at p. 55.

Within a few months, the UN had been able to conclude agreements with other specialized agencies such as the International Labour Organization (ILO), the United Nations Educational, Scientific and Cultural Organization (UNESCO), and the Food and Agriculture Organization (FAO). The Bank, however, was apparently convinced that the time was not ripe for even exploratory discussions on such an agreement. The Bank and its sister institution the IMF, considered themselves to be special cases among the specialized agencies, and after discussions between the two of them they produced a joint draft Relationship Agreement which they proposed to the UN.[2] That draft has been described as " . . . more of a declaration of independence from than cooperation with the United Nations".[3] The UN prepared a counter-draft,[4] and on August 15, 1947 – a year and a half after the process had begun – the actual negotiations between the ECOSOC negotiating committee and the Bank and Fund were conducted on the basis of these two documents.

After a tough day of negotiating, agreement was reached on the final language of the agreement between the UN and the Bank (hereinafter referred to as the "Relationship Agreement"). Richard H. Demuth, one of the principal authors of the Bank-Fund joint draft, observed later that "We took out a few of our declarations of independence, but not very many."[5]

The text which emerged did not truly resolve the dispute about the nature of the relationship between the Bank and the UN. In fact, two conflicting views of that relationship are reflected in the terms of the Relationship Agreement. That agreement notes that Bank members who are parties to the UN Charter have an obligation to carry out decisions of the Security Council through their action in the specialized agencies. The Bank also agrees, in somewhat ambiguous terms, to "have due regard" for decisions of the UN Security Council. But later in that same document the United Nations acknowledges that the action to be taken by the Bank on any loan is a matter to be

2 The Bank's version of the joint draft differed from that of the Fund in certain minor respects. The text of the Bank draft was sent by the Bank President to the UN with an accompanying letter dated July 21, 1947; UN document E/C.1/20, of July 22 1947.

3 MASON and ASHER, *op. cit.*, at p. 57.

4 See UN document E/C.1/35 of August 14, 1947.

5 MASON and ASHER, *op. cit.* at p. 57.

determined by the "independent exercise of the Bank's own judgment in accordance with its Articles of Agreement." And this was not the only "declaration of independence" which it contained.[6]

The next day, August 16, 1947 the Relationship Agreement was discussed by the ECOSOC, and approved by that body despite the opposition of some ECOSOC members who argued that it would undermine the authority of the UN and its ability to coordinate the work of the specialized agencies.[7] After approval by the Bank Board of Governors on September 16, 1947, and by the UNGA on November 15, 1947 the Relationship Agreement came into force.[8] The language of the Relationship Agreement, and the divergent interpretations of that language subsequently endorsed by officials of the Bank and of the UN,

6 Among the declarations of independence to be found in the Relationship Agreement; *UNTS*, Vol. 16, (1948), at p. 346, were the following:
(Article I)
"2. The Bank is a specialized agency established by agreement among its member Governments and having wide international responsibilities, as defined in its Articles of Agreement, in economic and related fields within the meaning of Article 57 of the Charter of the United Nations. By reason of the nature of its international responsibilities and the terms of its Articles of Agreement, the Bank is, and is required to function as, an independent international organization."
"3. The United Nations and the Bank are subject to certain necessary limitations for the safeguarding of confidential material furnished to them by their members or others, and nothing in this agreement shall be construed to require either of them to furnish any information the furnishing of which would, in its judgment, constitute a violation of the confidence of any of its members or anyone from whom it shall have received such information, or which would otherwise interfere with the orderly conduct of its operations."
(Article IV)
"3. The United Nations recognizes that the action to be taken by the Bank on any loan is a matter to be determined by the independent exercise of the Bank's own judgment in accordance with the Bank's Articles of Agreement. The United Nations recognizes, therefore, that it would be sound policy to refrain from making recommendations to the Bank with respect to particular loans or with respect to the terms and conditions of financing by the Bank. The Bank recognizes that the United Nations and its organs may appropriately make recommendations with respect to the technical aspects of reconstruction or development plants (sic) programmes or projects."

7 *Loc. cit.* For complete details see, "Draft Agreements between the United Nations and the International Bank for Reconstruction and Development and the International Monetary Fund", UN ESCOR, Fifth Session, 19 July–16 August 1947, pp. 266–276.

8 See the "Protocol concerning the entry into force of the agreement between the United Nations and the International Bank for Reconstruction and Development." Signed at New York, on 15 April 1948; *UNTS*, Vol. 16, (1948), at p. 344.

will be examined in greater detail below as part of the Southern Africa case study.

2. Bank Board of Governors 1951 Resolution regarding the Uniting for Peace Resolution

On September 13, 1951, soon after the UNGA had passed the "Uniting for Peace" resolution,[9] the Board of Governors of the Bank passed a brief resolution resolving:

> "That the Bank, in the conduct of its activities, shall have due regard for recommendations of the General Assembly made pursuant to said ["Uniting for Peace"] Resolution for the maintenance or restoration of international peace and security".[10] (Bracketed clarification added)

It is significant that in 1951, when the majority of UN members tended to support the Western viewpoint; and before the now familiar developing country majority came to dominate the voting on UNGA resolutions, the Bank was apparently positively disposed towards resolutions of that body. As will be seen below, the Bank's attitude towards the UNGA had evolved considerably by 1966.

It is interesting to note the rapidity with which the 1951 resolution was adopted. As was discussed above, the exact terms of the Relationship Agreement were agreed to only after difficult and extended negotiations between representatives of the Bank and of the UN. There is reason to believe that neither side was totally satisfied with the result.[11] The 1951 Bank Board resolution was passed after consultations between the UN Secretary General and the Bank lasting only about six months.[12] It was, in fact, adopted at the first full meeting of the Bank's

9 UNGA Resolution 377(V) of 13 September, 1951.

10 "United Nations Assembly Resolution 377 (V) Entitled 'Uniting for Peace' ", Resolution No. 64, Adopted on September 13, 1951 by the I.B.R.D. Board of Governors, in International Bank for Reconstruction and Development, *Summary Proceedings*: Sixth Annual Meeting of the Board of Governors, Washington D.C., September 10–14, 1951, at p. 26.

11 See the discussion of the relationship agreement, *supra.*, and MASON and ASHER, *op. cit.*, at pp. 56–59.

12 The UN Economic and Social Council had requested the Secretary General to consult with the specialized agencies concerning arrangements for assistance, pursuant to requests by the Security Council or the General Assembly, within the constitutional and budgetary limitations of the agencies; see

Board of Governors after adoption of the Uniting for Peace resolution by the UNGA. Since the Bank resolution does nothing more than to extend to some UNGA resolutions the same treatment which under the Relationship Agreement was already applicable to UNSC decisions, there was little need for more time to argue about the details.

By passing this resolution, the Bank's EDs in effect went on record as supporting the Uniting for Peace approach, an approach which both legally and politically was somewhat controversial at the time.[13] The Bank was under no legal obligation to take such a stand, but the support of the US and of its allies for the Uniting for Peace formula must have done a great deal to facilitate the Bank's decision.

As will be seen from the discussion below,[14] the legal significance of this resolution became a major point of contention when the UNGA finally did begin to make recommendations to the Bank, even though those recommendations were not taken pursuant to the "Uniting for Peace" formula.

B. CASE STUDIES ON POLITICS AND BANK DECISION-MAKING

1. The Membership of Poland and Czechoslovakia

Although the USSR never became a member of the Bank, two states in the Soviet political orbit, Poland and Czechoslovakia, were originally members. Almost from the very start Cold War politics affected the Bank's attitude towards them, but at the time the Bank had no difficulty justifying this on economic

Economic and Social Council resolution 363 (XII) of 14 March 1951, UN ESCOR, 12th Session, Supplement No. 1, UN Document E/1954, pp. 19–20. The relevant Bank Board of Governors resolution was adopted on the 13th of September 1951, or almost exactly six months later.

13 See, REICHER, H., "The Uniting for Peace Resolution on the Thirtieth Anniversary of its Passage", *Columbia Journal of Transnational Law*, Vol. 20, No. 1, (1981), at pp. 1–49 for a review of the history of that resolution and a summary of the arguments which the Soviet Union raised against it before its passage (at p. 26). For evidence that Soviet scholars have never fully accepted the validity of the Uniting for Peace formula; see TUNKIN, G.I., *Theory of International Law, op. cit.*, at pp. 322–323 ff. The Soviet Union, of course, has never been a member of the Bank.

14 See the Southern Africa Case Study, *infra*.

grounds. In 1946, the Bank's position on the link between economics and politics was expressed as follows:

> "Though the Bank is precluded from making or denying loans to achieve political objectives, there is an obvious and necessary interrelation and inter-action between political events and conditions in any country. The soundness of a loan depends fundamentally on the financial and economic prospects of the borrower. In so far as those prospects may be affected by the conditions of political instability or uncertainty in the borrowing country, those conditions must be taken into consideration."[15]

The Bank soon established a sort of linkage between participation by European countries in the Marshall Plan (officially known as the European Recovery Program or "ERP") and eligibility for Bank financing. Thus when in 1947 the Bank declined to make a loan which had been requested by Poland, Bank officials linked this decision to Poland's refusal to participate in the Paris Conference on European Recovery. Failure to attend was said to call into question Poland's independence from the USSR and therefore its status as a good credit risk.[16]

In its next Annual Report the Bank explained how the ERP was expected to facilitate the Bank's task in the reconstruction of Europe. With regard to Poland and Czechoslovakia who were not participants in that program, it was noted that:

> " . . . the Bank is not unmindful of the importance of the economic development of its member countries in Europe which are not participants in the ERP.
>
> "It is unfortunate but nonetheless true that *the existing political difficulties* and uncertainties in Europe present special problems which *have thus far prevented the Bank from making loans in those countries*. The Bank is fully cognizant of the injunction in its Articles of Agreement that its decisions shall be based only on economic considerations. *Political tensions and uncertainties* in or among its member countries, however, *have a direct effect on economic and fin-*

15 IBRD, *Second Annual Report*, Washington, 1947, at p. 17.
16 See "World Bank Loan to Poland Stymied", *New York Times*, November 5, 1947, at p. 43.

ancial conditions in those countries and upon their credit position.

"The Bank believes that there are substantial opportunities for the development of the productive resources of its member countries in Europe who are not participants in ERP. *It hopes, therefore, that the existing uncertainties can be clarified to an extent which will enable it to render financial assistance in the development of such countries,* which will not only be of benefit to them but to Europe generally, and it is continuing to explore such possibilities."[17] (emphasis added)

In spite of the Bank's expressed hopes, the situation was not to improve to the point where Bank loans to these countries would materialize. Poland withdrew in 1950 because by then it was clear that the Bank would not make any loans to Eastern Bloc countries. Czechoslovakia's membership in the Bank was formally terminated in 1954 after a dispute about the unpaid portion of its capital subscription.[18] Indeed it is understandable that a country which was deprived of benefits of membership saw little reason to contribute its share of gold or dollars.

This brief case study reveals that from the very beginning the Bank has recognized the linkages between economics and politics. These render it impossible, or at least impractical, for the Bank to ignore political developments which can be expected to affect the financial risks of a given loan. Although Cold War anti-communism undoubtedly influenced the development of this policy and its application to the Eastern European states,[19] it is important to note that an acceptable economic justification was always given.

2. The Southern Africa Case

Between 1961 and 1968 the UN General Assembly adopted a number of resolutions requesting the World Bank (along with

17 IBRD, *Third Annual Report*, (1948), at p. 14.

18 See MASON, E. S. and ASHER, R. E., *The World Bank Since Bretton Woods*, Washington, Brookings Institution (1973), at pp. 170–171.

19 According to the New York Times, Bank officials privately conceded in 1947 that the attitude of American investors towards loans to Poland and Czechoslovakia created great apprehension about loans to those countries. See "World Bank Loan to Poland Stymied", *op. cit.*

other specialized agencies) to deny technical, academic and other assistance to South Africa and Portugal because of their policies of *apartheid* and colonial rule (respectively) in southern Africa but the Bank continued lending to these regimes through 1966. During the course of the dispute which ensued, the Bank defined a rather precise legal position concerning the interpretation of the so called political activity prohibition in the Bank's Charter.

a) Resolutions Passed Prior to Consultations with the Bank

It was with regard to Portugal (at the time the colonial power in Angola and Mozambique) that the UNGA first began to solicit the assistance of the Bank. In 1960 the United Nations General Assembly adopted resolution 1514 (XV) which was entitled "Declaration on the Granting of Independence to Colonial Countries and Peoples". That resolution was essentially a condemnation of colonialism as contrary to the UN Charter, and a call for a transfer of power in all Trust and Non-Self-Governing Territories.

As a follow-up, UNGA resolution 1654 (XVI) adopted in November of 1961, created a "Special Committee" to examine the application of the earlier Declaration, and in its operative paragraph 8 requested the "specialized agencies concerned to assist the Special Committee in its work within their respective fields."[20] In March of 1962 a copy of this latter resolution was forwarded to the President of the Bank by the UN Secretariat, along with a letter drawing particular attention to operative paragraph 8. The Bank acknowledged receiving the letter a few days later, but took no further action at that time. Not surprisingly however, the UN was not content to let the matter rest.[21]

20 See, "The situation with regard to the implementation of the declaration on the granting of independence to colonial countries and peoples", UNGA Resolution 1654 (XVI), 27 November 1961, UN GAOR 16th Session, Supplement No. 17, UN Document A/5100, p. 65.

21 See "Consultation with the International Bank for Reconstruction and Development: Report of the Secretary-General, UN Document A/6825, of 15 September 1967, (hereinafter "Consultation with the IBRD") for an extensive account of the exchange of views between the Bank and the UN concerning possible Bank cooperation in applying UNGA resolutions on Southern Africa. While the report itself is quite brief, many of the relevant documents are reproduced as annexes to it.

As part of its mandate the Special Committee was supposed to examine and report on the implementation of the Declaration, and in order to do so more effectively, the Syrian representative to that committee requested the UN Secretary General to obtain information from the Bank concerning its loans to Portugal, and determine "whether or not a representative of the Bank could be invited to enlighten the Committee on this question." When requested to comment on the points raised, the Bank sent the requested information concerning its loans to Portugal, but declined to comment on the invitation it had received to send a representative to appear before the Special Committee.[22]

The Special Committee had decided on 3 July 1964, to study "the activities of foreign economic and other interests, which are impeding the implementation of the Declaration on the granting of independence in the Territories under Portuguese administration." When a letter from the UN Secretariat invited the Bank to comment on how it might assist in this task, the Bank stated that it had no information which could assist in that particular study.

Indeed, it would have been difficult for the Bank to give any other reply to a question which insinuated that the Bank itself might have been "impeding" the implementation of a UNGA resolution. Declining for the moment to send a representative before the Special Committee, the Bank presumably saw little point in attempting to justify its Portuguese lending policy before an essentially political body.

The situation was to develop considerably further in the course of the next two years due both to the activities of the UNGA and to those of the Bank. First of all, the UNGA and the Special Committee began to press the Bank with resolutions which appealed to the Bank by name, and specifically requested that it cease providing financial assistance to the Portuguese Government. Eventually, the same request was made concerning assistance to the Government of South Africa as well.

The Special Committee resolution of 10 June 1965 marked the beginning of this new phase. In addition to the expected

22 "The International Bank for Reconstruction and Development and implementation of United Nations General Assembly resolutions to withhold assistance of any kind to the Governments of Portugal and South Africa: memorandum by the UN Secretariat dated 3 March 1967", *Ibid.*, Annex I.

condemnations of Portugal's colonial policy, in this resolution the Committee:

> "6. Appeals to all the specialized agencies of the United Nations and *in particular the International Bank for Reconstruction and Development and the International Monetary Fund, and requests them to refrain from granting Portugal any financial, economic or technical assistance* so long as the Portuguese Government fails to renounce its colonial policy, which constitutes a flagrant violation of the provisions of the Charter of the United Nations". (emphasis added)

Meanwhile the UNGA was turning its attention to the *apartheid* policies of South Africa,[23] and on 15 December 1965 it adopted a resolution which drew attention to South Africa's *apartheid* policy as a violation of the UN Charter and a threat to international peace and security. That resolution also:

> "Invites the specialized agencies:
> "(a) To take the necessary steps to deny technical and economic assistance to the government of South Africa . . . "[24]

Resolution 2105 (XX) of 20 December 1965 referred to both the continuation of colonial rule and the practice of *apartheid* as threatening international peace and security and constituting a "crime against humanity". It then:

> "Requests all States and international institutions, including the specialized agencies of the United Nations, to withhold assistance of any kind to the governments of Portugal

23 Earlier resolutions concerning South Africa had followed more or less the same pattern as those discussed above concerning Portugal. UNGA resolution 1761 (XVII) of 6 November 1962 had established a Special Committee on the Policies of apartheid of the Government of South Africa to review and report to the UNGA on the situation, while UNGA resolution 1978 A(XVIII) of 16 December 1963 had invited "the specialized agencies and all Member States to give to the Special Committee their assistance and cooperation in the fulfillment of its mandate".

24 "The Policies of Apartheid of the Government of the Republic of South Africa", Resolution 2054A(XX) 15 December 1965, UN GAOR 20th Session, Supplement No. 14, UN Document A/6014, pp. 16–18.

and South Africa until they renounce their policy of colonial domination and racial discrimination''.[25]

Yet another relevant resolution was passed by the UNGA on 21 December 1965. It repeated the specific appeal which the Special Committee had made earlier to the specialized agencies, and in particular to the Bank and the IMF, to refrain from granting any financial or other assistance to the Government of Portugal as long as it failed to implement resolution 1514 (XV).[26]

Thus in December of 1965 three separate resolutions dealing with these matters were adopted, and all three of them were transmitted to the Bank during the month of January 1966. The Bank duly acknowledged receiving them, and replied that it had taken note of their contents.[27]

The Special Committee's mandate was to examine the application of the December 1960 Declaration, and once again it was not inclined to allow matters to rest where they were. It decided to follow up on the various requests and appeals which had been addressed to the specialized agencies in order to determine whether they had been brought before the decision-making bodies of those agencies, and whether any action pursuant to those requests and appeals had been taken or was contemplated. A letter was sent to the President of the Bank on 6 June 1966 requesting that he provide the Secretary-General with any relevant information.

According to the official reply of 5 July 1966 sent by the Bank's General Counsel, the three UNGA resolutions passed in December 1965 and mentioned above (2054 (XX), 2105 (XX), and 2107 (XX)) were circulated to the Bank's EDs on 21 March 1966.[28] Loan applications for projects in Portugal and South Africa were being studied by the Bank at that very moment, and the President of the Bank made a statement to the Bank's EDs on 29 March 1966. Among other things he stated:

The Bank's Articles provide that the Bank and its officers

25 ''Implementation of the Declaration on the Granting of Independence to Colonial Peoples and Territories'', Resolution 2105 (XX) of 20 December 1965, UN GAOR 20th Session, Supplement No. 14, UN Document A/6014.

26 ''Question of Territories under Portuguese Administration'', Resolution 2107 (XX) of 21 December 1965, UN GAOR 20th Session, Supplement No. 14, UN Document A/6014, pp. 3–4.

27 ''Consultation with the IBRD'', *op. cit.*, Annex I, paragraph 12.

28 ''Consultation with the IBRD'', *op. cit.*, Annex I, paragraph 15.

> shall not interfere in the political affairs of any member and that they shall not be influenced in their decisions by the political character of the member or the members concerned. Only economic considerations are to be relevant to their decisions. Therefore, *I propose to treat requests for loans from these countries in the same manner as applications for loans from other members.* . . . I am aware that the situation in Africa could affect the economic development, foreign trade and finances of Portugal and South Africa. It will therefore be necessary in reviewing the economic position of these countries to take account of the situation as it develops."[29] (emphasis added)

A full-blown dispute between the Bank and the UN became inevitable when, on 14 June 1966, the Bank entered into two loan agreements with Portuguese companies. These loans were guaranteed (since all Bank loans to private companies must be guaranteed by a Bank member) by two agreements with the Portuguese Government.[30]

In July of 1966, the Bank announced that it expected to enter into agreements to loan $US 20 Million to the South African Electricity Supply Commission, and on 8 September 1966 the loan agreement with that entity and the guarantee agreement with the South African Government were finalized. Eventually, the Bank agreed to send one of its officials to appear before a UN body to explain these decisions.

The General Counsel of the Bank (Mr. Broches) appeared before the Fourth Committee of the General Assembly on 28 November 1966 to explain why the Bank had continued to make loans for projects in Portugal and South Africa in spite of the UNGA resolutions requesting that it refrain from doing so. He asserted that Article IV, section 10 of the Bank's Charter made compliance with those resolutions impossible, since this would require that the Bank and its officers consider political matters

29 Quoted in the Statement of the IBRD General Counsel (Mr Broches) to the Fourth Committee of the UN General Assembly, 28 November 1966, reproduced in *International Legal Materials*, Vol. VI (1967), pp. 150–153, at p. 152 (hereinafter "Statement of the IBRD Counsel to the UN Fourth Committee").

30 The first was an agreement to lend $US 20 Million to Hydro-Electrica do Douro S.A.R.L. (Loan No. 452 P.O.), and the second was an agreement to lend $US 10 Million to Empresa Thermoelectrica Portugesa S.A.R.L. (Loan No. 453 P.O.). *Ibid.*, paragraph 14.

even if unrelated to economic factors. In making his point he stated:

> "I draw your attention to the fact that the provision is addressed to the Bank and its officers. The 'officers' are the President and the other senior members of the staff. The words 'the Bank' refer to the institution as such and to its organs, the Board of Governors and the Executive Directors."[31]

The Bank's General Counsel also explained that, in the Bank's view, the invitation for him to appear before the Committee was "a first step towards consultation by the United Nations with the Bank regarding recommendations to be addressed to the Bank" as provided for in Article IV of the Relationship Agreement. The lack of the prior consultation between the UN and the Bank which is called for in that agreement was offered by the Bank as a separate and independent legal justification for the Bank's not having given effect to the recommendations of the UNGA. He stressed the need for prior consultations as a means avoiding a situation where recommendations from one organization to the other might "run counter to the constitutional limitations of the recipient organization".[32]

In response to questions from the Fourth Committee, the Bank's representative further elaborated the Bank's position. He stated, for example, that "[w]hile the Bank could not be prompted by political considerations, it must always take into

31 Statement of the IBRD General Counsel to the Fourth Committee, *op. cit.*, at p. 152.

32 While this aspect of the dispute is for the most part only marginally related to this study, the connection which the Bank's General Counsel made between the requirement of prior consultation and the Bank's Charter is certainly of interest here. Referring to Article IV of the Relationship Agreement the Bank's Counsel stated (*Ibid.*, at p. 150) that:
"I may add, Sir, that in our view the provision for prior consultation has much more than merely formal significance. In such consultations the parties have an opportunity to test the *appropriateness of proposed recommendations against the respective constitutional provisions under which they operate and thus to avoid recommendations which run counter to the constitutional limitations* of the recipient organization, or are open to criticism for being contrary to existing agreements between the respective organizations." (emphasis added)

account any possible economic repercussions of political events and situations."[33]

The statements made by the Bank's Counsel touched on many related issues, including the possibility that Bank members might find themselves with conflicting obligations under the UN Charter and the Bank's Articles of Agreement. Article 103 of the UN Charter clearly provides that in the event of any such conflict the obligations of members under the UN Charter shall prevail, and it was acknowledged by Mr. Broches that in the Relationship Agreement, "[t]he Bank had taken notice of that obligation and of the fact that some of its members, despite their obligations under the Bank's Articles of Agreement, might be bound by superior obligations."[34]

One can sense in the replies of the Bank's Counsel a suggestion that the Bank's membership has a greater degree of flexibility than does the Bank itself in responding to and considering political factors, particularly when the members are acting as part of the broader UN system. This makes sense for a number of reasons. First of all, it is the Bank's Articles of Agreement which limit this type of activity, and those Articles can be expected to more effectively circumscribe the activities of the entity they create, i.e. the Bank, than those of its member states who exist and operate in many spheres independently of their membership in the Bank.[35] In addition, it is the members of the Bank, and not the Bank itself, who are bound by the UN Charter and its "superior obligations".

The statement which the President of the Bank had made to the Bank's EDs in March of 1966 was apparently intended to impress upon the EDs the idea that the Bank should not act upon the UNGA resolutions involved, and that statement had not been officially forwarded to the UN. When questioned about this, the Bank's Counsel noted that:

> "[h]e was sure . . . that the Executive Directors of the Bank, who represented the 105 member Governments,

33 UN Fourth Committee Discussion Following Statement of I.B.R.D. General Counsel, UNGA 21st Session, Fourth Committee, Provisional Summary Record of the 1645th meeting, New York, November 28, 1966, UN Document A/C.4/SR.1645 (November 30, 1966), reproduced in *International Legal Materials*, Vol. VI (1967), pp. 153–187, at p. 155.

34 *Ibid.*, at p. 158.

35 But see the discussion of member states as organs of international organization, in Chapter V, *supra*.

> had transmitted copies of the President's statement to their governments, so that *all the member Governments of the Bank must have been aware of it and have had the opportunity to instruct Executive Directors on the matter.*" (emphasis added)[36]

He thus implied that the responsibility for non-compliance with the UNGA resolutions lay primarily with the member Governments and not with the Bank itself.

A few days after the appearance of the Bank's General Counsel before the Fourth Committee the Legal Counsel of the United Nations (Mr. Stavropoulos) was asked to make a statement before that same committee concerning the dispute with the World Bank. While he agreed with the Bank's General Counsel that under the Relationship Agreement "reasonable prior consultation was required before either organization presented formal recommendations to the other",[37] he considered it "doubtful" that Article IV, Section 10 of the Bank's Charter precluded the Bank from considering the relevant UNGA resolutions.[38] In answer to questions from the Fourth Committee, he suggested that there should be further consultations between the UN and the Bank in order to explore possible ways of giving effect to the UNGA's resolutions.[39]

On December 8, 1966 the General Counsel of the Bank wrote to the Chairman of the Special Political Committee of the UNGA which was considering the policies of *apartheid* of the Government of South Africa. Since that Committee was considering matters relating to UNGA resolution 2054 A (XX) he considered it appropriate to point out that his statement to the Fourth

36 UN Fourth Committee Discussion Following Statement of I.B.R.D. General Counsel, *op. cit.* at p. 159.

37 Statement of U.N. Legal Counsel to the U.N. Fourth Committee and Discussion, UNGA, Twenty-first Session, Fourth Committee, Provisional Summary Record of the 1653rd meeting, New York, December 3, 1966, U.N. Document A/C.4/SR. 1653 (December 8, 1966), at p. 4.

38 *Ibid.*, at p. 5.

39 The UN Legal Counsel (Mr. Stavropoulos) was quite forthright in admitting before the Fourth Committee that the UN had erred by failing to initiate prior consultations before presenting recommendations to the Bank. At one point he received rather rough treatment from some members of the Committee for this principled attitude. The Soviet representative noted that "in saying that the United Nations had made a mistake, the Legal Counsel was certainly referring to the United Nations Secretariat." *Ibid.*, at p. 7.

Committee on November 28, 1966 was also applicable to the question of the Bank's loan operations in South Africa.[40]

b) Further Resolutions

Having become aware (through its Committees) of the technical requirement of prior consultations with the Bank, the UNGA continued, through further and more carefully worded resolutions, to press the Bank to cease assistance to Portugal and South Africa. Resolution 2184 (XXI) of December 12, 1966 repeats in its paragraph 9 the appeal to the specialized agencies in general and to the Bank in particular which is contained in resolution 2107 (XX), but the former also adds a new element. Paragraph 10 of this resolution:

> "Requests the Secretary-General to enter into consultation with the International Bank for Reconstruction and Development in order to secure its compliance with General Assembly resolutions 2105 (XX) of 20 December 1965 and 2107 (XX) of 21 December 1965 and with the present resolution."[41]

Resolution 2189 (XXI) of December 13, 1966 took the somewhat different approach of attempting to influence international institutions indirectly by addressing its requests for collective action to the member states. Paragraph 6 of this resolution repeats condemnations of colonial rule and of *apartheid* contained in the earlier resolution 2105 (XX). Later on, in paragraph 9 it:

> "Requests all States, directly and through action in the international institutions of which they are members, including the specialized agencies, to withhold assistance of any kind to the Governments of Portugal and South Africa . . . "[42]

40 Letter dated 8 December 1966 from the General Counsel of the International Bank for Reconstruction and Development to the Chairman of the Special Political Committee, UN Document A/SPC/115, reproduced in "Consultation with the IBRD", *op. cit.*, Annex I, Appendix 5.

41 UNGA resolution 2184 (XXI) of 12 December 1966, "Question of Territories under Portuguese administration", UNGAOR, Twenty-first session, Supplement No. 16.

42 UNGA resolution 2189 (XXI) of 13 December 1966, "Implementation of the Declaration on the Granting of Independence to Colonial Countries and Peoples", UNGAOR, Twenty-first session, Supplement No. 16.

The third in the series of resolutions passed in December of 1966 was resolution 2202 (XXI) passed on the 16th of that month. The condemnation contained in its first paragraph is limited to the policies of *apartheid* of the Government of South Africa, (this resolution does not directly refer to Portugal). The relevant portion of its paragraph 6:

> "Requests the Secretary-General:"
> "(d) To consult with the International Bank for Reconstruction and Development in order to obtain its compliance with the provisions of General Assembly resolutions 2105 (XX) of 20 December 1965 and 2107 (XX) of 21 December 1965 and with those of the present resolution, and to report to the General Assembly at its twenty-second session."[43]

Copies of UNGA resolutions 2184 (XXI) and 2202 (XXI) were independently sent by the Secretary General to the President of the Bank within days of their adoption.[44] The Secretary General and the Bank President met on December 20th and decided to proceed with a written exchange of views on the issues involved.[45]

As part of that exchange, the Legal Counsel of the UN sent to the General Counsel of the Bank, a memorandum prepared by the UN Secretariat and entitled "The International Bank for Reconstruction and Development and implementation of United States General Assembly resolutions to withhold assistance of any kind to the Governments of Portugal and South Africa".[46] In it, the UN Secretariat reviewed the chronology of those resolutions and of the dispute over compliance by the Bank, and set out its reply to the points which the Bank's General Counsel had made orally before the Fourth Committee.

The Legal Department of the Bank prepared a lengthy and detailed reply to the memorandum of the UN Secretariat. In his

43 UNGA resolution 2202 (XXI) of 16 December 1966, "The policies of Apartheid of the Government of the Republic of South Africa", UNGAOR, Twenty-first session, Supplement No. 16.

44 With regard to resolution 2184 (XXI) see the letter dated 15 December 1966 from the Secretary-General to the President of the IBRD, "Consultation with the IBRD", *op. cit.*, Annex I, appendix 7.

45 *Ibid.*, paragraph 23.

46 This memorandum, (hereinafter "UN Memorandum" or "Secretariat Memorandum") which was sent to the Bank on March 6th, 1967, is reproduced in full as Annex I to "Consultation with the IBRD", *op. cit.*

cover letter transmitting this reply to the UN, Mr. Broches, the Bank's General Counsel outlined his general conclusion about Article IV, Section 10:

> "I should like to add that, in my opinion, the prohibition contained in express terms in section 10 of article IV of the Articles of Agreement of the Bank is no more than a reflection of the technical and functional character of the Bank as it is established under its Articles of Agreement."[47]

Here, the Bank's General Counsel is explicitly endorsing a functionalist view of Article IV Section 10. This is a view which attributes to that section a considerably broader effect than would the alternative view endorsed by the UN Secretariat's memorandum.[48]

c) The Exchange of Memoranda between the Bank and the UN Secretariat

i) The Prior Consultation Issue

Part of the UN memorandum dealt with the question of prior consultation between the UN and the Bank under article IV of the Relationship Agreement. There is no need to dwell on this issue here. The UN did acknowledge that under that agreement some type of "reasonable prior consultation" was indeed a requirement before either the Bank or the UN could make formal recommendations to the other. At the same time it suggested that "reasonable prior consultation" might be considered to have taken place some time ago if one took into account the Fourth Committee's transmission of various resolutions to the Bank beginning in 1962 and the requests for information and invitations for the Bank to appear before that Committee. The memorandum passes to more substantive matters after noting that the definition of what constitutes reasonable prior consultation "is no longer at issue in the existing situation".[49]

47 The memorandum of the Legal Department of the Bank (hereinafter "Bank memorandum") was sent by the Bank's General Counsel to the UN Secretariat attached to a letter dated May 5, 1967. Parts of the letter, as well as the entire memorandum are reproduced as Annex II to "Consultation with the IBRD", *op. cit.*

48 Cf., the discussion of this article in Chapter V, supra.

49 *Ibid.*, paragraph 29.

While the Bank memorandum expressed some reservations about the Secretariat's position on the nature and timing of the consultation which should precede formal negotiations, it essentially agreed that "the issue does not appear to have practical importance at this juncture."[50]

The basic dispute concerned the scope of Article IV, Section 10 of the Bank's Charter and its applicability to the question of whether the Bank should make loans to colonial Portugal and the *apartheid* regime in South Africa in spite of UNGA requests that those governments be denied such support. The legal argument of the UN Secretariat was based on the language of that article, its drafting history, and the subsequent conduct of the Bank and its Board of Directors. In its reply, the Bank also addressed each of these points separately, and it is thus convenient to review the arguments of each side under these headings.

ii) The Language of Article IV, Section 10

The basic UN position on this section as elaborated in its memorandum was that "the sole purpose of section 10 is to prohibit interference in the internal political affairs of a Member State and discrimination against any member country because of the political character of its government."[51] According to this view, the last sentence of section 10 should not be regarded in isolation from the first sentence, because the language to the effect that only economic considerations are to be relevant "merely serves to elaborate and emphasize those factors which must be excluded from consideration (internal political affairs) by making express reference to certain factors (economic considerations) which obviously must be taken into consideration."[52]

The UN memorandum further noted that the UNGA resolutions in question were not concerned with internal political affairs but rather with situations threatening international peace and security arising due to the failure of Portugal and South Africa to observe their obligations under the UN Charter and

50 "Bank memorandum", at p. 3.
51 "UN Memorandum", paragraph 32, (emphasis added).
52 *Loc. cit.*

international law.[53] It then argued that since the UNGA has a function in connection with the maintenance of international peace and security and the observance of international law, resolutions such as these should carry great weight, and the Bank's Article IV, Section 10 (as properly interpreted) cannot justify the Bank's failure to comply with them.[54]

In reply, the Bank's central point was simply that "[t]here is no justification for imparting to the term 'political', as the Secretariat memorandum does, the qualification 'internal' ".[55] Based on the plain meaning of the words used in Article IV, Section 10, the Bank rejected the UN Secretariat's interpretation as wholly unfounded, while offering the view that:

> " . . . The contrast is between 'political' and 'economic' judgments and not between 'internal' and 'external' affairs. Section 10 thus confirms the non-political, technical, and functional nature of the Bank."[56]

iii) The Drafting History of Article IV, Section 10

The UN argued that its interpretation of Article IV, section 10 was supported by reference to the *travaux préparatoires* of the Bank's Charter. The preliminary draft referred to by the UN Memorandum states in pertinent part:

> "Section 11. Political Activity Prohibited
> "The Bank and its officers shall scrupulously avoid interference in the political affairs of any member. This provision shall not limit the right of an officer of the Bank to participate in the political life of his own country
> "The Bank shall not be influenced in its decisions with respect to applications for loans by the political character *of the government* of the member concerned with the loan.

53 The "UN Memorandum" (at paragraph 35) refers to the fact that not only the UNGA but also the Security Council had recognized the situation in South Africa and the situation resulting from the colonial policies of Portugal as seriously disturbing international peace and security. See, Security Council resolutions 180 of July 31, 1963 (appendix 10), 181 of August 7, 1963, 182 of December 4, 1963, 191 of June 18, 1964, and 218 of November 23, 1965 (appendix 11).

54 *Ibid.*, paragraphs 34–36.

55 "Bank memorandum", at p. 5.

56 *Ibid.*, at p. 7.

> Only economic considerations shall be relevant to the Bank's decisions."[57] (emphasis added)

It can readily be seen that this language is only marginally different from the ultimate wording of Article IV, Section 10. The UN memorandum reasoned that although the words "of the government" were for some reason eventually dropped, their original inclusion is evidence that the entire section relates only to the internal political life and/or political system of potential borrowers.[58]

The Bank's reply noted that the draft section 11 referred to by the UN memorandum does not utilize the term "internal", and in no way justifies the interposition of that term into the meaning of the existing section 10.

The UN argument based on this draft section is a very weak one. Even if we concede, for the sake of argument, that when Article IV, section 10 refers to the "political character" of a member this really means the political character of the government of a member, the overall interpretation of Article IV, section 10 advanced by the UN memorandum clearly contradicts the plain meaning of the rest of the text of that section.

Why does the UN memorandum stress such an unconvincing argument? Perhaps out of a need to identify something in this section which can definitely be said to relate only to the internal affairs of Bank members. It is easier to attribute a limited scope to the term "political character" than to the more general term "political affairs", and this may explain why the UN memorandum focuses upon the former and virtually ignores the latter, even though both figure prominently in the Bank's Article IV, Section 10. Having developed an argument (however unconvincing) to the effect that the first sentence of this section deals only with political interference in the internal affairs of potential borrowers, it can then be asserted that the broader and apparently unequivocal second sentence ("[o]nly economic considerations shall be relevant") must be interpreted in light of the

57 The quoted language was submitted to the Bretton Woods Conference in July 1944 as section 11 of the preliminary draft of the Bank's Articles of Agreement. See, Proceedings and Documents of the United Nations Monetary and Financial Conference, Vol. 1, (1948), at p. 202.

58 "UN Memorandum", *op. cit.*, paragraph 33.

first.[59] The argument is an imaginative one, but in the end it is far from persuasive.

iv) The Relationship Agreement as Subsequent Practice

With regard to subsequent practice, the UN argued first on the basis of Article VI of the Relationship Agreement between the Bank and the UN,[60] which reads as follows:

> "The Bank takes note of the obligation assumed, under paragraph 2 of Article 48 of the United Nations Charter, by such of its members as are also Members of the United Nations, to carry out the decisions of the Security Council through their action in the appropriate specialized agencies of which they are members, and will, in the conduct of its activities, have due regard for decisions of the Security Council under Articles 41 and 42 of the United Nations Charter."

According to the Secretariat memorandum, this language suggests that the Bank may take into account the international conduct of a member country which has violated its UN Charter obligations concerning the maintenance of international peace and security; and by agreeing to this language, the Bank has acknowledged that it is not precluded from considering such factors.[61]

59 The "UN Memorandum", *op. cit.*, puts it this way (at paragraph 32):
"It is submitted that, contrary to the position adopted by the Bank, the sole purpose of section 10 is to prohibit interference in the internal political affairs of a Member State and discrimination against any member country because of the political character of its government. This is probably one of the reasons why the section goes on to provide, in contradistinction, that only "economic considerations" shall be relevant to the decisions of the Bank and its officers. This latter provision, therefore, merely serves to elaborate and emphasize those factors which must be excluded from consideration (internal political affairs) by making express reference to certain factors (economic considerations) which obviously must be taken into consideration. Thus the last sentence of the section should not be regarded in isolation from the first sentence and interpreted as expressly confining the Bank to the consideration of nothing but the economic facts relevant to a particular loan and obliging it to disregard other material factors such as the international conduct of a member country and its repercussions upon international peace and security."

60 "Agreement Between the United Nations and the International Bank for Reconstruction and Development", *United Nations Treaty Series*, Vol. 16, (1948), pp. 346–356.

61 *Ibid.*, paragraphs 37–39.

Before addressing arguments which concern the above Article VI, the Bank cited two other parts of the Relationship Agreement in support of its claim to independence from UN control. Article I, section 2 of that Agreement contains a description of the Bank which ends with the following observation:

> " . . . By reason of the nature of its international responsibilities and the terms of its Articles of Agreement, the Bank is, and is required to function as, an independent international organization."

In a similar vein, Article IV, section 3 of the Relationship Agreement begins with this statement:

> "The United Nations recognizes that the action to be taken by the Bank on any loan is a matter to be determined by the independent exercise of the Bank's own judgment in accordance with its Articles of Agreement."

The Bank memorandum does not directly comment upon the language of these two sections, but by drawing attention to them it establishes that the Bank was conscious of its constitutional independence when entering into the Relationship Agreement, and perhaps more importantly that the UN recognized that independence.[62]

Next, the Bank presented an extended analysis of the legislative history of the Relationship Agreement which, as we have seen earlier, was agreed to only after difficult negotiations between the UN on the one hand and the Bank and Fund on the other. The length and difficulty of those negotiations, in which the Bank rejected a number of UN proposals, was said by the Bank to have resulted from the Bank's "inability to agree to any commitment which ran counter to the letter and spirit of its Articles of Agreement . . . "[63] According to the Bank memorandum, both the sides recognized this when the Relationship Agreement was negotiated.[64]

Against this background, the Bank proceeds to reply to the

62 But the independence of an entity, even a state, does not preclude its having or assuming obligations vis à vis the external world; and in this case, the independence of the World Bank as an organization does not negate the external obligations of the Bank's members under the UN Charter. See the discussion of Article VI of the relationship agreement, *infra*.

63 "Bank memorandum", at p. 14.

64 *Ibid.*, at p. 15.

UN Secretariat's arguments concerning the language of Article VI of the Relationship Agreement. Noting that the Agreements negotiated by the Bank and the Fund with the UN differ substantially from those between the UN and other specialized agencies, the Bank memorandum in essence argues that the Relationship Agreement constitutes evidence not of the Bank's obligation to follow UN political directives but of its constitutional inability to do so. In the ILO, FAO, UNESCO and ICAO Agreements, for example each of those organizations separately:

> " . . . *agrees to co-operate* with the Economic and Social Council in furnishing such information *and rendering such assistance to the Security Council as that Council may request, including assistance in carrying out decisions of the Security Council* for the maintenance or restoration of international peace and security."[65] (emphasis added)

The equivalent provision of the Bank's Relationship Agreement with the UN (Article VI) is weak in comparison:

> "The Bank *takes note* of the obligation assumed, under paragraph 2 of Article 48 of the United Nations Charter, by such of its members as are also members of the United Nations, to carry out the decisions of the Security Council through their action in the appropriate specialized agencies of which they are members, and will, in the conduct of its activities, have *due regard* for decisions of the Security Council under Articles 41 and 42 of the United Nations Charter." (emphasis added)

The Bank memorandum argues that the obvious difference between these agreements reflects the constitutional requirements of the Bank's Charter.[66] The statement that the Bank "takes note" of its members obligations does not entail the

65 Quoted *Ibid.*, at p. 17.

66 The Bank memorandum (*Ibid.*, at p. 16) cites a report to the General Assembly by the Economic and Social Council which supports this conclusion. While recommending the approval of the draft agreements with the Bank and the Fund that report notes (UN GAOR 2nd Session, Supplement No. 3, paragraph 162):
"As regards the draft agreements with the Bank and with the Fund, the Committee on Negotiations had regard to the responsibilities placed upon the two organizations by their articles of association with respect to the method and nature of their operations . . . "

direct assumption of an obligation by the Bank itself, and the agreement that the Bank will have "due regard" for certain Security Council decisions does not suggest any undertaking to "comply with" those decisions. Relying on the plain and ordinary meaning of the terms used in the Relationship Agreement, the Bank concludes that nothing in that Agreement is in the least inconsistent with a "functionalist" interpretation of the Bank's Article IV, Section 10.

From a legal-technical point of view the Bank's argument on the language of this agreement is basically sound. Nonetheless one cannot help but wonder what positive content, if any, there is to that part of Article VI which provides that the Bank will "have due regard for decisions of the Security Council under Articles 41 and 42 of the United Nations Charter." If, as the UN apparently believes, there is some such positive content to this language this has certainly not been acknowledged by the arguments in the Bank memorandum.

The first part of Article VI specifically "takes note" of the UN obligations assumed by the Bank's members; so what then is the purpose of the following clause stating that the Bank will have "due regard" for Security Council decisions? The Bank memorandum never attributes any positive meaning to this language.

v) The Relevance of the Bank's 1951 Board of Governors Resolution as Subsequent Practice

In the UN Secretariat's view, when the Bank's Board of Governors adopted a resolution in 1951 agreeing that the Bank would have "due regard" for recommendations of the UNGA made pursuant to the "Uniting for Peace" resolution,[67] this demonstrated that there was no constitutional obstacle to the Bank's complying with such resolutions.

As far as the Bank's internal legal order is concerned, the constitutional issues involved in the cases then at hand (colonial Portugal and South Africa) were said by the UN to be essentially the same as those which were raised by the "Uniting for Peace" resolution in 1951, thus the Secretariat memorandum suggests

67 "UN Memorandum", paragraphs 38 and 40. See also the background discussion of this resolution and its implications, *supra*.

that there is no reason why the Bank cannot comply with the relevant resolutions.[68]

The Bank memorandum notes that its analysis of Article VI of the Relationship Agreement applies equally as well to the 1951 Bank Board of Governors resolution. In the latter the Bank undertook to have "due regard" for UNGA recommendations pursuant to the "Uniting for Peace" resolution. As with the Relationship Agreement no undertaking "to comply" can be read into these words.[69]

Once again, the Bank's argument on the basis of this language is quite convincing, but in this case that same language was adopted by the Bank's Board of Governors under somewhat different conditions. The 1951 resolution was a statement of support by the Bank for the "Uniting for Peace" formula. While there were negotiations between the UN Secretary General and the Bank prior to the Bank's adoption of that resolution, the latter was a unilateral declaration, and was not adopted under the same kind of pressure for an agreement which prevailed before the negotiation of the Relationship Agreement.

Presumably, the Bank's Governors must have had some reason for adopting the 1951 resolution. Neither the Bank's Articles of Agreement, nor the UN Charter required or even anticipated such a resolution, so why, if no legal effect was intended, did the Bank's Governor's bother to adopt it? The UN may be correct in suggesting that the passing of this resolution by the Governors of the Bank demonstrates that they, as the organ expressly authorized to interpret the Bank's Charter, deemed it constitutionally permissible for the Bank to consider and act upon a politically oriented resolution of the UNGA.

The Bank memorandum avoids the issue of whether this resolution was intended to have any legal significance. It notes only that "[t]he willingness to have 'due regard' for 'Uniting for peace' recommendations has the same meaning and effect as the acceptance of the 'due regard' provision in article VI of the Relationship Agreement."[70] But since the Bank memorandum never attributed any effect to the "due regard" provision in the Relationship agreement, it still has not indicated in a positive way what it considers to be the meaning and effect of

68 *Ibid.*, paragraph 39.
69 "Bank memorandum", at p. 18.
70 "Bank memorandum", at p. 18.

this language. In this sense the Bank's position is unsatisfactory, since, as one commentator on this dispute has noted, the Secretariat memorandum assumes with some justification that the term "due regard" was intended to have some positive content.[71]

At the very least, this resolution constitutes evidence of a positive disposition of the Bank's membership towards the UNGA on September 13th, 1951, the date of its adoption. At that time, the Bank's member states were apparently willing to give "due regard" to a certain class of UNGA resolutions, i.e. those passed pursuant to the "Uniting for Peace" formula. Even though this undertaking to have "due regard" is not equivalent to a promise of compliance, it was at the very least a positive *political statement* in support of the "Uniting for Peace" approach. It is submitted that this was the real purpose of that resolution.

What legal effect, if any, should be ascribed to this political statement? The very fact that such a statement was made in 1951 indicates that the Bank's attitude towards political activity was less absolute in 1951 than it was in 1967 and thereafter. It is difficult to imagine the Bank adopting a resolution of this type today even as a political statement intended to be devoid of legal content. An evolution of the Bank's position regarding such matters is therefore evident. In fact, under the broad "functionalist" interpretation of the Article IV, Section 10 political activity prohibition which is advanced in the Bank Memorandum, it is arguable that the 1951 resolution is itself inconsistent with the Bank's Charter. It would in any case be a violation of "functionalist" principles (and a form of "positive politicization") for a technical agency such as the Bank to take a position on a political issue such as the controversial (in 1951) "Uniting for Peace" resolution.

The 1951 Bank Board of Governors resolution is evidence of organizational practice by the Bank inconsistent with the Bank's later view of Article IV, Section 10. As such, it does weaken the Bank's legal case for giving broad effect to that Section.

71 BLEICHER, S.A., "UN v. IBRD: A Dilemma of Functionalism", *International Organization*, Vol. 24, No. 1, (1970) at p. 39.

vi) Additional Arguments

As a last point, the UN memorandum suggests that the Bank, as a member of the United Nations family of institutions, would presumably not wish to ignore the virtually unanimous decision of the international community (working through the UN) in condemning the international conduct of Portugal and South Africa.[72]

The Bank memorandum does not attempt to rebut the above argument,[73] but as a last "functional" consideration, it stresses that economic considerations must prevail in the Bank's financial decisions and purely political factors must be excluded, because only this will reassure the investing public whose confidence is essential to the Bank's ability to raise private funds for development.[74]

d) UN Action After the Exchange of Memoranda

The exchange of memoranda did little to resolve the difference of opinion between the Bank and the UN on the essential issues. On December 18, 1968 the UNGA adopted a further resolution which noted with regret that some of the specialized agencies (the Bank and the IMF being named specifically) had not so far implemented resolution 2311 (XXII) and other relevant resolutions. The resolution repeated appeals to those agencies to withhold assistance to Portugal and South Africa, but then went further than past resolutions by making the following recommendation:

72 "UN Memorandum", paragraph 41.

73 The real "reply" to this appeal came in a letter dated August 18, 1967 from the President of the The International Bank for Reconstruction and Development to the Secretary-General of the United Nations which was sent at the end of the exchange of legal memoranda. ("Consultations with the IBRD", *op. cit.*, Annex IV). That letter ends with the following paragraph:
"In the circumstances, I should like at this point to leave legal argumentation aside and to assure you – and through you the various United Nations organs concerned – that the World Bank is keenly aware and proud of being part of the United Nations family. Its earnest desire is to co-operate with the United Nations by all legitimate means and, to the extent consistent with its Articles of Agreement, to avoid any action that might run counter to the fulfillment of the great purposes of the United Nations. I give you this assurance in the hope that it may be helpful in dissipating any misunderstanding of the Bank's attitude."

74 "Bank memorandum", at p. 19.

> "5. *Recommends* that the The International Bank for Reconstruction and Development *should withdraw the loans and credits it has granted to the governments of Portugal and South Africa,* which are being used by those governments to suppress the national liberation movements in the Portuguese colonies and in Namibia, and against the African population in South Africa;"[75] (emphasis added)

Before this resolution was actually passed by the UNGA[76] the Bank sent a letter commenting on the language of paragraph 5 to the UN Secretary General, and it was circulated in the UNGA prior to the vote. In comments submitted before the vote on this resolution the Bank noted that:

> . . . This new operative paragraph *would ask the Bank to act in contravention of formal loan agreements* which it has entered into and which are registered with the United Nations Secretariat. The Bank's General Counsel had advised me that under these agreements *the Bank could not legally do what the amendment would ask it to do*. I am further advised that if the Bank tried to act illegally in the manner suggested by the amendment, the borrowers in question could take legal action against the Bank before the international arbitral tribunals established by the loan agreements. I trust that the General Assembly would not wish to recommend to the Bank that it disregard the obligations it has undertaken in its loan agreements."[77] (emphasis added)

The legal points raised here are entirely straightforward and could not have been lost on the General Assembly. Nonetheless, the resolution, including the operative paragraph in question, was adopted by the UNGA by a vote of 82 in favor,

75 "Implementation of the Declaration on the Granting of Independence to Colonial Countries and Peoples by the specialized agencies and the international institutions associated with the United Nations", Resolution 2426 (XXIII), 18 December 1968, UN GAOR, 23rd Session, Supplement No. 18, UN Document A/7218.

76 The language of resolution 2426 (XXIII) was approved before its adoption by a report of the Fourth Committee to the UNGA, UN Document A/7424 of December 13, 1968.

77 Letter dated December 17, 1968 from the IBRD Special Representative for United Nations Organizations to the Secretary General Of the United Nations, UN Document A/7446 of December 17, 1968, reproduced in *International Legal Materials*, Vol. VIII, (1969), at p. 444.

and 7 against, with 25 abstentions.[78] Obviously those countries supporting this resolution did not consider the Bank's legal arguments to be decisive.

e) The Bank's Memorandum as the "Official" Bank View

While the Bank memorandum sets out in the clearest possible terms the views of the Bank legal staff on Article IV, Section 10 of the Bank's Charter, it is appropriate to ask whether these views were shared by the Bank's EDs and by the Board of Governors who have the constitutional authority to decide any questions of interpretation of that document. In a letter to the UN Secretary General dated August 18th, 1967 the President of the Bank suggested that the EDs did share these views. After acknowledging that disagreement persisted between the UN Legal Counsel and the Bank's General Counsel the letter stated that:

> " . . . the Executive Directors of the Bank who, as you know, are responsible for interpreting the Articles of Agreement, having carefully considered all the arguments advanced, have, although with some dissents, endorsed the position taken by the Bank's General Counsel. It seems to me unlikely that additional legal argumentation would change the situation."[79]

This appears to be an assertion that the Bank's EDs had actually made an interpretative decision under Article IX of the Bank's Charter. In fact no formal interpretation along these lines has ever been handed down by either the EDs or the Board of Governors.[80] Nonetheless, the EDs must have supported the position taken by the Bank in this dispute otherwise an interpretive decision would presumably have been forthcoming.

There is further evidence of support by the EDs for the pos-

78 A specific listing of the recorded vote can be found *Ibid.*, at p. 441.

79 Letter dated August 18, 1967 from Mr. Woods, the President of the The International Bank for Reconstruction and Development to Mr. U Thant, the Secretary-General of the United Nations, "Consultations with the IBRD", *op. cit.*, Annex IV.

80 In a private interview with the author of this study members of the Bank staff have confirmed that no such official interpretive decision has been made. Apparently the issue was never controversial enough *within* the Bank to merit such a decision.

ition taken by the Bank's General Counsel in this dispute. After the UNGA passed resolution 2426 (XXIII) Robert McNamara, who had only recently taken over as President of the Bank, sent a letter to U Thant, the then UN Secretary General, concerning the Bank's position on the various issues which are discussed above.[81] The final paragraph of the letter declares that "... the Executive Directors of the Bank ... have approved this letter."[82] Since McNamara's letter reconfirms every aspect of the Bank's prior position in this dispute,[83] the Bank's EDs did apparently approve of that position even if only "informally" and not in an official interpretive decision of the Bank's Charter.[84]

f) The Hidden Issues Involved in this Dispute

The history of this case study sheds some very important light upon the interpretation of Article IV, Section 10 of the Bank's Charter, but behind this largely technical issue were conflicts of another kind. After a review of the dispute, it is apparent that the argument had more to do with the independence of the Bank from the UN than with anything else.

The nature of the relationship between the United Nations Organization itself and the other specialized agencies which are

81 Letter of May 14, 1969 from Mr. Robert McNamara, President of the IBRD to Mr. U Thant, UN Secretary General replying to the UN on withdrawal of loans and credits from Portugal and South Africa, *International Legal Materials*, Vol. 8, (1969), at p. 1339, reproduced from UN Document A/AC.109/333 of July 3, 1969.

82 *loc. cit.*

83 McNamara's letter specifically confirmed that the Bank's position remained as set forth in a the letter of August 18, 1967 (quoted *supra.*). The earlier letter from Bank President Woods had concluded that under the terms of the Bank's Charter it could not comply with the UNGA's requests that it withhold economic assistance to Portugal and South Africa. (See Letter dated August 18, 1967 from Mr. Woods, the President of the Bank to Mr. U Thant, the Secretary-General of the United Nations, "Consultations with the IBRD", *op. cit.*, Annex IV.) McNamara's letter also explained that the Bank would have no legal grounds for withdrawing loans it had already granted to Portugal and South Africa, and that the Bank could not avail itself of the Secretary General's offer to assist the Bank in finding ways to implement the relevant UNGA resolutions on this matter. *loc. cit.*

84 Unlike the IMF, (whose Executive Board has a similar power of interpretation under Article XXIX of the IMF Articles of Agreement), the Bank does not publish any compilation of decisions by its EDs authoritatively interpreting its Charter. It is apparently the policy of the Bank to avoid formal interpretative decisions under Article IX of the Bank's Charter.

members of the "UN family" is left somewhat vague by the terms of the UN Charter. While it provides that the specialized agencies are to be brought into relationship with the UN, the terms of the agreements which are to accomplish this are not spelled out,[85] and as we have seen, they can vary a great deal. The Charter also calls for the UN to co-ordinate the activities of the specialized agencies by making recommendations to them but it does not define the legal effect of such recommendations.[86]

When it passed the resolutions involved in this dispute, the UNGA was merely attempting to fulfill this part of its mandate under the UN Charter. The Bank, however, is unusual among the specialized agencies in that it has generally considered independence from the political organs of the UN (in practice this may mean independence from all UN organs) to be indispensable if it is to accomplish its technical mission. It reacted defensively against what it may have perceived to be a direct attack upon its autonomy and independence.

While the potential conflict between the UNGA's role as political co-ordinator and the Bank's role as a technical institution could not have been fully anticipated by the drafters of the Charter, it is regrettable that the UN Secretariat did not appreciate the need for greater subtlety in its legal argumentation.

The UN's legal argument was based entirely upon its view that Article IV, Section 10 of the Bank's Charter applied only to the "internal affairs" of Bank members. This interpretation was unacceptable to the Bank not only because it was unjustified from a legal standpoint, but also because of the practical consequences which its acceptance would entail.

If the Bank were to accept such a limited interpretation of Article IV, Section 10 then the international political behavior of a potential borrower could be considered relevant to its loan decisions. Were this point to be conceded, the Bank would find itself under strong pressure to follow the UNGA's political directives on loans. Though the Bank would not be under a legal obligation to comply with such directives, how could it justify any failure to follow them? Since the Bank is not a political body, it would be expected to defer to the political judgment of the UNGA and the UNSC on such matters. The

85 See Articles 57 and 63 of the UN Charter.
86 *Ibid.*, Articles 58 and 63.

door, once opened, would be left wide open, and the Bank's autonomy would be seriously threatened.

g) The Failure to Address the Link between Political and Economic Factors

The most thorough legal analysis of this episode which can be found in the existing literature appears in an article by Samuel Bleicher. In that article Bleicher focuses upon what he sees as two distinct legal questions, i.e.:

(1) Must the Bank comply with the call of the General Assembly?
(2) May the Bank comply with the call of the General Assembly?

The Bank, he observes, argues that both of these questions must be answered in the negative.[87] After examining the legal contentions of both organizations he concludes that the answer to the first question "is clearly no", but that the Bank "is on shakier ground" in attempting to demonstrate that under its articles it is not legally permitted to consider UN recommendations.[88] He notes that the Bank has an interest in the preservation and strengthening of international law, and suggests that it could have chosen to consider Portugal and South Africa to be bad credit risks due to their failure to uphold their basic obligations under the Charter. This type of politically influenced economic decision would in Bleicher's opinion be consistent not only with the Bank's Charter, but also with the long term aim of the functionalist strategy, i.e. the strengthening of international institutions as a means to world order.[89]

As the next case study (Chile under Allende) reveals, the Bank has at times chosen to deny loans to a country because of the links believed to exist between certain political acts and their economic effects. It could then, have denied loans to *apartheid* South Africa and to colonial Portugal on the same grounds.

One reason it did not is because of the way the issues were raised by the UN. The UN memorandum did not even attempt to argue that economic consequences would follow the political

87 See BLEICHER, *op. cit.*, at pp. 36–37.
88 *Ibid.*, p. 37.
89 *Ibid.*, at pp. 42–46.

disputes involved, or to remind the Bank tactfully that it was perhaps ignoring this aspect of the economic analysis. It is quite possible that the Bank might have been open (or at least more susceptible) to this type of argument. Apparently, the Bank itself was not inclined to raise a point which would have weakened its position.

In this dispute, the Bank prevailed against political pressures by the use of careful legal arguments. But not all of the relevant legal issues were discussed. It is useful at this point to recall the following statement made by the President of the Bank to the EDs on March 29, 1966 at the beginning of this dispute:

> "I am aware that *the situation in Africa could affect the economic development, foreign trade and finances of Portugal and South Africa*. It will therefore be necessary in reviewing the economic position of these countries to take account of the situation as it develops."[90] (emphasis added)

The Bank's President acknowledged that the economic consequences of a political situation were properly relevant, yet the possible economic consequences of *apartheid* and of Portuguese colonial rule were never even raised as an issue in the exchange of views between the Bank and the UN. The Bank may have fought so successfully against politics that it ignored economics.

While the Bank refused to concede any of the legal points argued by the UN, it seems to have made an effort to avoid any further conflict with UN policies on Southern Africa. It has made no further loans to South Africa since those in 1966 which touched off this dispute, and resumed loans to Portugal only after that country withdrew from Angola and Mozambique in 1974–1975. At one point, when the Bank was contemplating loans to Botswana and Zambia, it demonstrated concern for the fact that those countries were continuing economic relations with Rhodesia, which at the time was the subject of economic sanctions imposed by the Security Council. In order to insure that there would be no adverse reaction from the Council it

90 Quoted in the "Statement of the IBRD Counsel to the UN Fourth Committee", *op. cit.*, *International Legal Materials*, Vol. VI (1967), at p. 152. See the discussion of the Bank General Counsel's appearance before that committee, supra.

required those states to consult with the UN about their special circumstances.[91]

Since the argument based on a link between economics and politics was not raised by the UN in this dispute, we must look to other case studies for evidence of practice on this matter.

3. The Chile Case, and the Bank's Policy towards Disputes over Compensation for Expropriation

a) The Bank and Allende's Chile: Evidence of a Politically Motivated Suspension of Bank Lending

Chile was a member of the World Bank upon its founding, and in 1948 was the first country to receive a development loan from the Bank. Since that time Chile has received $US 919.55 Million worth of loans and development credits from the World Bank Group. This overall figure, while somewhat interesting, tells us nothing about the possibility that political factors may have influenced lending to Chile. Before addressing this last issue, it may be useful to examine the pattern of Bank lending to that country. The table below shows the total loans authorized by the Bank for Chile between 1963 and 1985.

Although Bank lending to Chile has not followed any particular pattern it has, with one major exception, been more or less continuous since the early 1960's. The Bank loaned Chile $142.1 Million between 1961 to 1970, but did not approve a single loan to that country between 1971 and 1973. Lending resumed in 1974 increasing steadily for the next four years. What accounts for the three year hiatus between 1971 and 1973 when no new loans to Chile were authorized?

In September of 1970 Dr. Salvador Allende Gossens was elected President of Chile. President Allende was an avowed Marxist, and this eventually affected many aspects of the relations between the US government and the Chilean government. Ultimately, in September of 1973, President Allende's government was overthrown in a military coup in which US involvement is generally acknowledged.[92]

91 See MASON and ASHER, *op. cit.*, at p. 591.

92 The role of both the US government and of the US based company ITT in that coup has been well documented. See, US Senate, *Multinational Corporations and United States Foreign Policy*, 93rd Congress, 1st Session, Hearings

The Bank loaned Chile $19.3 Million in 1970, including a $10.8 Million loan in June of 1970, just a few months before Allende's election. No new Bank loans to Chile were authorized until January of 1974, a few months after the fall of Allende's government. It is reasonable to ask what link there was, if any, between the Allende government and the suspension of Bank lending to Chile.

IBRD loan authorizations to Chile between 1963 and 1985 (in $Millions)

Year	Total authorizations
1963	24.0
1964	0
1965	7.15
1966	60.0
1967	0
1968	11.6
1969	0
1970	19.3
1971	0
1972	0
1973	0
1974	13.5
1975	20.0
1976	33.0
1977	60.0
1978	0
1979	0
1980	116.0
1981	0
1982	0
1983	128.0
1984	136.0
1985	291.0

Source, World Bank Annual Reports 1963–1986

before the Subcommittee on Multinational Corporations of the Committee on Foreign Relations, Part 3, Washington, D.C., US Government Printing Office, 1973. For a debate on the degree of US involvement in that coup see also, "Chile: What was the US Role?" – an exchange between Elizabeth Farnsworth taking the position "More than Admitted", and Paul E. Sigmund saying "Less Than Charged", in *Foreign Policy* – Vol. XVI, (1974), pp. 126–156.

i) The Attitude of the US Government Towards Allende's Government in Chile

While most details of US policy towards the Allende government involve matters beyond the scope of this study, National Security Decision Memorandum (NSDM) 93 should be mentioned. This document, which established an official but unacknowledged US policy of applying economic pressure upon Chile, was issued by Henry Kissinger on behalf of President Richard M. Nixon on 9 November 1970; barely two months after Allende's election. Among other things, NSDM 93 provided that no new US economic or financial assistance was to be committed to Chile (except for humanitarian programs), and that assistance under existing arrangements was to be reduced or terminated if possible. The US was also to use its influence within the multilateral financial institutions to limit their aid to Chile.[93] Whether this actually affected the Bank's lending policy towards Chile will be discussed below.

ii) The Dispute Between Chile and the US over Compensation for Nationalized US Investments

Tensions between the US and Chile peaked after the Chilean Government expropriated US copper mining investments on July 16, 1971 and would not agree to provide the levels of compensation demanded by the US companies involved. US officials publicly linked Chile's policies on compensation for expropriation to the issue of development assistance. Upon learning of Chile's intention to subtract from compensation settlements what it considered to be "excess profits", US Secretary of State William P. Rogers made the following statement on October 13, 1971:

> "The Controller General of Chile announced his findings on October 11 that no compensation would be paid for the U.S. copper mining investments expropriated on July 16 except for modest amounts in the cases of two smaller properties.

93 For more about this directive (NSDM 93) see, DAVIS, N., *The Last Two Years of Salvador Allende*, London, Tauris & Co., (1985), at pp. 21–22, and KISSINGER, H., *The White House Years*, Boston, Little Brown, (1979), at p. 681.

> "The United States Government is deeply disappointed at this serious departure from accepted standards of international law. Under established principles of international law, the expropriation must be accompanied by reasonable provision for payment of just compensation.
>
> "Should Chile fail to meet its international obligations, it could jeopardize flows of private funds and *erode the base of support for foreign assistance*, with possible adverse effects on other developing countries. The course of action which the Chilean Government appears to have chosen, therefore, *could have an adverse effect on the international development process*."[94] (emphasis added)

When the above statement was made, the US had already severely reduced its official bilateral aid flows to Chile pursuant to the policy of NSDM 93, and the Bank had already declined to make loans to Chile during its first year under President Allende. Can the cutoff of Bank lending to Chile be linked to NSDM 93, to the dispute over Chilean nationalizations or both?

iii) The Suspension of World Bank Lending to Allende's Chile

The Allende government was convinced that the Bank's failure to approve new loans to Chile during this period was no coincidence, but was a direct result of US and World Bank attitudes towards Chile's policies on nationalization. At the annual meeting of the Bank in 1972 the Chilean Central Bank President observed that:

> "In the 22 months of the present administration, our country received not one new loan from the World Bank, in spite of having submitted elaborate projects for its consideration . . . These projects have the features of feasibility, financial return, and other technical conditions that fully comply with the requirements laid down in the Bank's Articles of Agreement and in its general operating

94 "U.S. Responds to Chilean Decision on Compensation for Expropriation", Statement by US Secretary of State William P. Rogers, *Department of State Bulletin*, Vol. LXV, No. 1688, November 1, 1971, at p. 478.

> policies. The projects are entirely in accordance with the purposes of development, which is stated by the Bank to be the primary objective, and in some cases their technical analysis has been completed in full by the management. And yet their presentation to the Bank's Board of Executive Directors has been held up.
>
> "The origin of this behavior is the situation resulting from the decision of the Government of Chile to nationalize five private U.S. enterprises which were exploiting our principal copper deposits, as senior representatives of the Bank have informed the authorities of my country, including myself . . .
>
> . . . "In acting as it did, the World Bank acted not as an independent multinational body at the service of the economic development of all its members, but in fact as a spokesman or instrument of private interests of one of its member countries . . .
>
> " . . . It is not possible to make declarations of multilateral convictions if, at the same time, what is actually done in practice appears to indicate that international financial instruments are being used for the foreign policy ends of a particular country."[95]

Soon thereafter, when the Bank President presented the Bank's annual report to the ECOSOC, a representative of Chile in that body made a similar point stating that "it seemed the Bank's current loan policy depended more on political ideology than on the content of the projects."[96]

The Bank, for its part, denied that it had cut off loans because of Chile's nationalization policies, and publicly attributed the cutoff to Chile's large external debt and lack of credit-worthiness.[97] Speaking before the ECOSOC, Bank President McNam-

95 Statement by Mr. Alfonso Inostroza, Governor of the IMF and the IBRD, to the 1972 Annual Meetings of the Boards of Governors, published in *Summary Proceedings: 1972 Annual Meetings of the Boards of Governors IBRD/IFC/IDA*, at pp. 53–59.

96 "Reports of the The International Bank for Reconstruction and Development, International Development Association and International Finance Corporation", *Yearbook of the United Nations*, Vol. 26, (1972), at p. 316.

97 See "Chile Criticizes World Bank Policy", *The New York Times*, September 29, 1972, *op. cit.*

ara specifically rejected the charges made by the Chilean representative.[98]

In spite of the Bank's denials, there is substantial circumstantial evidence of some type of link between the Allende government in Chile (and its policies on nationalization and compensation) and the suspension of Bank lending to that country. That evidence appears even stronger when the Bank's traditional attitude towards expropriation disputes is taken into consideration.

iv) The Bank's General Policy Towards Expropriation and Compensation Disputes

During the 1960s, countries that nationalized foreign owned property without paying compensation often found that the World Bank would not even consider their applications for loans.[99] The economic basis for this policy was explained by a 1969 Bank publication as follows:

> "The Bank is charged, under its articles of agreement, to encourage international investment. It has, therefore, a direct interest in the creation and maintenance of satisfactory relations between member countries and their external creditors. Accordingly, the normal practice is to inform governments who are involved in such disputes that the Bank or IDA will not assist them unless and until they

98 The summary record of his appearance records the following comment by Mr. McNamara ("Reports of the The International Bank for Reconstruction and Development, International Development Association and International Finance Corporation" (1972), *op. cit.* at p. 317):
"Continuing, the President said the charges made by the representative of Chile were false. . . . It was not the case that loans to Chile were denied because of the nationalization of certain property of nationals of the United States. The Bank had always followed a reasonable and consistent policy on nationalization of property, based on accepted principles of international law. The current problem arose because the Chilean economy was unfortunately in serious difficulties, the President of the Bank held."

99 MASON and ASHER, *op. cit.* at p. 747, mention the cases of Algeria (after 1964), the Democratic Republic of the Congo (now Zaire) (from 1961–1969), Indonesia (during the Sukarno regime), Iraq (in the mid 1960's), and the United Arab Republic (during most of the 1960's), all of which were faced with suspensions of Bank lending or refusals to lend linked with expropriation disputes.

make appropriate efforts to reach a fair and equitable settlement."[100]

In light of this well known policy of the Bank, it is somewhat surprising that Bank President McNamara did not openly acknowledge that compensation disputes were behind the cutoff of Bank loans to Allende's Chile. Couldn't the Bank have justified that cutoff in terms of the above-mentioned policy?

Perhaps not, since the official position of the Bank on this issue has always been somewhat flexible. A settlement need not necessarily have been reached, so long as "appropriate efforts" to this end are made by the potential borrower. During the years of the Allende government (1971–1973) Chile might well have qualified for World Bank loans under such a standard. Even after the Chilean government announced in October 1971 that no compensation would be paid to major US copper companies, it continued negotiating with the US in an effort to resolve the resulting dispute until the very day of the coup d'état.[101] Thus Allende's government never closed the door entirely to a more satisfactory resolution of the compensation issue.

Also of possible relevance is the fact that in June of 1971 the Bank had approved a $5.4 million loan to Guyana even though that country had not yet settled an investment dispute with a US corporation. (The US appointed ED abstained in the vote on that loan proposal.)[102] It would have been difficult for the Bank's management to justify the application of a stricter standard to the Chilean expropriations. These various factors help to explain the public denials of a link between Chilean policies on compensation for expropriation of foreign owned property

100 *Policies and Operations: The World Bank, International Development Association and International Finance Corporation*, Washington, D.C., IBRD, (1969) at p. 31.

101 There were legal appeals by the US companies involved to a five member Chilean Copper Tribunal, (the Chilean Government's decision was upheld in August 1972), followed almost immediately by negotiations between the US and Chilean governments in an attempt to reach a solution to the compensation dispute. According to Nathaniel Davis, US Ambassador to Chile from 1971–1973, these negotiations were still ongoing when the coup occurred. See, DAVIS, N., *The Last Two Years of Salvador Allende*, London, Tauris & Co., (1985), at pp. 99–107.

102 See, "Chile Criticizes World Bank Policy", The New York Times, September 29, 1972, at p. 61, column 2.

and the temporary cessation of Bank lending activity to that country.

v) Differences Between the US Government's Position on Nationalization and Expropriation Issues and that of the Bank

The US government has generally been stricter than the Bank in linking economic assistance to the satisfactory resolution of disputes over compensation for the expropriation of US foreign investments. This is partly because of the Gonzalez Amendment, a provision of US legislation which since 1972 has required US representatives to the Bank (and other MDB's) to vote against loans to countries which have expropriated US investments, unless the US President determines that arrangements for adequate compensation are being made.[103] Although that amendment does set out a flexible standard,[104] the judgments made by the US President have often been more demanding upon the potential borrowers than have those of the Bank management. Evidence of this can be found in the loan which the Bank made to Guyana in June of 1971 over the opposition of the US. Guyana had expropriated some US investments but discussions and legal procedures aimed at obtaining compensation were continuing. The US government did not consider that Guyana was doing enough to resolve the dispute, but the Bank management, and a majority of Bank EDs evidently disagreed.[105] The disagreement between the US and the Bank over standards in this area continues. Between October 1, 1979 and September 30, 1985 the Bank approved 9 loans which the US ED voted against due to disputes about uncompensated

103 The International Development Association Act as amended by Public Law 92-247 of March 10, 1972, Sec. 12; 22 U.S.C. Sec. 284j. A detailed discussion of the Gonzalez Amendment, and of other US legislation concerning the use of US voting power within the Bank, follows in Chapter VII, *infra*.

104 Under the Gonzalez Amendment compensation for the expropriated property need not necessarily have been paid in order for loans to be supported by the US, so long as "good faith negotiations are in progress aimed at providing prompt, adequate, and effective compensation under the applicable principles of international law". *Ibid*.

105 See, "Chile Criticizes World Bank Policy", *op. cit*.

expropriation of American investments. All 9 of these were concessional IDA credits for Ethiopia.[106]

vi) Evidence Suggesting that No Politically Motivated Cutoff Was Involved

In 1974 the Congressional Research Service (CRS) of the US Congress was requested by members of Congress to study whether the multilateral development banks (in this case the World Bank and the Inter-American Development Bank) had suspended lending to Allende's Chile for non-economic reasons. Jonathan E. Sanford of the CRS, who prepared the requested study,[107] was not given free access to the internal records of those international institutions.[108] Nonetheless, as a CRS researcher, he did have access to a number of generally unavailable sources, including "white papers" prepared separately by each of the two MDB's on its relations with Chile during the Allende period. The Bank's white paper, which presents its policies towards Allende's Chile in the best possible light, seems to have had a strong influence on Sanford's conclusion's, which read in part as follows:

> "The World Bank seems to have maintained a relatively consistent approach towards Chile during the entire 1961–1974 timespan. During the Frei Government, [1964–1970] this Bank was reluctant, (as it has been in other cases), to provide loans to Chile because of the inflation and economic instability which the country experienced late in the decade; economic conditions during the Allende period were also sufficiently problematic as to justify some hesitation.
>
> . . . The Bank's suspension of lending to Chile during the Allende period does not seem to be out of character

106 Between October 1, 1985 and September 30, 1987 the US did not invoke uncompensated expropriation as grounds for opposing any World Bank loans. See *International Finance*: The National Advisory Council on International Monetary and Financial Policies Annual Reports to the Congress, for fiscal years 1980–1987.

107 SANFORD, J.E., "The Multilateral Development Banks and the Suspension of Lending to Allende's Chile", Foreign Affairs Division, Congressional Research Service, The Library of Congress, August 6, 1974 (Revised December 13, 1974).

108 *Ibid.*, "Prefatory note".

with previous World Bank practice towards that country."[109] (bracketed clarification added)

Two primary considerations led Sanford to these conclusions. (1) Evidence of dismal Chilean economic conditions from 1961–1974, and of a continuing reluctance of the Bank to lend to Chile from late 1966 until the time of his study (1974). (2) Evidence, provided by the Bank, that beginning in March or April of 1973, the Bank and Chile began to normalize relations, and that during the summer of 1973, in the months before Allende's overthrow, Chile and the Bank's management had agreed in principle that Chile should receive the three small loans that the Bank did in fact made to Chile in the year after the 1973 coup.

A closer look at Bank loan authorizations for Chile during the 1961–1974 period does suggest that the Bank may have been less than enthusiastic about making loans to Chile even before Allende came to power. Between the end of 1966 and Allende's election in 1971, Bank lending to Chile had already slowed to a trickle, thus the "suspension" of lending between 1971 and 1973 could arguably be viewed as a continuation of that largely negative trend. Similarly, the resumption of lending in 1974 (the year of the CRS study), was at a low level ($US 13.5 Million), and so what occurred from 1971 to 1974 could be viewed as consistent with the entire course of Bank lending to Chile over the 1961–1974 period. The increase in Bank lending to Chile since 1974 is another story, but the possible implications of that will be discussed below.

There is evidence that the Bank intended to resume lending to Chile before the coup which overthrew Allende. Sanford's CRS study speaks of "World Bank preliminary notes of on the July 1973 meeting between Chilean Finance Minister Inostroza and Bank Vice-President Knapp" to which Sanford was apparently granted access.[110] The Bank's white paper describes this meeting in some detail, although it states that it took place in June and not July. In any case, it was apparently at that meeting that an agreement in principle on new loans was reached.

109 *Ibid.*, "Conclusions".
110 *Ibid.*, "The Banks and Chile Since Allende: Recent Employment".

vii) Evidence of Politicization of the EDs

Sanford seems to view these attempts by the Bank management to normalize relations with Allende's Chile as evidence that the Bank's management had not politicized its loan operations. But an agreement in principle between Allende's Finance Minister and the Bank's management cannot be equated with an effective resumption of Bank lending to Chile. Although the documentation concerning two of the three loans "agreed" upon was circulated to the Bank's EDs in August, they were not approved or even formally considered by that body until after the September coup. As the Bank's white paper states:

> "The papers circulated to the Board on August 7 regarding financing interest during construction on two outstanding loans were marked for consideration on September 4. *However, preliminary reactions* to these proposals which were expressed to the management of the Bank by several Executive Directors, *raised a serious question as to whether the proposals would command a favorable vote at that time*. Hence, after consultation with the Government of Chile, the management postponed indefinitely the placing of this item on the agenda of the Executive Directors, and this is how matters stood at the time that the Allende government was deposed."[111] (emphasis added)

Politicization of the Bank might have manifested itself in the refusal of the Bank's management to recommend Chilean loans to the EDs, or in a refusal of the EDs to approve such loans. The mere fact that the Bank management negotiated loans to Allende's Chile does not establish that the Bank's lending operations were not politicized.

Even assuming that Sanford was correct in concluding that the Bank's management maintained a consistent and essentially non-politicized approach to Chile between 1961 and 1974, the Bank's own white paper suggests that certain of the Banks EDs did not do likewise.

The last passage quoted above clearly indicates that as of

111 "Chile and the World Bank", White Paper prepared by the World Bank, Appendix to SANFORD, J.E., "The Multilateral Development Banks and the Suspension of Lending to Allende's Chile", *op. cit*. The quoted language appears in paragraph 32 of that appendix.

August 1973, the reason for delaying Bank loans to Chile was the opposition of certain unidentified EDs. That opposition was dropped within 5 months after the coup, since these same loans were ultimately approved by the EDs on February 7, 1974. Chile's economic situation had not had time to change much in the intervening months, but the political environment had been radically transformed.[112]

The increase in Bank lending to Chile since 1974 had not yet occurred when the CRS study was completed, but it does raise some important questions. Was that increase justified by economic factors? If not, does it indicate that only political factors, i.e. the Allende government and its clash with the US government, were behind the 1971–1973 suspension of Bank lending to Chile? These questions cannot be fully answered here, but it is worth noting that both Chile's economic policies and its attitude towards expropriation and compensation disputes changed dramatically after 1973. These two factors together might be seen as justifying a more positive evaluation by the Bank of Chile's creditworthiness after the coup.

It is interesting to note that Sanford's conclusions regarding the Inter-American Development Bank were quite different. He states that the evidence available to him:

> " . . . suggests that IDB management was actively avoiding a policy confrontation with the United States (and perhaps also with conservative Latin American governments such as Brazil) and that *U.S. influence on the Board of Executive Directors was sufficient to preclude IDB lending to Chile* as long as the United States (and perhaps other countries) desired to dissuade such lending. The IDB management seemed more willing to risk the dissatisfaction of several major Latin American member countries than to face a situation of direct policy conflict with the institutions major contributor."[113] (emphasis added)

112 As Sanford notes, "It is true, of course, that the new Chilean government quickly announced internal policy changes, and shifts in economic guidelines which external observers thought were more 'rational' and more 'sound' approaches to Chilean economic conditions. It was not clear at that point – or for some time thereafter – however, that these announcements would be translated into effective policy.", SANFORD, J.E., "The Multilateral Development Banks and the Suspension of Lending to Allende's Chile", *op. cit*.

113 Ibid., "Conclusions".

Sanford's study never discusses US government influence over the World Bank in this way.[114] Perhaps this is because the US has a higher percentage of the total voting power in the IDB than in the World Bank, and therefore presumably has more influence in the former. US influence within both institutions has always been great, and the management of each must have been aware of the fact that the Gonzalez Amendment could have been invoked by the US President at any time after the Chilean nationalizations, to require that the US appointed EDs vote against any proposed loans that country. The available evidence does not enable us to determine exactly to what extent the implied threat of US opposition may have discouraged the Bank management from proposing Chilean loans to the EDs,[115] but by the Bank's own admission, the opposition of certain EDs (unidentified by the Bank), caused an indefinite delay in formally proposing three loans to Allende's Chile in the last months before the coup which overthrew his government.[116] According to former US Ambassador to Chile Nathaniel Davis the Gonzalez Amendment was never invoked against Chile, "although multinational loans to Chile were blocked in informal ways."[117]

b) Conclusions Concerning the Chile Case

Our review of the pattern of Bank lending to Chile, and of other available documents has not uncovered conclusive proof that Bank lending (or non-lending) to Chile was politicized during Salvador Allende's presidency, but the circumstantial evidence

114 Sanford states at the beginning of his study that it "takes no position on the questions [sic] as to whether U.S. Government influence may have been responsible for the suspension of Bank lending to Chile during the period of Allende's presidency", and so it is somewhat surprising that he raises it in his discussion of the IDB. Quoted from *Ibid.*, "Prefatory Note".

115 With regard to the Gonzalez Amendment Lars Schoultz, ("Politics, Economics, and U.S. Participation in Multilateral Development Banks", *International Organization*, Vol. 36, No. 3, (1982) at p. 557) has aptly noted that: " . . . the law of anticipated reactions is by its nature difficult to observe in action. Thus it is impossible to ascertain whether the law has functioned to restrain Bank officials from processing applications that the United States could be expected to oppose."

116 "Chile and the World Bank", White Paper prepared by the World Bank, op. cit., paragraph 32.

117 DAVIS, N., The Last Two Years of Salvador Allende, London, Tauris & Co., (1985), at p. 73.

of such a politicization is very strong indeed. Clear evidence of the US government's willingness and intention to politicize the Bank on this issue can be found in NSDM 93. The President of the US decided on political grounds to use US influence in the Bank (and in other international financial institutions) to block loans or credits to Chile, and it is a fact that no Bank loans were made to Chile while this policy was in effect. But this does not suffice to prove that Bank lending to Chile was actually politicized. Since Chile's creditworthiness was very much in doubt during the years in question it may plausibly be argued that no such politicization was necessary to stop the flow of loans. Perhaps an uncreditworthy Chile did not qualify for loans during that period.[118] But the loans which the Bank made to Chile immediately before and after the Allende years, when Chile was similarly uncreditworthy, strongly suggest that consistent economic standards on eligibility were not applied to Chile by the Bank.

C. CASE STUDY ON RESTRICTIONS IMPOSED OR THREATENED BY THE US CONGRESS

1. Background discussion of the role of the US Congress in determining US Policy Towards the Bank

The United States is the largest contributor of funds to both the World Bank and the IDA (as well as to the IDB and the IMF). Given this fact it is perfectly normal that the US government should have developed procedures and passed legislation designed to ensure that the legitimate interests of the US as a

118 While acknowledging that President Nixon had ordered that the US should oppose loans to Chile by international financial institutions, Henry Kissinger suggests that no such loans would have been appropriate in any case. As he wrote in *The White House Years*, op. cit., at p. 681:

" . . . With the Chilean government's new policy of expropriation without compensation designed to discourage any private investment, with government fueled inflation reaching a level of some 350 percent (on the day of Allende's death) and destroying the middle class, and with default on its international debt repayments in 1971, the credit-worthiness of Chile would have dropped drastically between 1970 and 1973 whatever policy the United States pursued in international lending institutions. It would have been an imprudent financial institution, national or international, that extended substantial credit to someone who, in his national campaign declaration ('The Popular Government's First Forty Measures') had pledged to "renege the commitments with the International Monetary Fund" . . . "

Bank member are protected. As the largest holder of the Bank's capital stock the US could theoretically incur substantial financial liabilities if borrowers from the Bank failed to repay their loans.[119] While the need of the US government to protect important interests such as these is not in dispute, there has been a certain amount of disagreement between the executive and the legislature, over how this should be accomplished

The Constitution of the United States is based upon the principle of a fairly strict separation of powers between the legislative, executive and judicial branches of government[120] the powers of which are separately enumerated in the first, second and third articles of that document. The intention was to balance the power of each branch with the power of the others in order to assure that all three would cooperate for the common good of the nation. In practice this system has often led to confrontation between the branches, particularly between the legislative and executive branches, concerning the scope of their authority and powers. The determination of US foreign policy has often been at issue in these disputes, and since the early 1970's, the conflict has extended to the question of which branch shall determine US policy towards the MDB's.

Generally speaking, it is the President and the executive branch which are responsible for the conduct of US foreign policy,[121] but it is the Congress and the Congress alone which has the power to appropriate funds from the treasury. This explains why US participation in the Bank, IDA, IMF and similar agencies involving a pooling of national financial resources has required the approval of both chambers of Congress.[122]

119 Each member country's potential liability is limited to the unpaid portion of the issue price of the shares subscribed to as a Bank member (Bank Articles of Agreement, Article II, Section 6). Since only 10% of the Bank's capital is presently paid in, the maximum potential liability could be up to nine times again the amount already contributed.

120 The theoretical inspiration for this doctrine of separation of powers was largely provided by the French writer Charles Louis de Secondat, Baron de Montesquieu.

121 The role of the President in US foreign relations is clearly preeminent, but the US Constitution also grants to the Congress considerable powers in this field. For a detailed discussion of the constitutional issues involved see HENKIN, L., *Foreign Affairs and the Constitution*, New York, Norton and Co., 1972, especially chapters II–VII.

122 Only the approval of one chamber, the Senate, is needed to ratify treaties negotiated by the President. US Constitution, Art. II, Section 2(2). Concerning appropriations, see Art. I, Section 9(7).

The Bretton Woods Agreements Act of 1945 is the original US legislative authorization for the participation of that country in the Bank and the IMF. Under this Act a National Advisory Council on International Monetary and Financial Problems ("Council") was created "in order to coordinate the policies and operations of the representatives of the United States on the Fund and the Bank."[123] The Council is composed entirely of officials from the executive branch of the US government (most notably the Secretaries of the Treasury, of State and of Commerce), and is placed under the general direction of the President.[124] The Council was dissolved in 1965 and recreated in 1966 all by executive order of the US President,[125] and it still is the principal forum within the US government for coordinating the financial aspects of MDB issues. Since its creation in 1979 a separate panel, the Working Group on Multilateral Assistance ("WGMA"), has been the principal instrument for coordinating interagency views on loans and on operational and policy issues relating to the MDBs.[126]

Since 1972, Congress has moved to assert its own direct control over US policy towards these institutions. It has done so by including in its legislative authorizations for Bank and IDA funding certain policy directives for the US appointed EDs. The most important of those which apply to the Bank will be examined in Chapter VII below.

The case study immediately below involves efforts to assert Congressional control over the Bank itself and its activities, and not merely over US policy towards the Bank, and thus the threat of politicization was posed in the clearest possible terms. An examination and understanding of the legal arguments which were articulated in this series of disputes will contribute a great deal to the analysis of US national legislation which follows in the next chapter.

123 Bretton Woods Agreements Act of 1945, Public Law (hereinafter "PL") No. 79-171, Section 4(a), 59 Stat. 512 (1945); (22 U.S.C. Section 286(a)).

124 *Ibid.*, Section 4(b) (4); (22 U.S.C. Section 286(b)(4)).

125 Executive Order number 11269 of February 14th, 1966. The recreated Council is now called the National Advisory Council on International Monetary and Financial Policies.

126 See SANFORD, Jonathan, "The World Bank: Eighteen Questions and Answers", Congressional Research Service, The Library of Congress, Washington, D.C., June 27, 1986, at p. 34. (CRS reference 86-769F)

2. Disputes Over the Issue of Restrictions on US Contributions to the Bank

At times domestic interest groups within the United States have urged that country's government to "earmark" its financial contributions to the Bank. Earmarking would involve the placing of direct restrictions upon the uses to which US contributed funds could be applied by the Bank. This practice would create a real problem for the Bank because according to Article VII, Section 6 of the Bank's Charter, the Bank's assets are to be free from restrictions, regulations or controls of any nature.[127] Bank officials have consistently maintained that because of this section the Bank is constitutionally unable to accept restricted funds, but this interpretation has not always been accepted by the US Congress.

The dispute over earmarking and restrictions has involved US contributions to other multilateral development banks (MDB's) as well. In 1975 members of the US Senate appropriations subcommittee on foreign operations were impatient because the Inter-American Development Bank (IDB) was not doing enough to promote cooperatives, credit unions, and saving and loan associations despite repeated urgings of that subcommittee that they do so. As a result, the legislation embodying the fiscal year 1975 appropriation for the IDB's concessional loan fund (the Fund for Special Operations) provided that $50 million of the $350 million appropriated should be used only for these purposes.[128] The IDB refused to accept the earmarked funds, on the grounds that to do so would constitute a violation of its Charter.[129]

127 Article VII, Section 6 of the Bank's Charter reads as follows:
"Section 6. Freedom of assets from restrictions
To the extent necessary to carry out the operations provided for in this Agreement and subject to the provisions of this Agreement, all property and assets of the Bank shall be free from restrictions, regulations, controls and moratoria of any nature."

128 Public Law 94–11, Title III, March 26, 1975, 89 Stat 23.

129 Article XI, Sec. 5 of the IDB Charter, (which is analogous to IBRD Art. VII, Section 6), provides that:
"To the extent necessary to carry out the purpose and functions of the Bank and to conduct its operations in accordance with this Agreement, *all Property and other assets of the Bank shall be free from restrictions, regulations, controls and moratoria of any nature*, except as may otherwise be provided in this Agreement." (emphasis added)

a) Proposals for Restrictions in the Foreign Aid Appropriations Bill for 1978

On June 23, 1977 the US House of Representatives approved a version of the Foreign Aid Appropriations Bill for 1978 ("H.R. 7797") which among other things was intended to govern the terms of US participation in the various MDB's, including the Bank and the IDA.[130] Although this version of that bill was never approved by the US Senate or signed into law by the President it provided the occasion for an extended debate within the US government, and between the US government and the MDBs, concerning the legality of any attempts by the US to earmark its contributions to the MDB's. The bill provided for the US to accept a commitment to the IDA's 5th Replenishment,[131] and for the US to subscribe to an increase in the capital stock of the Bank and the IFC, but in doing so it would have placed "country-specific" restrictions on the use of the funds to be contributed.[132] Section 107 of that bill provided that:

> "None of the funds appropriated or otherwise made available pursuant to this Act shall be obligated or expended to finance directly or indirectly any assistance or reparations to Uganda, Cambodia, Laos, or the Socialist Republic of Vietnam."[133]

The amendment incorporating these country-specific restrictions was proposed by Congressman C.W. "Bill" Young, and is sometimes referred to as the "Young Amendment". Another part of the bill (Section 509) would have prevented the use of US contributed funds to finance certain commodities.

> "None of the funds appropriated or made available to

130 US Congress, House, *Foreign Assistance and Related Appropriations Bill*, 1978, (H.R. 7797), as passed by the House of Representatives on June 23, 1977. (hereinafter "H.R. 7797")

131 In order to prevent the Bank's soft-loans affiliate, the IDA, from exhausting its available financial resources, new contributions to that organization are needed every few years. This is accomplished under the terms of so-called replenishment agreements under which IDA donor governments jointly pledge to contribute.

132 Restrictions are said to be "country-specific" when they apply only to certain countries which are specifically named.

133 H.R. 7797, *op. cit.*, Section 107. Section 114 of this same bill contained a similar prohibition on assistance to Mozambique and Angola, while Section 510 barred assistance to Cuba.

> International Financial Institutions pursuant to this Act shall be used by the United States representatives to those institutions for the purpose of establishing or expanding production of sugar, palm oil or citrus crops if the United States is a producer of the same, similar or competing agricultural commodity."[134]

The US Senate and President Jimmy Carter opposed these restrictions, arguing that the MDB's could not accept restricted funds, and that therefore to enact the House version of the bill would mean the end of US participation in those institutions. There was nonetheless a period of a few months during which the US Congress remained deadlocked on the issue of whether or not to accept the House language. During this time a number of letters and memoranda were exchanged, some of the most important of which will be discussed here.

b) McNamara's Letter to the US Secretary of the Treasury

Robert McNamara, President of the Bank, wrote to the US Secretary of the Treasury on July 5, 1977 explaining that it would be impossible for the Bank or its affiliates to accept restricted funds or commitments. Referring to sections 107 and 509 of the House Bill the letter observes that:

> " . . . if these provisions become law the United States would have to condition its commitment and its subscriptions on a requirement that these funds not be used to finance loans to certain countries or for certain agricultural commodities. The question arises, therefore, whether IDA could accept United States commitment to the Fifth Replenishment and the Bank and IFC could accept United States subscriptions to their capital stock if they were made subject to such conditions or others of a similar nature.

134 *Ibid.*, Section 509.

"The answer is that IDA, the Bank and IFC could not accept the funds, so conditioned . . . "[135]

McNamara then explains that for the US to condition its commitment to the Fifth IDA Replenishment would prevent the agreement for that Replenishment from becoming effective. This would mean the end of IDA operations since the IDA's existing resources were already fully committed to borrowers.

The letter reaches a similar conclusion about restrictions upon subscriptions to the Bank's capital stock.

" . . . Any subscription which is made subject to the conditions referred to above would not be consistent with the terms on which subscriptions can be made or with the obligations of shareholders to the Bank under the Articles of Agreement and would therefore not be acceptable. The use of funds paid by shareholders for their stock cannot be conditioned in that way and, similarly, no condition can be imposed which would restrict the power of the Bank to make calls upon the callable portion of Bank stock so as to enable the Bank, if necessary, to make payment on its borrowings or guarantees."[136]

c) The First Opinion of the Bank's General Counsel

In August of 1977 the US appointed ED at the Bank requested an opinion from the Bank's General Counsel on the question of whether the Bank and its affiliates could accept the US contributions contemplated by the HR 7797 subject to the conditions contained in that bill. In an office memorandum dated August 29, 1977 the Bank's General Counsel, Mr. Broches expressed

135 Letter dated July 5, 1977 from Robert McNamara, President of the International Bank For Reconstruction and Development, to W. Michael Blumenthal, Secretary of the Treasury of the United States, (Hereinafter "July 5, 1977 McNamara letter"). Reproduced in United States House of Representatives, (hearings), *Foreign Assistance and Related Appropriations for 1979*, hearings, Ninety-Fifth Congress, Second Session, before the Subcommittee on Foreign Operations and Related Agencies of the Committee on Appropriations of the US House of Representatives (hereinafter "Foreign Operations Hearings, 1979") at pp. 492–493.

136 *Loc. cit.*

his view that the "the institutions could not accept the funds, so conditioned".[137]

Mr. Broches then proceeded to explain that "[t]he terms and conditions of both subscriptions to the capital of the Bank and IFC and of subscriptions and contributions to IDA . . . are governed by . . . the constituent instruments of these institutions, and by the Resolutions of their Boards of Governors which authorize these subscriptions and contributions."

Only one paragraph of this memorandum was concerned with the Articles of Agreement of the Bank. It made two points about the conditions and restrictions which HR 7797 would impose upon US participation in the Bank. The first is that such restrictions would be inconsistent with the right of the Bank to use the funds paid by shareholder members in accordance with the Bank's Charter.[138] The second point is that such conditions might restrict the Bank's essential right, under Article II, Section 5(ii) of its Charter, to call in payment of the unpaid portion of its subscribed capital if this is needed to meet the obligations of the Bank.[139] Article II, Section 3(b) of the Bank's Charter authorizes the Bank to prescribe the rules laying down the conditions under which members may subscribe to its capital stock. The Charters of the IDA and the IFC contain similar language.[140]

The bulk of the August 29 memorandum consists of an exegesis of various resolutions of the Boards of Governors of

137 Internal World Bank memorandum dated August 29, 1977 from Mr. A. Broches, Vice President and General Counsel of the Bank, to Mr. Edward R. Fried, Executive Director (US appointed). Reproduced in "Foreign Operations Hearings, 1979", *op. cit.*, at p. 537–538.

138 "The use by the Bank of funds paid by shareholder members is governed by the Articles of Agreement. Restrictions such as those contained in HR 7797 would be inconsistent with the Bank's right to use such funds and therefore unacceptable.", *loc. cit.*

139 " . . . under the Articles a subscription gives rise to an obligation on the part of a subscribing member to make payment of the paid-in portion of the subscription price . . . and to respond to calls made by the Bank on the remaining portion of the subscription price left uncalled. . . . no condition can be imposed which would restrict the power of the Bank to make calls on the callable portion of Bank subscriptions when, as stipulated in Article II, Section 5(ii) of the Articles, such calls are required to meet the obligations of the Bank arising out of its borrowings or guarantees.", loc. cit.

140 See IDA Articles of Agreement, Article III, Section 1(b), and IFC Articles of Agreement, Article II, Section 3(d).

the Bank, IDA and IFC which were adopted pursuant to this authority. The final paragraph of that memorandum states that:

> "10. In conclusion, none of the Resolutions permit the institutions concerned to accept from a member subscriptions or contributions subject to a condition that the funds subscribed or contributed are not to be used for loans to certain countries or for projects for certain agricultural commodities."[141]

d) The Bank General Counsel's Second Opinion

The US appointed ED received the above mentioned memorandum as the dispute over earmarking was being argued between the House of Representatives (in favor of earmarking), and the Senate and the Executive branch (opposed). Those in the House who felt most strongly about the need to restrict contributions saw a loophole in the argument of the Bank's General Counsel. If, as he had argued, the terms of subscriptions and contributions were governed by resolutions of the Boards of Governors, they reasoned that it should be possible to amend those resolutions so as to authorize acceptance of restricted or earmarked contributions. The US ED then requested a further opinion from the Bank's General Counsel on whether this could indeed resolve the problem and eliminate all obstacles to the acceptance of restricted subscriptions and contributions. This was given in second memorandum to the US ED dated September 28, 1977.[142]

The second opinion from the Bank's Counsel concludes that:

> " . . . *While the Executive Directors have considerable latitude*

141 Loc. cit.

142 Internal World Bank memorandum dated September 28, 1977 from Mr. A. Broches, Vice President and General Counsel of the Bank, to Mr. Edward R. Fried, Executive Director (US appointed), (Hereinafter "Second IBRD Opinion"). Reproduced in "Foreign Operations Hearings, 1979", *op. cit.*, at p. 539–540. The issue to be addressed in this second opinion is framed by the Bank's Counsel in the following language (*loc. cit.*):
"3. When writing to you on August 29, 1977 I did not address the hypothetical question whether, if the Executive Directors of the institutions were willing as a matter of policy to recommend to the Boards of Governors to amend the Resolutions above referred to so as to authorize acceptance of the conditions sought to be imposed by HR 7797, the Bank and IDA could properly do so consistently with the institutions' respective Articles of Agreement."

in the exercise of their powers of interpretation they may not use it so as to in effect amend the Articles of Agreement. In my opinion . . . the Executive Directors could not properly as a matter of law adopt interpretative decisions which would permit these institutions to accept U.S. contributions subject to conditions as proposed in H.R. 7797.''[143] (emphasis added)

i) The Bank's Articles of Agreement

This opinion cites certain provisions of the Bank and IDA Charters as the basis for the conclusions above, stating that those provisions, among others, "would be violated by acceptance of the conditions referred to." The first section referred to is Article I of the Bank's Charter which states the Bank's purposes, and in particular paragraphs (i) and (iii) of that Article. There it is stated that the "encouragement of productive facilities and resources in less developed countries" (paragraph (i)) and "to promote the long-range balanced growth in international trade" (paragraph (iii)) are purposes of the Bank. The opinion does not elaborate upon how the House bill would violate these purposes, but the implication that the restrictions in that bill would conflict with them is quite reasonable. Those restrictions have as their purpose to *discourage* aid to the targeted developing countries, and to *prevent* the long term growth of international trade in the certain commodities by developing countries. These objectives are inconsistent with those of the Bank and the IDA.[144]

The two sentences of the so-called "political activity prohibition"[145] are mentioned separately in this opinion as the two other parts of the Bank and IDA Charters which would be violated by the restrictions in H.R. 7797. In the opinion of the

143 *Loc. cit.*

144 Although the statement of purposes of the IDA found in Article I of its Charter is relatively brief and does not contain all of the language referred to, it does provide that the IDA is to further "the developmental objectives of the International Bank for Reconstruction and Development". It is no doubt on this basis that the second opinion asserts that "These purposes must be deemed to be incorporated by reference in IDA's statement of purposes (Article I).", *loc. cit.*

145 The political activity prohibition is contained in Article IV, Section 10 of the Bank's Charter, and in Article V, Section 6 of the IDA's Charter. See the detailed discussion of this prohibition, its purpose and effect, *supra.*

Bank's Counsel, the injunctions in their Charters that these institutions shall not be influenced by the political character of the member or members concerned, "do not permit the exclusion of certain members from the circle of potential borrowers on political grounds."[146]

It can hardly be disputed that H.R. 7797 was intended to exclude the targeted states on political grounds and, as the Southern Africa case study demonstrates, the Bank has consistently maintained that this section of its Charter forbids any such exclusion. It would have been surprising had the Bank's Counsel taken any other position on this matter.

But this opinion goes somewhat further in its interpretation of the Bank's Article IV, Section 10. The second sentence of that section provides that "only economic considerations shall be relevant" to the Bank's decisions, and that "these considerations shall be weighed impartially in order to achieve the purposes stated in Article I." The opinion refers to this language as "excluding the intrusion of national commercial considerations."[147]

ii) An Exclusion of National Commercial Considerations?

This is a very broad interpretation of the language involved. Here, for the first time, a Bank official claims that this section does more than exclude political considerations, and declares that it also excludes economic considerations which are not directly related to the Bank's stated purposes. Thus in his view, the Bank's Charter requires that "national commercial considerations", such as those in the parts of H.R. 7797 intended to protect US producers of certain commodities, may not be considered when loan decisions are made.[148]

Acceptance of such a view of this section would have a number of implications, some of them quite far-reaching. One

146 "Second IBRD Opinion", *op. cit.*

147 *Loc. cit.*

148 Apparently the Bank's General Counsel reached his conclusion based on the last part of Article IV, Section 10 which states that "Only economic considerations shall be relevant to their decisions, *and these shall be weighed impartially in order to achieve the purposes stated in Article I.*" (emphasis added). Since Article I of the Bank's Charter does not mention any negative and narrowly national goals such as protecting one state's producers from foreign competition, it could be argued that consideration of such goals should be excluded from the decision-making process.

potential problem is that there will not always be a clear line between national commercial considerations and other types of economic considerations which must be considered relevant to the Bank's decision-making. In some cases national commercial considerations will be relevant to the question of whether a particular loan is economically viable. In the case of H.R. 7797, for example, it might be argued that the US experience with the production of sugar, palm oil and citrus crops has demonstrated that in the international marketplace there is no demand for further production of the same, similar or competing products. In the Admissions Case the ICJ made a very similar point when it noted with regard to the UN Charter that:

> "Article 4 does not forbid the taking into account of *any factor which it is possible reasonably and in good faith to connect with the conditions* laid down in that Article."[149] (emphasis added).

The same might be said of Article IV(10) of the Bank's Charter, especially since the Bank has always maintained that the economic consequences of the political situation in a country are properly relevant to its decisions. Such an argument could not, however, suffice to establish the acceptability of the commodity restrictions in H.R. 7797. Ultimately, any *a priori* restriction on the Bank's use of funds to finance the production of these products would be a clear violation of the Bank's Article VII, Section 6 (IDA Article VIII, Section 6) which provides that the Bank's assets "shall be free from restrictions, regulations, controls and moratoria of any nature." This would appear to be the clearest basis for concluding that the Bank could not accept funds subject to continuing restrictions of any kind. For some reason, this section is not mentioned in either of the opinions given by the Bank's Counsel on H.R. 7797.

The argument that the Article IV, Section 10 of the Bank's Charter excludes national commercial considerations may be a bit radical, but it appears more or less harmless when applied to H.R. 7797. But if that section does exclude these considerations, then the same limitation must also be applied to the EDs in all their decision-making. This would mean that while

149 Advisory opinion on Conditions of Admission of a State to Membership in the United Nations, *ICJ Reports* (1947–1948), p. 63. See the discussion of this case in Chapter V, *supra*.

fulfilling his duty as ED even an appointed ED could not properly (that is to say legally) consider the unilateral economic interests of the member which appointed him. This would reduce the EDs to the status of international civil servants, leaving little legal scope for the *de facto* role of the appointed EDs as national representatives.[150]

Broadening Article IV, Section 10 into a prohibition on the consideration of national commercial considerations would be in the spirit of international cooperation, but this interpretation goes well beyond what has actually been agreed to in the Bank's Charter. The only considerations which are explicitly excluded by that section are those of a political nature. What then is the meaning of that section's requirement that economic considerations "are to be weighed impartially in order to achieve the purposes stated in Article I"? It is submitted that it limits the way in which national economic considerations can be taken into account without excluding them completely.

The Bank and its organs may take national commercial considerations into account when they are relevant to the economic analysis of a loan proposal, but their decisions (including the votes of the EDs) must be made according to a broader analysis of all the relevant economic considerations. As long as the consideration of national economic interests is not inconsistent with a decision reflecting the broader economic merits involved, the decision-making process within the Bank can legally take heed of these narrower interests.[151] The fundamental standard of "good faith" is applicable here.

150 See the discussion of the role of the EDs, *supra*.

151 A more recent opinion by the Bank's General Counsel seems to support this view. Speaking of those who elected or appointed a ED as his "constituency", this opinion concludes that an Executive Director "may express the views of such a 'constituency' and vote on its instructions . . . However, he is not to act simply as an ambassador of the government or governments which appointed or elected him and is expected to exercise his individual judgment in the interest of the Bank and its members as a whole." "Prohibition of Political Activities Under the IBRD Articles of Agreement and its Relevance to the Work of the Executive Directors", legal opinion by Ibrahim F.I. Shihata, Vice President and General Counsel of the World Bank, section M87-1409, at p. 8 (December 23, 1987), (unpublished). Quoted in SHIHATA, I.F.I., "The World Bank and Human Rights: An Analysis of the Legal Issues and the Record of Achievements", *Denver Journal of International Law and Policy*, Vol. 17, No. 1, (1988), at p. 46.

iii) Restrictions on the Callable Portion of Capital Subscriptions

The second opinion ends by returning to what may have been the most important point in the earlier opinion, i.e. that it would be totally unacceptable to subject the callable portion of the Bank's capital to any condition, since this would destroy confidence in the Bank's financial structure.

> ". . . If H.R. 7797 were to be interpreted as applying the conditions laid down therein to the callable portion of the U.S. subscription to the Bank's capital, that alone would make the conditions unacceptable as violating the obligation imposed by the Articles on members to respond to calls on the callable portion of the capital. As you know, these unconditional obligations of the members are relied upon by investors in the IBRD's debt obligations."[152] (emphasis added)

iv) Possible Limits Upon the Interpretative Authority of The EDs

Under the terms of the Bank's Charter it is to the EDs that any question of interpretation of that Charter is to be submitted.[153] The only appeal from an interpretative decision by the EDs is to the Bank's Board of Governors, and any decision by that board is to be final.

In considering the issue of the proper role of the EDs and Governors within the Bank, their degree of independence, the legal limits to their discretion, etc., it is somewhat strange to think that this very issue could be authoritatively decided, (perhaps on a largely political basis), by those same EDs and governors.

The existing literature concerning the operation and legal significance of this interpretive procedure relates for the most part not to the Bank but to its sister institution the IMF. (Article IX of the Bank's Charter which outlines this procedure largely parallels Article XXIX of the IMF's charter.) F. A. Mann has argued that a non-judicial body cannot render a judicial decision, and that therefore interpretations by the EDs and/or

152 "Second IBRD Opinion", *op. cit.*
153 Article IX, Section a.

the Governors of the IMF are not a judicial act.[154] Even if one does not accept this conclusion,[155] it is clear that the Bank's EDs do not have the power to legislate, and that therefore their interpretations, if inconsistent with the Articles of Agreement, can in no way alter or increase the obligations of a member.[156]

Courts of Bank members have sometimes acknowledged that the interpretations of the EDs of the Bank or IMF are binding upon their governments. The Federal Communications Commission of the US has, in a judicial ruling, expressly recognized that the interpretations by the EDs are binding on the US;[157] and the Court of Appeal of Louisiana (4th Circuit) has observed, by way of *dictum*, that the Fund's interpretative decisions are "binding on all of its members".[158] But these two decisions do not tell us anything new about the interpretation of the Bank's Charter, and in any case they are not the best authority.[159]

Of course, the Bank and the Fund are separate institutions despite the similarities of their decision-making structures and procedures. The Bank's EDs rarely make formal decisions interpreting the IBRD Charter, and the Bank does not publish its interpretative decisions as the Fund does. In practice, however, the Bank's EDs do make their decisions on the basis of some interpretation of the Bank Charter which is acceptable to them. Thus interpretations by the EDs may determine fundamental Bank policy even when they are informal.

As we have seen, the second opinion asserted that "[w]hile

154 See, MANN, F.A., "The 'Interpretation' of the Constitutions of International Financial Organizations", *B.Y.I.L.*, 1968–1969, pp. 1–19. In comments equally applicable to the Bank he goes on to note that "a system such as the weighted voting system is totally alien to the judicial process." (at p. 7), and concludes that "Neither the Executive Directors nor the Governors have the exclusive right or duty of deciding a question of interpretation." (p. 17)

155 Sir Joseph Gold has expressed the view that "there can be little doubt that an international tribunal would regard itself as concluded (sic) by an interpretation" under this internal procedure. GOLD, J., *Interpretation by the Fund*, Washington, International Monetary Fund Pamphlet Series, No. 11, 1968, at p. 47.

156 MANN, *op. cit.*, at p. 13.

157 See 17 FCC 450 (1953), cited in SCHWEBEL, S.M. ed., *The Effectiveness of International Decisions*, Leyden, Sijthoff, (1971), at pp. 124–126.

158 *Theye y Ajuria v. Pan American Life Insurance Company*, 154 So. 2nd 450, 453 (1963), reversed on other grounds, 161 So. 2nd 70 (1964).

159 While citing these two decisions, Mann dismisses them as "hardly observations which may claim to originate from close analysis or to carry such authority as to add much to the discussion." MANN, *op. cit.*, at p. 14.

the Executive Directors have considerable latitude in the exercise of their powers of interpretation they may not use it so as to amend, in effect, the Articles of Agreement." This is quite significant from a legal point of view. It is an assertion by the Bank's General Counsel of a limitation upon the power of the EDs. As we have seen above, the procedure which entrusts the power of interpretation to the EDs has at times been criticized as essentially non-legal and even political. Here the Bank's Counsel endorses the idea that when the EDs exercise their interpretative function, (a function which may be considered quasi-judicial), the EDs are subject to substantive constitutional restraints inherent in the language of the Bank's Charter.

The Bank's EDs must logically be bound by the Bank's Charter, but their apparently exclusive right to interpret that Charter raises the question of how they could ever be called to task should they decide to exceed the limits of the "considerable latitude" they enjoy in exercising their powers of interpretation. While the individual ED may be held accountable by the government or governments which appointed or elected him, this type of political constraint is no guarantee that their actions will remain within the applicable legal limits.

What remedy would be available if the EDs were to exceed those limits in exercising their power of interpretation? If, for example, the US had managed to push through an interpretation to the effect that restricted subscriptions and contributions were permitted under the Articles of Agreement, under the Bank's Charter the only appeal of that decision would have been to the Bank's full Board of Governors.[160] That Charter provides for external review of disputes only under certain circumstances, and never when the dispute is with an active member of the Bank.[161]

e) Political Maneuverings within the US Government to Forestall Legislative Restriction of US Contributions

In the event, the potential problems posed by H.R. 7797 never fully materialized due to a political compromise worked out

160 Article IX, Section (b) of the IBRD Charter.

161 Article IX, Section (c) provides for external arbitration of disputes only when the dispute is between the Bank and a former member, or between the Bank and a member during the permanent suspension of the Bank.

between the US President and the House Subcommittee on Foreign Operations of the Committee on Appropriations. President Carter sent a letter to the Chairman of that subcommittee promising to "instruct the U.S. Executive Directors in the banks to oppose and vote against, throughout fiscal year 1978, any loans to the seven countries mentioned in the House amendments", and that US "representatives will also oppose and vote against loans for the production of the three commodities where such production is for export and could injure producers in the United States."[162] Largely on the basis of this letter the US House and Senate were together able to agree to a version of the Foreign Aid Appropriations Bill for 1978 which did not apply conditions or restrictions to the US participation in the MDB's.[163] This did not, however, mean that the US Congress had abandoned attempts to restrict the use of its contribution to the MDB's.

The same issues were debated again one year later when Congressman Young proposed a somewhat different list of target countries.[164] The House rejected that proposal, and then adopted another proposal which targeted only Vietnam. A similar amendment barring the use of US funds for MDB aid to Cuba was also accepted by the House, but both these restrictions were deleted from the final version of the 1979 foreign assistance appropriations bill due to strong Senate opposition.[165]

The most difficult moment for the Bank came during the discussion by the US Congress of the foreign aid appropriations bill for fiscal year 1980. Once again the House had adopted by a large majority amendments which would prohibit the use of US contributed funds for MDB loans to Vietnam or Cuba. This time the Senate hesitated before expressing its opposition to

162 Letter dated October 6, 1977 from Jimmy Carter, President of the United States, to Clarence D. Long, Chairman, Subcommittee on Foreign Operations, Committee on Appropriations of the US House of Representatives. Reproduced in the *Congressional Record*, (House), Vol. 123, (October 18, 1977), at p. 34093.

163 PL 95-148, approved October 31, 1977.

164 This time the proposed targets included seven-right wing repressive regimes.

165 For a detailed analysis of the political maneuverings involved in the various attempts to impose these restrictions, see SCHOULTZ, L., "Politics, Economics, and U.S. Participation in Multilateral Development Banks", *International Organization*, Vol. 36, No. 3, (1982), especially at pp. 566–571; and SANFORD, J.E., *U.S. Foreign Policy and Multilateral Development Banks*, Boulder, Colorado, Westview Press, 1982, especially at pp. 135–145.

these restrictive provisions regarding the MDB's, and it seemed quite possible that this time it might accept the House view and approve them. Among the factors complicating the decision was the growing Vietnamese military involvement in Cambodia (which was just beginning), and the emotional reflexes left by the earlier US involvement in Vietnam.

A conference committee composed of members of both the House and the Senate met twice to try to reach agreement on a single version of this bill, but those Congressmen who insisted that no US funds should be used for loans to Vietnam resisted any compromise which did not accommodate their viewpoint. This time, agreement by President Carter that he would oppose such loans would not satisfy them. IBRD President McNamara took the unusual step of meeting with a group of Congressmen to assure them that the proposed restrictions were unnecessary since no further Bank or IDA loans to Vietnam were contemplated, but even this did not satisfy the hard-liners in the House.

In the conference committee, those favoring the restrictions focused to a large degree on emotional charges of atrocities by the Vietnamese, while others repeated the Carter administration's argument that the restrictions would end US participation in the Bank and the other MDB's. The legal argument, i.e. that the proposed restrictions would be illegal, was certainly not decisive. One conservative Senator reportedly responded to the legal argument by saying: "Let's forget about these legal niceties. Even if we're wrong, lets do it anyway. Lets stop the killing . . . "[166]

f) World Bank President McNamara's Written Promise to the US Congress

A way out of the impasse was suggested by two Congressmen who were sympathetic to the Bank's position on earmarking. Since McNamara had already stated that the Bank did not intend to make any further loans to Vietnam, these legislators proposed that he sign a letter to that effect, addressed to the

166 See, "Freeze on Vietnam Loans Ends Effort to Restrict U.S. Funds for World Bank", *Congressional Quarterly*, November 3, 1979, at p. 2504, where the debate in this conference committee is summarized. (The quoted phrase is attributed to Jake Garn, Republican Senator from Utah.)

chairman of the relevant House subcommittee. The letter was drafted not by McNamara himself, but by supporters of the Bank within the US government. It was then presented to him as he got off a plane in Washington on November 1, 1979, and he quickly signed it.[167] As a friend and former colleague of McNamara was later to explain, the letter was signed "[i]n circumstances of maximum confusion and haste".[168] The letter read as follows:

> "In response to your inquiry, I would like you to know that events over the past year have raised a very serious question about Vietnam's current commitment to a rational development policy. These questions were considered sufficiently fundamental to warrant a suspension of new lending to Vietnam
>
> "Under current conditions it would not be possible to invest funds there with a high probability that investment objectives would be realized or with assurances that the project would benefit the masses of the people. Consequently, I cannot recommend a loan to the Board in FY [fiscal year] 1980 and therefore the Bank Group will not be providing a loan to Vietnam in FY 1980."[169] (bracketed clarification added)

This was nothing less than a written promise that, at least for the time being, the Bank would not be making any more loans to Vietnam. As such, it satisfied those leaders in the House of Representatives who had wanted to restrict the Bank's operations. The letter was a great victory for them since it committed the Bank not to use *anyone's* money for loans to Vietnam, whereas HR 7797 would only have restricted the use of US contributed funds. After it was received, the House-

167 See "Washington Watch", *The New York Times*, November 5, 1979 at p. D2.

168 CLARK, W., "Robert McNamara at the World Bank", *Foreign Affairs*, Vol. 60, (1981), at p. 181.

169 Letter dated November, 1, 1979 from IBRD President Robert McNamara to Clarence Long, Chairman of the Subcommittee on Foreign Operations and Related Agencies, of the Committee on Appropriations of the US House of Representatives, (hereinafter "McNamara letter of November 1, 1979"). Reproduced in the *Congressional Record*, (House), (December 3, 1979), at p. 34415, and excerpted in SANFORD, J.E., *U.S. Foreign Policy and Multilateral Development Banks*, *op. cit.*, at p. 143, in SCHOULTZ, *op. cit.*, at p. 570 and in "Washington Watch", *The New York Times*, Monday, November 5, 1979, at p. D2.

Senate conference committee agreed to recommend that there not be any restrictions on US contributions to the World Bank Group. For the moment the conflict in the US Congress over this issue had ended, but the Bank's claim to be an autonomous international institution had been seriously compromised.

McNamara soon realized that he had erred. On the same day he sent a second letter to G. William Miller the US Secretary of the Treasury in which he apologized for dealing directly with the US Congress instead of working through the officially designated channels, i.e. the US Department of the Treasury. The text of that letter was as follows:

> "Owing to the extreme urgency of the matter and the lateness of the hour, this afternoon, I addressed the appended letter directly to the Chairman, Subcommittee on Foreign Operations, U.S. House of Representatives, thus deviating from the rule I have invariably followed of communicating with member governments only through officially designated channels, in your case, through the Treasury . . . While I know you will in the circumstances understand the compelling reasons for this departure from our fixed rule, I nevertheless ask you to accept my apologies."[170]

Apologies to the US Treasury were probably unnecessary. C. Fred Bergsten, Assistant US Secretary of the Treasury for International Affairs, and acting US appointed ED of the Bank, had supervised the drafting of the "offending" letter, which was more a product of Carter Administration officials than of McNamara himself.[171] Officials of both the US Congress and the US Treasury had approved it before it was presented to him for signature, but he might not have been aware of this when he sent his apology to the US Treasury.

The strongest reaction to the letter came from within the Bank itself. William Clark, who at the time was Vice President for External Relations of the World Bank, has described the internal Bank reaction to this letter as follows:

170 Letter dated November, 1, 1979 from IBRD President Robert McNamara to G. William Miller, US Secretary of the Treasury. Reproduced in the *Congressional Record*, (House), (December 3, 1979), at p. 34415.

171 See, "Freeze on Vietnam Loans Ends Effort to Restrict U.S. Funds for World Bank", *op. cit.*, at p. 2504.

> "Then the storm burst. The Bank's Board of Executive Directors – long disturbed by American attitudes – joined unanimously to protest both the bypassing of the Board and the clear breach of the established practice that the President of the Bank dealt only with the executive authorities of member governments; *to them McNamara's action underlined the determination of the United States to politicize the multilateral institutions*. The episode really shook the confidence of the Board in their chairman's capacity to defend them against what they perceived as a hostile America. To make matters worse, even after McNamara's personal reassurance Congress did not appropriate new funds for IDA and did not do so during the remainder of his term of office."[172] (emphasis added)

It was not so much what the letter said that was controversial. Apparently the Bank had already imposed a sort of "unofficial" freeze on lending to Vietnam after the Vietnamese invasion of Cambodia in September of 1979, and McNamara had made this point orally in his earlier meeting with Congressmen.[173] The problem was that McNamara's action encroached upon the prerogatives of the EDs, and severely compromised the independence of the Bank from the US Congress. Although the EDs did not decide to countermand McNamara's action, he was sharply rebuked by them, and this added fuel to other criticisms of his performance during his last year as President.[174]

In this case Congress demonstrated its ability to politicize the Bank without actually incorporating politically oriented directives or restrictions in the statute books. This time the *threat* of such legislation was more than adequate to permit Congress to impose its will upon the Bank. The resulting suspension of Bank lending to Vietnam is much like the sanction which the UNGA asked the Bank to impose against South Africa and Portugal in the 1960s.

172 CLARK, *op. cit.*, at p. 181.

173 *loc. cit.*

174 See, SCHEIBLA, S.H., "McNamara's Band Sour – Directors, Staff Critical of World Bank Operations", *Barrons*, December 3, 1979, at p. 1.

7

POLITICIZING LEGISLATION AND INTERNATIONAL LEGAL STANDARDS: A REVIEW OF SELECTED US NATIONAL LEGISLATION CONCERNING THE WORLD BANK

One of the greatest difficulties involved in evaluating the legality of votes cast by a state within an intergovernmental organization stems from the fact that in most cases, it is impossible, to determine "the reasons which, in the mind of a Member, may prompt its vote. Such reasons, which enter into a mental process, are obviously subject to no control."[1] Taking note of this difficulty, the Advisory Opinion on Conditions of Admission was careful to declare that the opinion given in that case only concerned cases where a member has explicitly stated that its vote will be cast pursuant to certain criteria.[2]

States are under no obligation to declare the motivations for the votes they cast in the World Bank, and thus it is ordinarily impossible to build more than a circumstantial case to the effect that votes in that organization have been cast according to inappropriate political criteria. Politicization cannot be proven except in those cases where the political motivations behind a given vote have been admitted. This chapter evaluates legislation passed by the US, some of which constitutes an explicit statement of political directives motivating the use of US voting power within that organization.

1 Advisory opinion on Conditions of Admission of a State to Membership in the United Nations, *ICJ Reports* (1947–1948), at p. 63

2 *Ibid.*, at p. 60. See the discussion of this case in Chapter V, *supra*.

A. THE LEGISLATION

1. Political Forces behind this Legislation

In the US, as in other industrialized countries, foreign aid has little or no domestic constituency of any political importance. As we have seen in an earlier Chapter of this study,[3] expenditures for foreign aid, whether through bilateral or multilateral channels, must continually be justified in terms of promoting the national interest. Inevitably, disputes arise within the US about whether a particular foreign aid project is truly justifiable from this point of view. Frequently, one or more of the many interest groups which characterize the domestic political scene in the US will attempt to mobilize opposition to foreign aid. The goal may be to protect the global environment, to promote respect for human rights, to protect US export interests, or simply to prevent aid to certain disfavored recipient countries. The legislation reviewed in this Chapter is one result of this process. Both the President and the Congress are subject to these political pressures, but the two are not always equally responsive to them. At times they disagree about US foreign aid policy as they do about other aspects of US foreign policy.

There has often been competition between the legislative and executive branches of the US government concerning the scope of the authority and power of each in the determination of US foreign policy. Under the US Constitution the President is responsible for the conduct of US foreign policy, while the Congress retains control of the "spending power."[4] In practice Congress often finds it appropriate to delegate some of this spending power to the President, particularly in areas such as foreign aid, where considerations of foreign policy and of spending policy meet. But in foreign relations, as in other fields, Congress has often voted to attach various types of conditions or restrictions to the use of the funds it appropriates.

Although the focus of our inquiry is upon US multilateral aid

3 See Chapter III, *supra*.

4 See the Constitution of the United States of America, Article I Section 8 (concerning the Congressional spending power), and Article II Sections 2 and 3 (concerning the President's conduct of foreign policy). HENKIN, (*Foreign Affairs and the Constitution*, (hereinafter "*Foreign Affairs*") New York, Norton and Co., 1972, at pp. 39 ff.) points out that the US President's powers in foreign affairs go well beyond what is explicitly stated in the Constitution.

policy, it is worth noting here that the Congress has long restricted the use of bilateral aid funds which it has appropriated.[5] The First Hickenlooper Amendment, originally enacted in 1962, is perhaps the best known of these restrictions.[6] It is still in effect, and forbids the granting of bilateral US assistance to countries which have nationalized US properties without prompt, adequate and effective compensation.

Eventually, Congress turned its attention to the use of multilateral aid funds contributed by the US. As we have seen in Chapter VI's case study on restrictions, attempts by Congress to earmark or to restrict the use of these funds in the same way that it restricts the use of bilateral US aid have led to crisis and confrontation in the past. For the moment, Congress seems to have abandoned attempts to follow this dangerous course. This means that, once these funds are contributed to a MDB such as the World Bank, they pass beyond the direct control of Congress. Nonetheless, Congress does have a way to influence, if not control, the use of MDB funds. It does this by passing legislation which includes policy directives for the US appointed EDs within the Bank and the other MDBs.

No one could question the right of Congress, under US law, to refuse to appropriate funds, but opinions are divided concerning the constitutionality of add-on clauses to US appropriations bills and other legislation (known as "riders"), which purport to instruct delegations to international conferences.[7] Henkin suggests that conditions imposed by Congress should not invade Presidential prerogatives at least when they are only incidental to the actual spending authorized,[8] and he specifically questions the power of Congress to instruct US delegates to international organizations.[9] In any case, Congress has not hesi-

5 See the various Foreign Assistance, and Foreign Assistance Appropriations Acts passed by Congress, especially the Foreign Assistance Act of 1961, P.L. 87–195, 75 Stat. 424, approved September 4, 1961, as amended.

6 The Foreign Assistance Act of 1961, *op. cit.*, as amended, Sec. 620(e). This amendment was first enacted by the Foreign Assistance Act of 1962, P.L. 87-565, 76 Stat. 255, approved August 1, 1962, Sec. 301(d)(3), and the present version is codified at 22 USC Sec. 2370(e)(1).

7 HENKIN, *Foreign Affairs, op. cit.* at p. 113, and pp. 360–361 note 74.

8 *Ibid.*, at p.115.

9 Commenting upon legislation which forbids US representatives to certain international organizations from committing the US to pay more than 33.33 % of the budget of those organizations, Henkin concludes that "The power of Congress to instruct delegates to international organizations in this respect is as questionable as in respect to any other international act or negotiation." *Ibid.*, p. 362, note 79.

tated to pass numerous legislative amendments purporting to do exactly that, and the courts of the United States have never been asked to pass upon their constitutionality.[10]

In 1972 the US Congress for the first time passed legislation instructing the US EDs to the Bank and IDA to vote against loans to certain categories of countries, i.e., those which had nationalized or appropriated the property of US citizens without making satisfactory arrangements for compensation, or those which had failed to take adequate steps to prevent illegal drugs from passing from their territory to the US or to US servicemen abroad (these were known as the "Gonzalez Amendment" and the "Rangel Amendment", respectively).[11] Since then, quite a bit of further legislation has been enacted requiring negative votes by the US on Bank and IDA loan applications.

This chapter will review a broad range of legislation most of which concerns the use of US voting power in the Bank/IDA. A few legislative provisions which apply only to US policy in another international financial institution such as the IMF or the ADB have also been included because they illustrate the

10 Until 1983 the Congress commonly used a so called "legislative veto" as a method for limiting the use of discretionary power which it delegated to the executive branch. Legislation delegating a broad discretionary power to the executive branch, would at the same time stipulate that one House of Congress (or in some cases both) could, by majority vote, disapprove of any particular use of that discretion, and in effect veto it. This device was frequently used by Congress to limit its delegations of authority to the Executive in matters involving spending for foreign affairs and other purposes. In 1983 the Supreme Court of the United States held that the use of the legislative veto was unconstitutional. The Court reasoned that the Congressional resolutions of disapproval were essentially legislative in effect, and thus the Constitution required that they be passed by both Houses and then presented to the President for his signature or veto. *Immigration and Naturalization Service v. Chada*, 462 U.S. 919 (1983). US foreign relations law, which relied heavily upon the legislative veto in the past, has been shaken up by this ruling. See, FRANCK, T.M., and BOB, C.A., "The Return of Humpty-Dumpty: Foreign Relations Law after the Chada Case", *American Journal of International Law*, Vol. 79, No. 4, (1985), at pp. 912–960.

11 The IDA Third Replenishment Act, Public Law (hereinafter "PL") 92–247, approved March 10, 1972 adding Sections 11 – 13 to the International Development Association Act, PL 86–565 (22 USC Sections 284i–284k). As early as 1965 US legislation had been passed requiring that the US vote to disapprove certain loans by the Inter-American Development Bank to countries where the US had suspended its bilateral aid program due to uncompensated expropriation of US foreign investments. PL 89-6, approved March 24, 1965, adding Section 15(c) to the Inter-American Development Bank Act, PL 86-147, (22 USC Section 283l(c)) approved 7 August 1959.

pursuit by the US of objectives which are particularly unusual or interesting. (See Annex B, #1, #2 & #3)

The table in Annex B gives details concerning the legislation discussed in this chapter. That same body of legislation is then classified analytically in the chart found in Annex C. The structure of that chart is based on the typology which follows.

2. Typology of Legislation (Details and exact references can be found in Annex B.)

a) Types of Considerations Reflected

i) Political Unilateral

Although there is a strong argument to the effect that absolutely no political considerations should be allowed to influence Bank decision-making, it is the intrusion of considerations which may be classified as political/unilateral which conflicts the most with the letter and spirit of the Bank's Charter. Not only are these matters political rather than economic (and thus *prima facie* in conflict with the Bank's Charter), they also respond to interests which the US cannot claim to share with the international community at large. Under this rubric fall those US laws which link US policy within the Bank (and often the vote of the US appointed ED) to unilateral political considerations of the US.

(a) Type of government of recipient At present, no legislation concerning US policy in the Bank attempts to fix the US EDs position on proposed loans according to the type of government of the prospective borrower. An example of how such considerations might be reflected in legislation is provided by an act passed in 1983 requiring the US ED in the IMF to oppose credits by that institution to any "communist dictatorship" or to "any country practicing apartheid" unless certain conditions are met. (Annex B, #1 and #2) Although not directly relevant to the World Bank, these directives are of some interest particularly in light of the fact that the US Congress has passed relatively little politically motivated legislation concerning US policy within the IMF.

(b) Country specific legislation Very rarely does any of the legislation examined in this study refer by name to a certain country (or group of them) which is to be given special (either favorable or unfavorable) treatment. Such country-specific policies seem particularly inappropriate because they are invariably based on political and not economic considerations.

The two country-specific references which have been identified for purposes of this study are quite different in terms of their operation and purposes. The first (#3), concerns the membership of Taiwan in the ADB. It expresses the sense of the Congress that Taiwan should remain a member of the ADB, and gives notice that the US "will not countenance attempts to expel Taiwan" from the ADB. The threat is implicit that US contributions to the ADB and its soft-loan affiliate might be jeopardized if Taiwan were to be expelled. This was passed because it was apparently feared that Taiwan would be expelled when the Peoples Republic of China (PRC), the more generally recognized government of China, was eventually admitted.

While this legislative policy statement has no legal effect, it is a clearly expressed threat which carries political weight. Taiwan, of course, will not object to being offered this political protection, and is not likely to consider that statement to be a coercive act or a hostile intervention in Taiwanese affairs. It is the ADB itself and not Taiwan which is the target of the coercion implied here. Since The PRC, Taiwan and the US government all agree that there is only one China (which includes Taiwan), the support for the separate Taiwan government which this legislation provides might well be considered to constitute an intervention in the internal affairs of the PRC. The result so far has been a "two China policy" by the ADB which now counts both "Chinas" among its membership.[12]

Certain legislative language which is only partially country specific (#26) should also be mentioned here. It expresses the sense of Congress that World Bank and IMF financial assistance to any nation, and "in particular to El Salvador and Nicaragua", should be used to assist the private sector. The direct effect of this language upon loans to these countries is likely to be minimal, but in light of the troubled relations between the present US and Nicaraguan governments, this legislation can be seen

12 On March 10, 1986 China became the 47th member of the ADB. Taiwan, which has been a member since 1966 remains a member under the name of Taipei-China.

as part of the US diplomatic and military initiative in Central America.

The only other country-specific legislation which has been identified provides that the US appointed EDs in the Bank and other MDBs, when considering their votes on proposed loans to three countries; Vietnam, Laos and Cambodia; are to take into account the responsiveness of those countries in providing a more substantial accounting of US servicemen missing in action from the war in Indo-China (#20). In contrast to the Taiwan membership provisions discussed above, the countries referred to here are being identified as potential targets of coercion. This legislation puts them on notice that certain political acts on their part are likely to influence the support they can get from the US in various MDBs.

Neither of these country specific acts provides for a mandatory no-vote, and thus their impact is somewhat limited. Nonetheless the adoption of legislative statements of US policy towards the Bank which explicitly refer to specific countries is notable as one of the crudest and most transparent means of injecting political issues into Bank decision-making.

(c) Policy on American MIA's The legislation discussed immediately above concerning Vietnam, Laos and Cambodia (#20) stresses that US policy towards proposed loans to these countries by the MDBs should be influenced by the degree to which they have been responsive to US concerns on the sensitive and emotional issue of US servicemen missing in action from the war in Indo-China. Within the US there is a strong desire to identify and repatriate the remains of as many of these missing soldiers as possible, and many Americans are suspicious that these three countries have not been forthcoming on this humanitarian issue. Thus it appears among a list of considerations which US appointed EDs in the MDBs are to take into account when considering how to vote on loans to these countries.

ii) Political, Related to Upholding International Norms

The legislation reviewed in this section is concerned with what are essentially political issues, and in this sense it may be in conflict with the ideal of the Bank as a non-political institution.

But it is probably unrealistic to expect that the operations and decision-making of the Bank can be isolated from all political influences. When the political influences which do intrude have the purpose and effect of promoting respect for international norms, this may arguably justify their intrusion. At the very least, this may be seen as a mitigating factor rendering that intrusion less onerous, and less of a threat to international law and order.

(a) Human Rights violations The human rights issue may have many dimensions; ethical, legal, political and even economic. But for purposes of this typological classification of US legislative acts relative to the Bank, those raising considerations of human rights may be seen as primarily political rather than economic.

It is true, however, that those legislative amendments which are intended to cut off or reduce Bank loans to countries violating human rights may arguably have an economic purpose, since such violations may prevent the effective mobilization of human resources for development. According to this argument the above considerations could be justified as relating to the "creditworthiness" of the borrower which under the Articles of Agreement of the Bank is one of the primary conditions of financing which must be given due regard in every case.[13]

The Bank itself has consistently acknowledged that "conditions of political instability or uncertainty in the borrowing country . . . must be taken into consideration" insofar as these affect the financial and economic prospects of the borrower.[14] A failure to respect human rights may well have an effect upon the economic prospects of a country, and thus Bank policy should not necessarily exclude such considerations from that institution's economic analyses of potential borrowers.

But there is still some disagreement about whether considerations of human rights are properly relevant to decisions on World Bank lending. Both Robert McNamara, speaking as the Bank's President in 1978,[15] and Barber Conable, the Bank's cur-

13 Bank Articles of Agreement, Article III, Section 4(v).

14 IBRD, Second Annual Report, Washington, 1947, at p. 17.

15 In a 1978 interview ("McNamara on the Biggest Issue: World Economy", *New York Times*, Sunday April 2, 1978, at p. E3), McNamara was asked whether the Bank could deal with the human rights issue in its operations. In his answer he stated:

rent President,[16] have publicly suggested that the Bank should not make its decisions on the basis of human rights considerations.

Some of the US legislative provisions concerning the Bank and human rights are intended merely to promote the development of a viable human rights standard which can then be applied to decision-making in the Bank and other international financial institutions. The Young Amendment (#4) instructs US Governors to the MDBs to consult with other Governors concerning the adoption of Charter amendments in those organizations which would set human rights standards applicable to loan decisions. There can be nothing illegal about proposing to discuss an issue such as this. Any member government has the right to propose international consultations on the possible amendment of the Bank's Charter even though such consultations could effectively lead to the discussion of a political issue within the Bank. The amendment calling for consultations on a

---

"Among the most fundamental of human rights are the rights to minimum acceptable levels of nutrition; health and education. Hundreds of millions of people in developing countries, through no fault of their own, are denied these rights today. The Bank, perhaps more than any other institution in the world, is helping large numbers of these people move out of absolute poverty toward a more decent life. *What we are not capable of is action directly related to civil rights. Such action is prohibited by our charter,* it would require information and competence which we lack, and there is no agreement between our member governments on acceptable standards for civil rights in a wide variety of circumstances found in developing countries.

"Many governments, both developed and developing, resent the efforts of the United States to force its own values and its own standards of conduct on other states through international institutions which by tradition have operated on the basis of consensus. Even more, they resent being asked to apply those standards except when the United States decides that its own security interests or other national interests dictate otherwise." . . . *"We do not, we have not in this institution allowed our lending policy to be determined by civil rights considerations, whether they be civil rights considerations of leftist or rightist governments.* And our lending policies in Chile have been dictated, both under Allende and under Pinochet, entirely by economic considerations." (emphasis added)

16 On Thursday November 20, 1986, the Bank's Board approved a $250 Million loan to Chile which was opposed by various human rights groups and Democratic members of the US Congress. The US ED abstained in that vote. The day before the vote Barber Conable Jr., said he was aware that Chile was a "controversial case", but that it "has a good adjustment program and we are anxious to avoid politicizing this institution." Farnsworth, C., "Despite Dissent, World Bank Gives Loan to Chile", *International Herald Tribune*, Saturday-Sunday, November 22–23, 1986, p. 3. (From the The New York Times Service).

standard for meeting basic human needs and protecting human rights (#5) is equally innocuous.

The Harkin Amendment (#6) approach to the human rights issue goes considerably further. It focuses upon countries "whose governments engage in a consistent pattern of gross violations of human rights", and thus it is based on the idea that adequate human rights standards already exist, and should be applied by the US EDs in the various MDBs. It expresses a US policy that funds should be channeled towards countries other than those which are responsible for such a pattern of violations. The US EDs in the Bank and other MDBs are "authorized and instructed" to oppose loans or assistance to these countries unless assistance is directed specifically to programs which serve the basic human needs of their citizens.

Finally, human rights issues figure among the list of matters which US EDs are expected to take into consideration whenever participating in Bank (or other MDB) decision-making (#20). They are specifically instructed to take into consideration any actions by either the executive branch or the Congress on individual bilateral assistance programs because of human rights considerations. Thus if US bilateral aid has been suspended or reduced because of human rights violations the US EDs are to reflect upon whether multilateral aid should not be opposed as well.

(b) Drug trade While there is an obvious economic aspect to the international traffic in illegal narcotic drugs, this issue too, when raised in the context of Bank decision-making, seems to be primarily a moral and political one.

The Rangel Amendment (#7) requires that the US EDs oppose loans to countries which have failed to take adequate steps against the illegal traffic from or through their territory of narcotic drugs reaching either US territory or US personnel within the jurisdiction of those countries. The international community deplores the traffic of illegal narcotic drugs because of the death and corruption which it spreads, and in this sense the Rangel Amendment may be seen as upholding international norms as expressed in numerous treaties and resolutions. There is, however, a very clear element of unilateralism in this amendment in that its focus is limited to the traffic in illegal drugs which reach either US territory or certain US personnel abroad

Much the same can be said of the more recent anti-drug legislation (#29) which combines a "no vote" directive like that in the Rangel Amendment with a directive that the US Eds are to propose a change in Bank lending priorities including a new emphasis on drug eradication and drug crop substitution programs. Support for programs such as these would be consistent with the Bank's Charter.

(c) Policy towards hijackers The Harkin Amendment (#6 discussed above) applies to countries whose governments provide refuge to aircraft hijackers the same treatment which it mandates for those which consistently engage in human rights violations. First it expresses a US policy that funds should be channeled towards countries other than those whose governments provide refuge to individual hijackers. It also mandates that US EDs in the Bank and other MDBs oppose loans or assistance to these countries unless assistance is directed specifically to programs which serve the basic human needs of their citizens.

iii) Political Military

Military questions involve one of the most sensitive areas of high politics. Because these matters are directly linked to the sovereignty and vital interests of states, it is important that the Bank avoid any appearance of interfering in them, either by giving support for them or withholding support because of them. But to the extent that military spending programs affect the financial status or "creditworthiness" of a potential borrower they ought logically to have some indirect impact upon loan decisions by the Bank.

The US Congress has, at times, passed legislation which links US votes on MDB loans to military considerations. While no such legislation is presently applicable to US voting in the Bank, two examples are given below of how this type of consideration has been applied to US participation in MDBs.

(a) Purchase of heavy military equipment Article I of the Bank's Charter provides that all of the Bank's lending operations are to be guided by the purposes set forth in that Article, and those purposes effectively preclude the direct use of Bank financing for military purposes.[17] This situation is the same for all of the MDBs. Nonetheless, the point has been made that financial assistance even for non-military projects, may help a borrowing country to increase, or at least maintain, its military spending. Following this logic, a legislative amendment has been passed (it is applicable only to the IDB and not to the World Bank) which requires that the US vote against any proposed loan "which might assist the recipient country directly or indirectly to acquire sophisticated or heavy military equipment" (#8). This amendment is either superfluous, given that MDB loans cannot be directly used for such purposes, or impossibly broad since any country acquiring this type of equipment might be indirectly aided in that enterprise by IDB loans.

(b) Nuclear weapons policy From 1974 to 1976, following the directive contained in the first "Long Amendment" (#9), the US opposed IDA financing for any country which developed a nuclear explosive device unless the country was a party to the Treaty on Nuclear Non-Proliferation or agreed to become a party to that treaty. The US voted against 26 consecutive credits for India before the legislation requiring these negative votes was repealed in 1977. India was apparently the specific target, and in fact the only target, of that legislation. Every IDA credit for India which the US opposed due to this legislation was nonetheless approved without the support of the US[18] and this suggests that the coercive impact of the legislation was minimal. This may be one reason why it was repealed in 1977.

Even though the original Long Amendment has been repealed, under one current section of the International Financial Institutions Act (#20) it is US policy to take the nuclear weapons policy of a recipient state into consideration when voting on proposed MDB loans. The question of whether a recipient country has detonated a nuclear device, is not a State party to the Treaty on Nuclear Non-Proliferation or both is

17 Among those stated purposes of the Bank which are most relevant here are the following: reconstruction after WW II, the development of productive resources and facilities and their reconversion to peacetime needs, the promotion of international trade and investment, and assistance in bringing about a smooth transition from a wartime to a peacetime economy. IBRD Charter, Article I

18 SCHOULTZ, "Politics, Economics, and US Participation in Multilateral Development Banks", *International Organization*, Vol. 36, (1982), p.558.

included among the list of factors which US EDs in all MDBs are instructed to take into consideration when casting the US vote. An economic justification for this policy would stress the fact that nuclear weapons programs may waste the scarce funds available to a country to finance its economic development.

iv) Economic, National/Unilateral

As we saw in Chapter VI, the General Counsel of the Bank once argued in a confidential written opinion that Article IV, Section 10 of the Bank's Charter, in addition to prohibiting political activity, also excluded "the intrusion of national commercial considerations" into decision-making by the Bank.[19] If this very controversial idea is accepted then certain types of unilateral economic considerations may also be seen as improperly politicizing the Bank. Two general types of national or unilateral economic considerations which have been reflected in US legislation on the Bank are considered below.

(a) Expropriation of US investments The Gonzalez Amendment (#10) which has been in force since 1972, states that the US is to oppose MDB loans to countries which have expropriated US investments without taking adequate steps towards compensation. Is there any way in which this can be seen as in conflict with the letter or the spirit of the Bank's Charter?

The Bank and IDA have long had a policy of discouraging the expropriation of foreign investment without adequate compensation.[20] One could certainly argue that uncompensated expropriation of this type is a violation of international law and that it will have negative economic implications for the expropriating country. But by singling out as targets of US negative votes only those countries which have expropriated the property of US nationals the US Congress is pursuing a unilateral interest of the US. It would be easier to justify US

19 See the discussion of the Restriction Case Study, supra., and the second legal opinion sent by the Bank's General Counsel to the US appointed ED in the course of that affair ("Second IBRD Opinion", reproduced in "Foreign Operations Hearings, 1979", *op. cit.*, at p. 539–540).

20 This is in pursuance of one of the basic purposes of the Bank as stated in Article I, section (ii) of its Articles of Agreement, i.e., the promotion of private foreign investment. See the discussion of the expropriation issue in the discussion of the Chile Case Study, *supra*.

legislation relating to this issue if it required negative votes against all expropriating countries which failed to give adequate compensation regardless of whose property was involved. The unilateral nature of this legislation suggests that its primary basis is political rather than economic.

(b) US national economic considerations One section of the International Financial Institutions Act requires that consultations between the US Treasury and ranking Congressional leaders should be held both before and during any international negotiations involving potential increases in the contribution or subscription of the US to any MDB (#11). This is entirely an internal matter for the US government, and not an attempt to legislate concerning loan decisions in the Bank or any other MDB. It is quite natural for the different branches of the US government to develop procedures for coordinating the US position in international negotiations, and there can be no grounds for objecting to a legislative provision of this sort.

Unlike the above, the Mathis/Moore Amendment (#12) raises serious questions about whether US legislation, passed with the clear intention of promoting the economic interests of the US, can nonetheless be in conflict with the spirit, and perhaps even the letter, of the Bank's Charter. This amendment requires US EDs in all of the MDBs to oppose any loan or financial assistance by these organizations if it will establish or expand production for export of certain agricultural commodities (palm oil, sugar, or citrus crops), and thereby cause injury to US producers of the same or competing products. It also contains a statement of Congressional policy to the effect that the US should use its voice and vote in the MDBs to combat hunger and encourage development in developing countries by seeking to channel assistance for agriculturally related development to projects fulfilling the domestic food and nutrition needs and alleviating hunger in the recipient country.

This amendment is intended to protect the narrow economic interests of US exporters of the listed commodities, even though the declaration of Congressional policy articulates a more humane formal objective. Although the policy it mandates may arguably (though not necessarily) serve the economic interests of the US, it is not consistent with Article IV, Section 10 of the Bank's Charter. The analysis of this issue in Chapter VI concluded that as long as the consideration of national economic interests is not inconsistent with a decision reflecting the broader economic merits involved, the decision-making process within the Bank can legally take heed of these narrower interests. The Mathis/Moore Amendment does not leave any room for the consideration of these broader economic considerations, thus any vote cast pursuant to this amendment would be in conflict with the international obligations of the US.

The same considerations apply to the Obey Amendment (#13) under which the US EDs in all MDBs are to oppose any use of MDB funds for the production for export of any commodity which is in surplus on world markets, if the assistance would cause "substantial injury" to US producers of the same or competing commodities. US opposition to MDB loans which would increase the production of products already in surplus could easily be defended as a simple expression of economic good sense. But as is the case with many of the amendments discussed here, the unilateral (if understandable) focus upon preventing damage to private US economic enterprises raises concern about the use of the Bank as an instrument for serving the narrow economic interests of one of its members.

(c) Salaries of Bank employees and EDs The Helms Amendment (#14) directs US EDs in all international financial institutions fostering international development to take all appropriate action to keep salaries and benefits of employees to levels comparable to what is received by those holding comparable positions in the private sector or in the US government. The adoption of this amendment reflects the belief of many in the US Congress that international civil servants are overpaid, and that too large a portion of funds contributed to multilateral development assistance goes towards paying these salaries. Regardless of whether one considers this to be a real problem, the Congress is within its rights in expressing concern about this aspect of the Bank's operation, and the directive which is given to the US EDs ("to take all appropriate actions") is unobjectionable. The use of US government salaries and benefits as a standard may seem a bit presumptuous to some and rather parsimonious to others. In any case it is doubtful whether this amendment has had any significant effect upon Bank salaries and benefits.

A more bizarre situation has resulted from an amendment to various appropriations acts which mandates that no US contribution can be made to any MDB whose US ED or alternate receives a salary greater than that received by a US government employee of a certain (presumably corresponding) grade (#15). Congress must have hoped that this would lead to a cap being placed upon the salaries of all the EDs concerned, but this has not been the result. What has been achieved is that the US ED in the World Bank is actually paid less than the other EDs.

v) Other Considerations

(a) US access to records/documents of the MDB Under this category fall two legislative provisions aimed at ensuring that the US "representative" to each MDB has access to all of the institution's documents (#16) and financial records (#17). These are superfluous since the EDs of each MDB have always had access to these records. They do serve the purpose of putting the MDBs on notice that future US contributions are directly contingent upon continued US access to the records of the organization.

It is somewhat ironic that these amendments provide direct access only for the US executive branch since the US EDs are directly answerable to the President and not to the Congress. Those EDs (who are essentially civil servants in the US government) have refused to grant Congress full access to these records. Minutes of the meetings of the Executive Board, for example, have never been provided to Congress. Nonetheless, Congress does succeed in gaining access to many of the Bank's internal records.[21]

(b) Basic human needs Two separate Congressional policy statements have been identified concerning MDBs and basic human needs. One states that the US is to use its voice and vote in the MDBs to seek to channel assistance to projects which address basic human needs of the people of the recipient country (#18). The other proclaims that both US bilateral assistance and US participation in multilateral institutions are to

21 The experience of the author in preparing this study can bear this out to some extent. Several of the internal Bank documents used to document the case studies were most easily obtainable in the US Congressional Record.

emphasize programs in support of countries pursuing development strategies designed to meet basic human needs and self-sustaining growth with equity (#19). The significance of policy statements of this kind will be discussed below.

The legislation reviewed here refers to the promotion of basic human needs in a number of other contexts as well. Notable among these is the Harkin Amendment (#6) which provides for an exception, where basic human needs will be served, from the general "no" vote requirements of that amendment. Another statute requires the US to initiate international consultations in the MDBs on establishing a viable standard for meeting basic human needs (#5).

(c) Environmental reform of the MDBs With the passage of the legislation referred to here in late 1985 (#28), the US Congress began a crusade for environmental reform of the MDBs. So far no directives requiring a "no" vote have been enacted as part of this effort. The main thrust of the statute which has been enacted is to have the US encourage the MDBs to involve the Environmental and Health Ministries of MDB member countries in project development and planning, while also strengthening the expertise of the Bank's professional staff on environmental issues.

As a member of and contributor to the Bank, the US is certainly within its rights in calling for an improvement in this aspect of the Bank's performance. A clear link exists between environmental concerns and the traditional economic objectives of the Bank. In economic terms the pollution and environmental damage which result from Bank financed projects can be classified as externalities, i.e. costs which have not been factored into project planning and which are not borne by those responsible for incurring them. According to the free market economic theory generally favored by the Bank, externalities such as these should be internalized both in terms of decision-making and of financial responsibility. Since the adoption of this legislation the World Bank and the other MDBs have significantly improved their capacity to evaluate the environmental aspects of the projects they finance, but further improvement in this area is still needed.

(d) Miscellaneous The existence of a legislatively enacted list of factors which US EDs are to take into consideration when carrying out their MDB duties (#20) has already been referred to above as the various items on the list were discussed separately. All of them appear to be more political than economic. Two of these factors relate to the issue of cutting off aid to governments which violate human rights. One consideration is the nature and extent of any specific action which the US government has already taken for human rights reasons on individual bilateral assistance programs. The second factor is the extent to which any multilateral aid would directly benefit the needy people in the recipient country.

The third factor is whether the recipient country has detonated a nuclear device, is not a party to the nuclear non-proliferation treaty or both. The fourth and last political consideration listed is "country-specific". In relation to assistance for the Socialist Republic of Vietnam, the People's Democratic Republic of Laos and Democratic Kampuchea (Cambodia) the US appointed ED is to consider the extent to which the governments of those countries have been responsive in providing a more substantial account of Americans missing in action from the days of the war in Vietnam.

A number of other legislative provisions must also be mentioned here. A new Long Amendment (#21) directs that the US is to use its voice and vote in the MDBs to promote the development and utilization of light capital technologies, while another amendment (#22) orders US representatives to all international organizations to encourage and promote the integration of women into both national economies and into professional and policy-making positions within the international organizations themselves.

Congress has also adopted a general statement of US multilateral aid policy which declares that where development requires major infrastructure projects, any US assistance should be furnished in a multilateral framework with significant contributions of other donor countries (#25). It also states that infrastructure projects should be complemented by other measures to ensure that the benefits of the infrastructure reach the poor.

b) Means through which the Legislation Attempts to Affect Bank Policy

Having reviewed the different types of political considerations reflected in this body of legislation, it is now essential to distinguish between the different means through which it attempts to influence Bank policy. Just as some objectives are more justifiable and acceptable than others, it is only certain of the various means discussed below which raise serious legal and political problems.

i) Non-Binding Statements of Policy and Policy Directives

(a) Statements of policy It is fairly common for US legislative acts to begin with a statement of policy. Legislative statements of US foreign aid policy reflect the general strategy and objectives of US foreign assistance as articulated by Congress. It is probably useful for Congress to focus consciously upon these matters from time to time, though the policy statements which result have little direct legal effect. These policy statements are probably the least objectionable of all the means used by Congress to influence Bank policy.

(b) Vague directives In practical terms these vague directives normally have no more legal effect than the policy statements discussed earlier, but the former tend to be addressed to specific officials such as the US appointed ED of the Bank, or to those members of the US executive branch such as the Secretary of the Treasury or even the President himself, to whom the US ED is answerable. These directives may state that certain factors are to be taken into consideration, or that decisions are to be made with certain goals in view, without mandating any specific action (such as a "no vote"). The Helms Amendment on salaries in international financial institutions (#14), two of the amendments about the need to address basic human needs (#18 and #19), and the list of "considerations" which US EDs are to take into account (#20) all attempt to influence the voting and other activities of US EDs only through the use of such directives.

The advantage of the vague directive is that it expresses to the ultimate decision-maker (the US ED) a Congressional preference about what factors should be considered, without ever actually tying that decision-maker's hands on any specific decision. From the point of view of the Bank's need to preserve a certain autonomy from the US Congress, these directives are clearly preferable to more rigid "no vote" directives.

(c) Obligations to consult The obligation to consult represents a third category of non-binding policy statement or policy directive. To speak of an "obligation" to consult as a "non-binding" policy directive seems to be somewhat contradictory, since at least legally speaking a true obligation cannot be non-binding. But an obligation to consult is more procedural than substantive. One who is obliged to consult may not actually be obliged to reach any result in those consultations.[22]

The Young Amendment (#4) is one example. Under the terms of this amendment the President is to instruct the US Governors to the various MDBs to consult with the other Governors concerning the possibility of amending the Charters of these institutions so as to set and apply human rights criteria to future loan decisions. Thus far, this has not led to the amendment of the Bank's Charter nor that of any other MDB. While this amendment does create a loose obligation for US representatives to the MDBs, it does not create a true obligation to consult.

A true obligation to consult exists vis à vis another party with a corresponding right to be consulted. Such an obligation is created by that legislative provision which requires internal consultations within the US government under certain circumstances. This measure (#11) requires the Secretary of the Treasury or his designee to consult with Congressional leaders both before and during any international negotiations which involve potential increases in the US contributions to any of the MDBs. The purpose is quite evidently to insure Congressional input in these negotiations from the start, and thus to help reconcile US Executive and Congressional positions before possible increases in US contributions are discussed in international

22 The distinction is that between an *obligation de moyen* and an *obligation de resultat*. The obligation to consult found in the legislation discussed here is merely an *obligation de moyen*.

negotiations. This is entirely a question of improving the coordination and functioning of the US government in multilateral negotiations, and thus it is quite appropriate (from both a legal and a political standpoint) that it should be regulated by the internal law of the US.

(d) Obligations to promote a specific policy One of the most direct and efficient ways in which the US Congress can influence MDB policies is to direct the US ED to promote a specific policy change. Legislation requiring US EDs to "vigorously promote" the environmental reform of all the MDBs, was passed by Congress at the end of 1985 (#28). When the US ED raised the issue before the World Bank's Executive Board it turned out that there was a great deal of support for these reforms among the Bank's other EDs. By the end of 1988 both the World Bank and the IDB had taken a number of steps to improve their environmental performance, and the process of environmental reform is still underway in both institutions. While a number of factors have contributed to that result, the legislation was an important catalyst. A separate legislative provision making use of this same device (#29 regarding anti-drug policy) has yet to produce such dramatic results.

To an even greater extent than the vague directives mentioned above, this type of legislation directly involves the US Congress in an MDB's internal policy debates. When it proposes specific policies which are consistent with the Bank's essential purposes Congress can make a positive, and potentially effective, contribution to those debates. This is something which it cannot generally do by using the "no" vote directive discussed below.

ii) "No" Vote Directives

(a) Directives which allow for considerable Presidential discretion or flexibility

Many so called "no" vote directives passed by Congress contain such loopholes that they still leave the Executive branch with very broad discretion in determining how the US vote in the Bank will be used. In practice, when this much discretion is left to the President, the only real limitation is one of "good faith", since there is no effective review of the determinations (made by the Executive) upon which the application of the "no" vote directive depends.

Perhaps the most significant example of how this flexibility can be used or abused, is provided by the history of the Harkin Amendment (#6) and its application. That amendment requires the US EDs to oppose any MDB assistance to countries whose governments engage in a consistent pattern of gross violations of human rights, unless the assistance is specifically directed to meeting the basic human needs of the citizens of that country. It is left up to the executive branch to determine: 1) whether the government of each potential recipient country is to be considered as guilty of such a pattern of human rights violations, and if so, 2) whether any particular MDB loan which has been proposed is directed towards the basic human needs of citizens.

It is interesting to note that in applying the Harkin amendment's human rights provisions, the US EDs have not actually voted against proposed loans to violating countries, but instead have been content to abstain on those loans. In the view of the Treasury Department, which gives instructions to the US ED, this Amendment apparently creates something less than a true "no" vote directive. The first part of that Amendment does use rather flexible language, stating that in the MDBs the US "shall advance the cause of human rights, including by seeking to channel assistance towards countries other than those whose governments" are consistent human rights violators. Other parts of that amendment state more directly that the US EDs are "authorized and instructed to oppose" any loan or other assistance to offending countries, but this requirement is apparently being ignored.[23]

Under the Carter administration, this amendment was often invoked, and the US voted against many proposed MDB loans to countries with bad human rights records. Between October 1977 when the amendment was passed and January 1981 when President Carter left office, the US abstained for human rights reasons on a total of 112 loan proposals in all of the MDBs

23 Quoted from 22 USC Sec. 262d(a) and (f).

combined. Of these 112 votes 61 were against repressive conservative governments in Latin America.[24]

During the first seven years of the Reagan Administration (January 1981–January 1988), with the same Harkin Amendment in effect, the US abstained on human rights grounds only 47 times in those same institutions.[25] It is useful to note the identity of the borrowers affected in those few cases where the Reagan administration actually opposed loans (or rather abstained) on human rights grounds. Of the 47 votes mentioned above, 35 were cast on loans to states considered by the US to be strongly pro-Soviet.[26] This suggests that political criteria (including factors other than human rights) were applied in exercising executive discretion under the Harkin Amendment.[27]

The Gonzalez Amendment (#10) is another important enactment which in practice leaves the President free to determine whether or not to oppose loans pursuant to a Congressional "no vote" directive. The Executive branch makes the decision about whether potential MDB borrowers which have expropriated US investments have taken "adequate steps" towards compensation. Standards concerning the compensation of foreigners for the expropriation of their property have long been a subject of dispute, but the standard to be applied under this amendment is still surprisingly vague. It is left to the executive to determine not merely whether "adequate" compensation has been paid, but more broadly whether "adequate steps" in that direction have been taken. In practice this means that despite the amendment the US ED is free to support MDB loans to a

24 See *International Finance*: The Annual Report to the President and Congress of the (US) National Council on International Monetary and Financial Policies, for fiscal years 1978–1981.

25 Ibid., for fiscal years 1981 – 1988.

26 The targets viewed as pro-Soviet by the US when it abstained on human rights grounds were as follows, Yemen P.D.R. (13 times), Angola (8), Benin (5), Syria (4), Uganda (under President Obote, 3 times), and Laos (2). *Loc. cit.*

27 Under the Reagan administration the US did abstain a few times to protest loans to countries it did not believe to be pro-Soviet. At first, bureaucratic inertia brought about a continuation of the Carter policy, thus in 1981 the US abstained due to human rights on four loans, one to each of the following countries; Guatemala, the Philippines, Paraguay and Bolivia. Other than the votes against pro-Soviet states enumerated in the footnote above, no other loan was opposed by the US on human rights grounds until 1985 when the US began to abstain on loans to Chile. By September 1987 the US had abstained on these grounds 8 times on MDB loans to Chile. *Loc. cit.*

country which has expropriated US investments, even if all that country's government has done is express a willingness to discuss compensation in the future. The President could hardly ask for more flexibility.

Two separate legislative amendments are designed to protect US commodity producers from MDB financed competition, but they are marginally different in the degree of discretion they leave to the Executive. The Obey Amendment (#13) mandates a US "no" vote on any proposed use of MDB funds which would cause "substantial injury" to US producers of competing commodities. Because it is so difficult to determine exactly when such a threshold of "substantiality" has been crossed, this language leaves room for a lot of Executive discretion.

The Mathis/Moore Amendment (#12) (which applies only to agricultural commodities) mandates a US "no" vote on any proposed MDB assistance which will cause injury to competing US producers whether that injury is substantial or not. Less discretion is left to the Executive under this language, and thus this amendment might more appropriately be classified under the category discussed immediately below, i.e. as an effectively mandatory "no" vote directive.

(b) Effectively mandatory "No" votes

Decisions on US voting in the Bank which fall within the scope of the Congressional directives discussed above may in the final analysis be attributable more to the President (who as Chief Executive has the final say in exercising Executive discretion) than to legislation passed by Congress. The Congress may favor policies which are in conflict with the letter or the spirit of the Bank's Charter, and may enshrine its preferences in legislation, but as long as the votes of the US ED are not necessarily and finally determined by these legislative enactments, the latter are not in real and effective conflict with the international institutional law of the Bank.

Thus, it is with the mandatory legislative directive that the real possibility of conflict between US legislation and international law emerges. The Mathis/Moore Amendment (#12), discussed in the preceding section, is the closest thing to a truly mandatory "no" vote directive which can be found in current US legislation concerning the Bank. In the past another considerably more absolute "no" vote directive was applicable to

US voting on concessional loans by the Bank's soft loan affiliate the IDA. The original Long Amendment (#9) which was in effect from 1974 through the time it was repealed in 1977 required the US to oppose concessional loans to countries which developed nuclear weapons and which had not signed the Nuclear Non-proliferation treaty. It left room for absolutely no discretion, and 26 consecutive votes by the US ED in opposition to IDA credits for India were directly and effectively legislated by Congress. If these votes were in conflict with the Bank's Charter,[28] responsibility must be laid at the door of Congress and not the US Executive branch.

iii) Congressional Declarations that None of the Funds Appropriated shall be used for Certain Purposes

It was the threatened use of this particular device which was at the center of the dispute between 1977 and 1979 over Congressional efforts to bar the use of the US contributed funds for IDA loans to Vietnam.[29] Since Article VII, Section 6 of Bank's Charter states that all Bank assets shall be free from restrictions, the Bank cannot accept restricted funds. As the case study on restrictions demonstrates, the mere threat of restricted contributions has on at least one occasion been enough to compromise the independence of the Bank in the eyes of some observers. From the Bank's point of view, the threat or use of these restrictions by its largest (and indispensable) contributor, is extremely troubling whenever it occurs. It represents a greater threat to the Bank than do the largely ineffective directives ordering US EDs to cast a negative vote for one reason or another. Only rarely has the Congress attempted to use this device as a means of asserting control over Bank lending policies.

Two of the foreign assistance appropriations acts included in Annex B provide for some restrictions upon US contributions to the Bank, (#16 and #17) but they have no real effect. All that they require is that the Bank provide US representatives to these institutions with access to documents and other infor-

28 As has been noted above, there is a plausible economic justification for opposing loans to developing countries which spend scarce financial resources on the development of nuclear weapons, thus the Long Amendment is not in clear conflict with the Bank's Charter.

29 This dispute is discussed in Chapter VI, supra. as the "Case Study on Restrictions Imposed or Threatened by the US Congress".

mation about its operations. The US ED has access to this information in any case. Moreover, the Bank can accept the funds because the apparent restriction is not intended to apply to use of the funds *after* they have been made available to the Bank. The restrictions involved here are actually conditions to be met before the funds appropriated are actually made available to the Bank. What the Bank cannot accept is funds which are subject to restrictions applicable after their transfer to the Bank.

B. THE EVIDENCE OF INTENT

As we have seen, the element of intent or of an impermissible objective can be an important part of the analysis of legal phenomena such as politicization, intervention, economic coercion, and the abuse of rights. The difficulty which is generally involved in proving intent, and in identifying the actual objectives of governments has already been discussed. We can now attempt to examine and to evaluate the evidence which is available.

1. The Legislation Itself as Evidence of Congressional Intent

Congressional efforts to influence US policy towards the Bank and IDA have, for the most part, taken the form of amendments to legislation appropriating funds for the US contribution to these (and other) institutions. As a result, there is a concrete record of congressionally mandated policy towards them. This record, in the form of US legislation, reveals a definite policy of attempting to use US voting power in the Bank and the IDA as a means of exerting pressure upon certain states for political purposes. The objectives of Congress in enacting various policy directives for US appointed EDs are fairly clear from the face of the legislation concerned. That legislation is thus the logical place to look for evidence concerning the intentions of the US Congress which passed it.

Sometimes legislative acts and amendments in the US (and elsewhere) contain an explicit statement of their formal objectives. These can be useful in determining the intentions of the Congress in adopting the acts in question. Often, however, no truly formal objectives are identified by a legislative act or, even if some are identified, other potentially more significant objectives are left unstated. In either of these cases, it can be useful to consider whether certain additional objectives are not implicit in the measures enacted.

For example the Mathis/Moore Amendment (#12), formally and explicitly expresses the desire of Congress:

> "to combat hunger and malnutrition and to encourage economic development in the developing countries . . . by seeking to channel assistance for agriculturally related development to projects that would aid in fulfilling domestic food and nutrition needs and in alleviating hunger and nutrition in the recipient country."[30]

But the more fundamental objectives of Congress in passing that amendment are suggested by its operative language.

> "The United States representatives to the institutions named in this section shall oppose any loan or other financial assistance for establishing or expanding production for export of palm oil, sugar, or citrus crops if such loan or assistance will cause injury to United States producers of the same, similar or competing agricultural commodities."[31]

The objective, of course, is to protect the US producers of the stated agricultural commodities from any new foreign competition financed by the MDBs.

In a similar fashion, those provisions of US legislation which mandate the way in which the US is to use its voting power in the Bank, identify fairly clearly, if only implicitly, the objectives behind certain seemingly "politicized" or "coercive" votes by the US within these institutions. In light of the original Long Amendment (#9) for example, it is clear that between 1974 and 1977 when that amendment was in effect the US voted against many IDA loans to India because it had detonated a nuclear explosion without signing and ratifying the Treaty on Nuclear Non-Proliferation ("NPT"). It is reasonable to conclude that the objective of that amendment was to punish India for its actions and/or to pressure it to do something it has resisted doing in the past, i.e. ratify the NPT. An element of international

30 International Financial Institutions Act, Section 901, 22 USC Section 262g.
31 *Loc. cit.*

coercion was therefore almost certainly present. But as we have seen, a economic justification for these votes was also available.

2. Statements of the Executive Branch

In addition to the legislative evidence discussed above, at times there have also been public statements by officials of the executive branch mentioning for example that the US would oppose a given loan application for certain stated reasons. Some such statements have suggested that the US intends to use the Bank (or its voting power in the Bank) as a means of applying economic pressure, but normally some arguably economic justification is given.

For example, in July of 1983, James Conrow, then the Director of the US Treasury's Office of Multilateral Banks (and now a high official at the IDB), publicly announced that the US would oppose any loan to Nicaragua by the World Bank or the Inter-American Development Bank until the Sandinista Government took steps to "revitalize the private sector" and "improve the efficiency of the public sector".[32] The formally expressed justification is economic, but given the state of relations between Nicaragua and the US at that time, there is every reason to believe that Nicaragua was singled out for political reasons which were implicit but left unstated.

It is difficult to establish with certainty the true motivation behind US negative votes on loan applications within the Bank and the IDA,[33] and this is especially true when the decision concerning those votes is made exclusively by the Executive branch of the US government. At least when those votes are cast pursuant to legislative directives the latter will provide concrete evidence of the factors motivating the negative vote.

C. THE POTENTIAL LEGAL CONFLICT BETWEEN US LEGISLATION AND THE BANK'S CHARTER

1. The Bank's Charter under US Law

The Bank's Charter is an international agreement which sets out the rights and obligations of member states in a quasi-

32 International Herald Tribune, Saturday-Sunday, 2–3 July 1983, p. 5.

33 The Annual Report of the National Advisory Council on International Monetary and Financial Policies for each fiscal year does identify the *formal* reason for every US negative vote in the various MDBs.

constitutional fashion. The US accepted that Charter according to its laws, and therefore has agreed to be bound by that agreement. The Bank and IDA Charters have never been ratified by the US Senate as treaties, but acceptance by the US President of membership, and of the obligations it entails, was authorized by the US Congress pursuant to legislation.[34] This method of accepting membership is fully consistent with the Charters of the Bank and the IDA.[35] As a matter of the constitutional law of the US, the acceptance of an international agreement in this way is generally considered to have the same legal effect as ratification by the Senate.[36] This means that the obligations of the US under the Bank Charter are full treaty obligations.

But what is the effect of treaty obligations according to the internal law of the US? Article VI, Section 2 of the US Constitution states that:

> "This Constitution, and the laws of the United States which shall be made in pursuance thereof; and all treaties made, or which shall be made, under the authority of the United States, shall be the supreme law of the land; and the judges in every state shall be bound thereby, anything in the Constitution or laws of any state notwithstanding." (emphasis added)

Thus "all treaties made" are "the supreme law of the land", and at least in this sense seem to be on the same footing as the legislative acts of Congress. But how, if at all, does this rule relate to a situation where a legislative act of Congress seems to be in conflict with a treaty obligation? It is well established that as a matter of internal US law, any act of Congress can override the effect of a treaty or other international agreement entered into earlier.[37] This means that a treaty obligation of the

34 See the Bretton Woods Agreement Act, PL 79-171, 59 Stat. 512, approved July 31, 1945, 22 USC Sec. 286 (IBRD); and the IDA Act, PL 86-565, 74 Stat. 293, approved June 30, 1960, 22 USC Sec. 284 (IDA).

35 See IBRD Charter Art. XI, Sec. 2; IDA Charter, Art. XI, Sec. 2.

36 See, MCDOUGAL, M.S., and LANS, A., "Treaties and Congressional-Executive or Presidential Agreements: Interchangeable Instruments of National Policy", *Yale Law Journal*, Vol. 54, (1945), pp. 181–351.

37 In 1888 the US Supreme Court, in the case of *Whitney v. Robertson*, (124 U.S. 190, 194) stated that:.
"By the Constitution a treaty is placed on the same footing, and made of like obligation, with an act of legislation. Both are declared to be the

US can in no way restrict the power of the US President and Congress to enact conflicting legislation.[38]

2. The Relation between the Internal Laws of the US and its International Obligations

While subsequently adopted and conflicting legislation may create some doubt about the exact status of the Bank's Charter under US law, there can be little doubt about the status of US legislation under international law. As the Permanent Court of International Justice observed in the case of *Certain German Interests in Polish Upper Silesia*, "[f]rom the standpoint of International Law and of the Court which is its organ municipal laws are merely facts which express the will and constitute the activities of States".[39] Thus when questions arise about the international legality of actions taken by a state pursuant to its municipal law, the municipal law itself may constitute evidence of conduct in violation of international law.[40]

Of course while legislative acts of the US Congress may potentially have some evidential value, they can in no way diminish the international legal obligations of the US. It is a well established principle of international law that a state cannot justify a violation of its international legal obligations by invoking the provisions of its own municipal law.[41] Thus we see that

supreme law of the land, and no supreme efficacy is given to either over the other. When the two relate to the same subject, the courts will always endeavor to construe them so as to give effect to both, if that can be done without violating the language of either; but if the two are inconsistent, the one last in date will control the other, provided always the stipulation of the treaty on the subject is self-executing."

For more on conflicts between treaties and legislative acts see HENKIN, *Foreign Affairs, op. cit.*, at pp. 163–164 and associated notes; See also Brownlie p. 52-53.

38 Henkin, *Foreign Affairs, op. cit.*, at p. 151, notes that:

"A treaty, moreover, does not dispose of constitutional power: internationally the United States retains the power (not the right) to violate its treaty obligations; constitutionally, the President and Congress can exercise their powers even in violation of a treaty undertaking."

39 *Certain German Interests in Polish Upper Silesia*, P.C.I.J., Ser. A, no. 7, p. 19.

40 *Loc. cit.*, see also Brownlie, op. cit., at p. 42.

41 See the *Free Zones* case, (1932), P.C.I.J., Ser. A/B, No. 46, p. 167; *Greco-Bulgarian Communities* case, (1930), P.C.I.J., Ser. B, no. 17, p. 32. See also Article 27 of the Vienna Convention on the Law of Treaties which states that "A party may not invoke the provisions of its internal law as justification for its failure to perform a treaty."

if there is a conflict between US municipal law and international law governing the activities of member states within the World Bank, the resulting legal situation will appear to be quite different depending upon whether it is viewed from the perspective of international law or that of the municipal law of the US.

D. THE LEGAL CLASH BETWEEN THIS LEGISLATION AND INTERNATIONAL LAW

1. Specific Areas of Conflict Reviewed

a) The Possibility that this Legislation may Require an ED within the Bank to Engage in a Form of "Political Activity" Prohibited by the Bank's Charter

In examining the issue of whether any of this legislation has engendered "political activity" by the US ED which is in conflict with the Bank's Charter, one must again make reference to the different means used to influence Bank policy.[42] Because of their non-binding nature and generally limited effect, mere statements of policy do not oblige the Bank's EDs to act contrary to the Bank's Charter. Legislative declarations restricting the Bank's use of US contributed funds could potentially be in conflict with the Bank's Charter, but as we have seen above no effective declarations of this type are currently in effect.[43]

At present the possibility of an acute conflict between US legislation and the Bank's Charter is posed primarily by legislative "no" vote directives as discussed above. These are intended to direct the activities of the US appointed ED within the Bank. At the same time, of course, the activities of EDs are also governed by the Bank's Charter.

42 It is also possible that political activity in conflict with the Bank's Charter could result from the discretionary policy of the executive branch. See the cases discussed in Chapter VI, *supra* concerning the cutoff of World Bank lending to Poland, Czechoslovakia and Chile.

43 See the discussion of these declarations earlier in this Chapter. The discussion in Chapter VI of the dispute over restricted contributions to the Bank indicates how the mere threat of legislative restrictions on US contributions to the Bank was on at least one occasion sufficient to compromise respect for the Bank's Charter. This was an extremely serious development, and there is no way of knowing if Congress will go down this road again in the future. Only once, however, has Congress actually adopted legislation attempting to impose continuing (and therefore unacceptable) restrictions on the use of the US contribution to a MDB. This was in 1975 and the MDB involved, the IDB, refused to accept the restricted funds.

This matter has been discussed in detail in an earlier chapter.[44] It is sufficient to recall here that Article IV, Section 10 of the Bank's Charter, the so-called "political activity prohibition", requires that political considerations be excluded from Bank decision-making, while Article I states that the Bank's decisions are to be guided by the purposes expressed in that article (which are economic).

The overall effect of these provisions of the Bank's Charter is to place legal limits upon the scope of the decision-making discretion enjoyed by the Bank's Governors and EDs. The idea that such limits may apply to the use of voting power within an international organization was endorsed by the ICJ in its Advisory Opinion on the Conditions of Admission.[45] Although that opinion dealt with the UN Charter and not with the Bank, the same logic should nonetheless apply.

Some of the legislation examined imposes (or at least proposes) criteria for decision-making by the US ED which appear to fall outside the essentially economic parameters permitted by the Bank's Charter. That Charter is legally binding upon the US, and to the extent that US legislation requires an ED of the Bank to exceed the limits of his legally held discretion, that legislation is in conflict with the international legal obligations of the US.[46]

44 See Chapter V, *supra*.

45 Advisory Opinion on Conditions of Admission of a State to Membership in the United Nations, *ICJ Reports*, (1947–1948), p. 57. This opinion, and its relevance to the issues examined here is discussed further in Chapter V, *supra*.

46 Cf. "Prohibition of Political Activities Under the IBRD Articles of Agreement and its Relevance to the Work of the Executive Directors", legal opinion by Ibrahim F.I. Shihata, Vice President and General Counsel of the World Bank, section M87-1409, at p. 8 (December 23, 1987), (unpublished). Quoted in SHIHATA, I.F.I., "The World Bank and Human Rights: An Analysis of the Legal Issues and the Record of Achievements", *Denver Journal of International Law and Policy*, Vol. 17, No. 1, (1988), at p. 46. This opinion supports the view that member states are under a legal obligation not to politicize the votes of the EDs. While the opinion acknowledges that as a general matter EDs may vote upon the instructions of the countries which they represent, it concludes that the ED:
"is not to act simply as an ambassador of the government or governments which appointed or elected him and is expected to exercise his individual judgment in the interest of the Bank and its members as a whole. Members of the Bank are under an obligation not to influence the Bank's President and staff in the discharge of their duties, and the Executive Directors are under a duty not to act as the instrumentality of members to exert such prohibited influence."

Still, the question of legality is complicated by the fact that there is often a connection between economic considerations and political issues. Because of this, prudence and logic may require that certain political matters be taken into account even in an essentially economic analysis. The Harkin Amendment's (#6) directive that the US should oppose Bank loans to countries whose governments engage in a consistent pattern of gross violations of human rights might thus be justified by the observation that such violations are likely to undermine the economic health of the prospective borrower. Similarly, the original Long Amendment (#9) and its mandatory "no" vote on concessional loans to countries developing nuclear weapons makes a certain amount of economic sense. Nuclear weapons programs are enormously expensive and from a purely economic point of view could be seen as wasting funds which could be used more productively.

But the fact that one can conceive of an economic pretext for the Long Amendment should not blind us to its essentially political thrust. The object was to punish India for exploding a nuclear device and pressure that country to ratify the NPT, and the 26 votes cast for this purpose constituted a politicization of the Bank, and a form of illegal political activity by the US ED in the Bank (IDA).

The Gonzalez Amendment (#10) which orders a US no vote on loans to countries which have expropriated US investments without compensation is based on criteria which are both political and economic. Nationalization of foreign investments is a political act which may well have economic consequences. The Bank itself has recognized that this is true, and has consistently refused to make loans to countries expropriating foreign investments "unless and until they make appropriate efforts to reach a fair and equitable settlement."[47]

Article IV Section 10 of the Bank's Charter directs not only that its decisions are to be made according to economic considerations, but also that the economic considerations are to be "weighed impartially" in order to achieve the agreed purposes

47 *Policies and Operations: The World Bank, International Development Association and International Finance Corporation*, Washington, D.C., IBRD, (1969) at p. 31. See also the more detailed discussion of the Bank's general policies towards expropriation and compensation disputes which is included in the Chile Case Study, in Chapter VI, *supra*.

of the Bank set out in Article I of that Charter. Thus even if the record of potential borrowers concerning human rights violations or the uncompensated expropriation of foreign owned property are viewed as essentially economic considerations, the way in which the Harkin and Gonzalez amendments have been applied[48] establishes that the economic considerations involved have been applied in an essentially political way, and for political purposes. This amounts to prohibited political activity within the Bank.

The availability of an economic justification for US "no" votes cast pursuant to the Gonzalez Amendment still leaves open another important question about possible conflicts between US law and the Bank's Charter. That Amendment only applies to loans to countries which have nationalized US investments without adequate compensation. To what extent, if any, does the Bank's Charter exclude the intrusion into Bank decision-making of economic considerations such as this which concern only the interests of the US and which thus have a national or unilateral character? This issue is raised even more squarely by the Mathis/Moore and Obey Amendments (#12 & #13 respectively), which mandate a US "no" vote on MDB loans for financing the production of commodities for export whenever the increased foreign competition would result in injury to US commodity producers.

These amendments reflect an economic nationalism which is in conflict with the spirit of international economic cooperation upon which the Bank is based, but this does not necessarily mean that they require the US ED to act outside of the legal limits of his discretion. The September 28, 1977 opinion of the Bank's General Counsel notwithstanding, the language of Article IV, Section 10 does not unequivocally bar national commercial considerations from being taken into account in World Bank decision-making. As long as the consideration of national economic interests is not inconsistent with a decision reflecting the broader economic merits involved, the decision-making process within the Bank can legally take heed of these narrower

48 The Harkin Amendment on human rights (#6), and the Gonzalez Amendment on uncompensated expropriation (#10) have been selectively applied. It is loans to pro-Soviet states which have been the target of US opposition votes cast pursuant to these two amendments. See the more detailed discussion of these amendments, *supra*. this same chapter.

interests. Accordingly, the Gonzalez and Obey Amendments, which call for using the US vote to serve the national economic interests of the US, are not in legal conflict with the Bank's Charter because they could, according to their terms, be applied in a manner consistent with the Bank's broader economic goals.

The policy of the Gonzalez Amendment (#10) is to oppose loans to countries which have expropriated US property without adequate steps towards compensation. This parallels the policy of the Bank on this issue, and promotes the Bank's goal of encouraging foreign investment.[49] There is no inherent conflict between the directives of this Amendment and the Bank's Charter. Nonetheless, as has been noted above, the consistently political application of the Gonzalez Amendment can be seen as a form of prohibited political activity.

The Obey Amendment (#13) is intended to prevent the MDBs from financing the production of commodities for export when this would result in injury to competing US producers. If the amendment required a US "no" vote whenever this injury was likely to result from a proposed loan it would be inconsistent with the Bank's Charter. A loan which injured US producers might nonetheless be economically sound. But the Obey Amendment only requires the US ED to oppose such loans in cases where the commodity to be produced is already in surplus on world markets. The fact of such a surplus provides adequate economic grounds for opposing such a loan regardless of the effect upon competing US producers. Thus the Obey Amendment does not mandate any action by the US ED which is inconsistent with the Bank's Charter.

Like the Obey Amendment, the Mathis/Moore Amendment (#12) mandates a US "no" vote on loans intended to finance the production for export of certain agricultural commodities where the loan would cause injury to producers of competing commodities in the US. Unlike the Obey Amendment, however, its application is not limited to cases where the commodity to be produced is already in surplus on world markets. Under this amendment, loans which would result in harm to certain US producers are to be opposed regardless of other considerations. It is in conflict with the Bank's Charter because on its face it does not allow for the consideration of any economic factors

49 According to Article I(ii) of the Bank's Charter one of its agreed purposes is to "promote private foreign investment".

other than the effects which the proposed loan would have upon US producers.

Do any of the other "no" vote directives reviewed here clearly require the US ED to act contrary to the Bank's Charter? Two such directives remain to be discussed here; the Rangel Amendment on the illegal drug trade (#7 and #29), and that aspect of the Harkin Amendment (#6) which deals with refuge for hijackers. While it is perfectly comprehensible, from a political point of view, that the US should want to take action to discourage both the illegal traffic of narcotic drugs to US territory and the granting of refuge to those who hijack aircraft, only through the most creative of arguments could either of these considerations be classified as "economic."[50]

Though these two amendments are difficult to justify economically, both of them leave room for considerable executive discretion in their application. The Rangel Amendment's "no" vote requirement applies only when the prospective borrower "fails to take adequate steps" against illegal drug traffic. It has been noted above that this is a flexible standard. In fact, while all US "no" votes or abstentions in the MDBs and the reasons why they were cast are reported to the US Congress annually, so far the failure of a prospective borrower to take such steps against the drug trade has never been stated as the reason for such a vote.

That part of the Harkin Amendment being considered here requires a "no" vote on loans to countries giving refuge to hijackers except when the loans are specifically directed to programs which serve the basic human needs of the citizens of that country. This standard is somewhat less flexible than that contained in the Rangel Amendment, but again not once has a

50 Of course one could argue that the traffic in illegal narcotics is a form of economic activity, and that it is detrimental to the economic health of a country (although this has not been proven). Even more creatively, one could say that since aircraft hijacking discourages international travel and communications, granting refuge to hijackers may have a negative effect upon the world economy. In the Admissions Case (*ICJ Reports* 1947–1948 at p. 63) the ICJ concluded that in voting on admissions UN members were justified in "taking into account of any factor which it is possible reasonably and in good faith to connect" with the criteria for decision set out in Article 4 of the UN Charter. Applying that same test here would allow human rights, the drug trade, and refuge for hijackers to be linked to the Bank's economic purposes, so long as the linkage was made in good faith. See the discussion of the Admissions Case in Chapter V, *supra*.

"no" vote or abstention by a US ED ever been justified to Congress on the basis that the borrower gave refuge to hijackers.

None of the legislation reviewed in this section has been effective in politicizing the outcome of the Bank's decision-making on loan proposals. The loans concerned have all been approved in spite of the many "no" votes cast pursuant to legislative directive. Regardless of the effect created, some of this legislation does require the US ED to cast politically motivated negative votes within the World Bank; and those provisions which do so are in conflict with Article IV Section 10 of the Bank's Charter. By using the US ED as an instrument for the exertion of prohibited political influence within the Bank, the US has violated its legal obligations under that Charter.[51]

b) The Possibility that this Legislation may Encourage an Abuse of Rights by the US or by its Appointed Executive Director

Doubts persist about whether the doctrine of abuse of rights is part of international law,[52] but if it is it would seem to be applicable to some of the "no" votes mandated by the legislation reviewed above. As we have seen, an abuse of rights involves three elements: 1) the abusing state must be acting within its apparent rights; 2) that state must exercise its rights so as to impede the enjoyment by other states of their own rights, or must exercise it in order to accomplish some other improper purpose; and 3) this must result in injury to another state.

Much of the US legislation which concerns the use of US voting power within the Bank is geared toward ends other than those mentioned in the Bank's Charter, and may also be seen as an attempt to impede the enjoyment by other states of their own rights as members of the Bank.[53] Two of the essential elements of abuse of rights are thus present at least in those cases where "no" votes have been cast pursuant to directives based on political factors. First of all the US is using its legally held voting power under the Bank's Charter, and at the same

51 See SHIHATA, "The World Bank and Human Rights", *op. cit.*, at p. 46.

52 See the discussion of this doctrine, and its status as part of international law, in Chapter V, *supra*.

53 When a negative vote is cast by the US ED pursuant to a legislative directive, the legislation in which that directive is embodied provides ample evidence of the intention or purpose behind the casting of that vote.

time that power is intentionally being used for purposes which are improper under the terms of that Charter. These votes clearly constitute politicization, but they will only amount to an abuse of rights if they cause injury to another state.

Had any of the many US negative votes cast pursuant to the original Long Amendment (#9) sufficed to prevent a loan from being approved, this would have been sufficient to establish an abuse of rights attributable to legislative directive. Similarly, a "no" vote pursuant to the Mathis-Moore Amendment (#12) would clearly constitute an abuse of rights if it succeeded in causing injury to another state. One could argue that the same is true of the Harkin Amendment (#6), and the Rangel Amendment (#7 or #29).[54] But the third necessary element in an abuse of rights, actual injury to another state, has not often been present. This is because of the fact that US opposition rarely suffices to prevent the approval of loans by the Bank. While the US has in fact abused its rights in following the policy of certain of these legislative amendments, the failure of that abuse to cause identifiable injury prevents it from being legally recognizable as such.

The only cases in which US legislative policy seems to have been effective in preventing loans by the Bank, (and thus in causing injury to another member state), concerned more than simple "no" votes pursuant to legislative directive. These include the suspension of Bank lending to Chile from 1971 to 1973 while the Allende government was in power, and the suspension of Bank lending to Vietnam in 1979 under a threat by Congress to restrict US contributions to the Bank and IDA. The documented use of threats and coercion in these two cases constituted both illegal acts of politicization and an abuse of rights, even though in these cases no legislative amendments adopted by the US government could be linked to the "abuses" in question.

54 Although neither human rights considerations nor action against the international drug trade have traditionally been considered relevant to the Bank's economic mission, a consensus linking them to the Bank's agreed purposes may develop as international concern about these two problems grows.

The concept of *détournement de pouvoir* is applicable to actions by the Bank's organs (including the EDs) much as abuse of rights is applicable to actions by member states. Thus an abuse of rights by the US through the use of its voting power implies a *détournement de pouvoir* by its appointed Executive Director.

c) The Legislation and Standards of Non-Intervention

We must now consider whether actions taken pursuant to this legislation have resulted in illegal economic intervention or illegal economic coercion of a target state. As we have seen, international legal standards in this area are disputed,[55] and the consideration of this issue is a rather complex question depending upon many factors.

According to the standard of intervention proposed in Chapter IV of this study, US "no votes" in the Bank cannot be considered to constitute illegal intervention through economic coercion unless two distinct elements are present. There must be a coercive or interventionistic objective, and there must also be an effect on the target sufficient to threaten its independence and freedom of action.

In economic intervention as with certain other rules of international law relevant to this study, the intentions of the US are fully as important as the actions it has taken. Could the intentions behind any of this US legislation be considered to be improperly interventionistic or coercive?[56] When the Congress mandates a US "no" vote on proposed loans to countries following or not following a certain policy, this should normally be interpreted as an attempt to persuade potential borrowers not to pursue the policy in question. When a credible and non-interventionistic economic justification for opposing that policy is available, it will be difficult to establish that an unacceptably interventionistic political motive is present. Many of the "no" vote directives reviewed here (such as #9 on nuclear weapons and #10 on expropriation without compensation) involve an arguably proper economic motive, but the available justifications are not particularly credible. Thus these "no" vote directives do constitute an attempt to subordinate the sovereign rights of borrowers.

The intent to intervene or to coerce can be inferred from the circumstances surrounding a number of the provisions discussed. Most notably among these are #6 on human rights, #7 and #29 on the drug trade, #9 on nuclear non-proliferation, #10 on expropriation of US investments, and #12 and #13 on

55 See Chapter IV, *supra*.

56 This question is asked with regard to the purposes implicit in this legislation, since no clear statements of an improper purpose are contained in the legislation itself. See the discussion of this issue, *supra*.

the protection of US producers of certain commodities from MDB financed competition.[57] Nonetheless, it is doubtful whether opposition by the US to loans as mandated by this body of legislation has ever had an effect sufficient to threaten the independence or freedom of action of the state targeted. Although that opposition falls within the modern political definition of intervention, it will qualify as illegal intervention (under the standard proposed in Chapter IV) only to the extent that it has a real effect of some kind upon the state or states targeted. The apparent ineffectiveness of US "no" votes and abstentions in the Bank does not establish the absence of such a real effect. The successful efforts by the US to block Bank loans to Chile under Allende and to Vietnam were accomplished without the use of legislatively mandated "no" votes. These two episodes clearly did constitute illegal intervention. Other undocumented cases, tied to this legislation, may well exist. It has not been possible to document any more such cases for purposes of the present study, but further research in this area may prove to be of interest to scholars in the future.

The formal purpose of the Harkin Amendment(#6) is to promote respect for international human rights norms, and this helps to justify the coercive intent which is apparently behind that particular piece of legislation. Since human rights violations are now considered to be a matter of international concern, the application of that amendment could be viewed as a legitimate, if unilateral sanction. This argument is undermined by the fact that in practice (at least under the Reagan administration) it was invoked principally against states considered by the US to be pro-Soviet.

2. A General Assessment of Whether the Bank has been Illegally Politicized by this Legislation

Much of the legislation discussed has an essentially economic purpose, is consistent with the policy and practice of the Bank,

57 Even more clearly interventionistic is the legislation requiring a negative vote to be cast solely because of the type of political system of the target state. At present it is not with regard to the Bank but only the IMF that such a legislative directive is in effect, (the "communist dictatorships" amendment (#1)).

and therefore cannot be said to politicize that institution.[58] On the other hand, some of these legislative amendments involve factors which may be seen as essentially political such as nuclear arms tests and policy towards hijackers. Amendments such as these do tend to inject political matters into Bank councils and decision-making, but that alone is not enough to constitute legally significant politicization. This can be said to occur only when the rights of Bank member states are detrimentally affected or when a member state takes politicizing actions in material violation of its obligations under the Bank's Charter.

This legislation is more notable for its inefficacy than for its consistency with the principles and objectives of the Bank's Charter. At times the US executive branch has used the discretion it is granted under some of these legislative enactments to avoid casting "no" votes based on political considerations. Even when the US has opposed loans on political grounds the effect has generally been minimal. It is because of this inefficacy that politicizing legislation has not had a more detrimental effect upon the rights of the Bank's members or upon the Bank's ability to function effectively.

All 112 MDB loans which the Carter administration opposed because of human rights considerations pursuant to the Harkin Amendment (#6) were nonetheless approved. One analyst of this situation has suggested that the real purpose of legislation such as this is not to halt any particular loan, but to communicate a message of concern to the MDBs and the recipient governments.[59] In this light the Harkin Amendment appears as little more than a political statement. It may well be seen as politicizing the Bank, but not in the legal sense of detrimentally affecting the concrete legal rights of the member governments targeted by that amendment. The same observation can be made with regard to the completely ineffective application of the original

58 But it should be recalled that selective concern for human rights, or the application of a double standard on any issue has sometimes been identified with politicization. By implication then, the uneven application of even purely economic criteria can constitute politicization. See the discussion in Chapter II, *supra*.

59 SCHOULTZ, *op. cit.*, p. 565, note 70, put it this way:
"the goal of the U.S. government was not to halt any particular loan, but to communicate a message of concern to the MDBs and the recipient governments. In some cases, (IDB loans to Pinochet's Chile, for example) the message appears to have had the effect of halting the processing of additional loans to repressive governments, but these cases are very few."

Long Amendment (#9) between 1974 and 1977. Because of India's nuclear weapons policy the US voted against 26 consecutive IDA credits for India, every one of which was nonetheless approved. The record indicates that legislatively mandated "no" votes by US EDs have been notoriously ineffective. Because of this the actual damage to the legal rights of other Bank member states has been minimal.

Has the US violated the its obligations under the Bank's Charter by using its ED as the instrument of prohibited political activity within the Bank? On many occasions it has. Both through the legislatively mandated no votes discussed in this Chapter, and through the policies discussed in Chapter VI's case studies, the US has violated its obligation not to politicize the Bank; an obligation which results from Article IV, Section 10 of the Bank's Charter.

The basic reason for concern about this type of legislation is the fear that it might force the Bank to act according to criteria distinct from or even inconsistent with those provided for in its Charter. This fear does not seem to be justified given the established ineffectiveness of these various amendments in influencing the Bank's ultimate decisions on loan applications. There is, of course, the possibility that the legislation may have a sort of "hidden effectiveness" which is not evident from reports of the negative votes cast and the loans approved. The Chile case study and the case study on restrictions indicate how at different times the US, by making known its opposition was apparently able to prevent loans to a country from even being presented to the EDs for their approval. But when acting (and voting) without support from other Bank members the US cannot often accomplish this feat. It should be remembered that the US alone does not have the voting power necessary to defeat a proposed loan once it has been presented to the Bank's EDs.[60] The effectiveness of US opposition will usually depend upon the ability of that country to rally other member states to join it in opposing loans to its disfavored targets. The fact that so many loans are approved despite the opposition of the US

60 The US does have sufficient voting power to single-handedly prevent many of the loans it opposes in the IDB (those made by its soft-loan Fund for Special Operations), and in that institution it has been possible for the US to halt the processing of new loans to certain borrowers. See the quotation in the immediately preceding footnote.

demonstrates that the US legislative policies behind that opposition have little support among other Bank members. More specifically, it demonstrates that other Bank member states do not share the view that it is legal for a member state to cast its vote within the World Bank according to political criteria.

8

SUMMARY AND CONCLUSIONS

A. THE POLITICIZATION PHENOMENON IN THE WORLD BANK

1. The Search for Legal Standards Limiting Politicization

The concept of politicization is related to many legal doctrines, but the key as it has emerged in this study is the need to preserve respect for the constitutional order which structures international economic cooperation within the World Bank. If the Bank is to retain the reputation and status which have permitted it to be an effective instrument of international cooperation, it is important to ensure that when a decision is taken on the use of the Bank's resources it will be taken in accordance with the terms of the Bank's Charter. In recognition of this an attempt has been made here to define a legal concept of politicization which is applicable to the Bank.

Although there is a need for legal standards limiting the politicization of the Bank, there are serious obstacles to their development and effective application. One problem is that within the Bank there has been a lack of consensus on related issues from the very start. When the Charter of the Bank was negotiated at Bretton Woods the two key countries involved strongly disagreed about the role of the Executive Directors who would run the Bank. The UK argued that they should be like international civil servants owing their allegiance only to the Bank, while the US insisted that they should be subject to government control. The Bank's Charter as subsequently adopted did not clearly resolve this issue, and the initial lack of consensus on this point continues to haunt the organization.

In any case, both as part of a Bank organ and as representatives of governments which are parties to the Bank's Charter, the EDs are under a legal obligation to respect Article IV section 10 of that Charter which mandates that they are to make their decisions according to economic criteria applied impartially in order to achieve the Bank's economic purposes.

Curiously enough, our attempts to define legal standards on the politicization of the Bank are complicated by the ineffectiveness of many of the politicizing actions which have been taken. It is a simple matter for the US to politicize the vote of its own appointed representative, but without the support of Executive Directors elected or appointed by other contributors to the Bank, the US Executive Director alone cannot block or defeat loan proposals which are otherwise acceptable to that institution. The US government has been notoriously unsuccessful in enlisting the support of other Bank members for its politically inspired "no" vote positions, and because of this there has been little if any actual injury to the rights of the states targeted by those votes. As long as politicization does not substantially affect the legal rights of the target states, it remains primarily a political phenomenon.

But negative votes do not tell the whole story. Ordinarily, the Bank's staff does not present a loan proposal to the Executive Directors until there is a consensus for approval; and most Bank loans are approved by consensus rather than by a formal vote. Thus the most effective politicizing actions are those which succeed in blocking loans before they are presented to the Bank's Executive Directors.[1] Where the politicizing influence is applied subtly and behind the scenes, it is more difficult to monitor and to regulate.

Another problem is that politicizing actions are sometimes identifiable as such only when the motivations of the actor are known. If it could be established beyond a reasonable doubt that a World Bank member state had deliberately acted to coerce and threaten the independence or freedom of action of another member state, or had consciously abused its voting power

1 Three such cases which have been identified are discussed below as well as in Chapter VI, *supra*. They are the blocking of loans to Poland and Czechoslovakia in the 1950s, the suspension of lending to Chile in the early 1970s and the promise exacted from Bank President McNamara that no loans would be made to Vietnam during fiscal year 1980.

under the Bank's Charter, it would be easy to conclude that it had acted illegally. In practice, the evidence concerning the true motives of a state is usually only circumstantial and inconclusive. In law, the bad motives of a state cannot lightly be presumed, and this constitutes a further problem with the implementation of an effective legal standard.

2. A "Minimal" Standard Formulated

What then are the legal standards applicable to the issue of politicization, and to what extent have they been violated by the practices of the US which have been reviewed here? So far, the Bank's members have found it difficult to reach a consensus on acceptable and yet effective legal standards in this area. *Nonetheless, the past practice of the Bank and its member states has reflected a clear but limited consensus to the effect that members are not to use their voting rights in that organization as a political tool for the pursuit of objectives unrelated to the Bank's purposes*. Over the last two decades the United States has publicly challenged that consensus, primarily pursuant to legislative directive, but this cannot excuse the violation of the political activity prohibition in the Bank's Charter.

Many states may feel a desire to mobilize the power and influence of the Bank in support of causes they consider to be just, but the US is in a unique position among Bank member states. It has a greater say in Bank decision-making than any other state due both to its weighted share of the voting power (over 18% of the total) and to the similarly high proportion which it contributes to the resources of the Bank and IDA. Decision-makers in the US Congress are aware of this power, as are the leaders of political pressure groups who attempt to influence the US Congress. Both have been involved in a rather blunt attempt to assert full Congressional control over the Bank, and to embroil that institution in efforts to enforce American political judgments abroad.

In many cases the American political judgments concerned may be fully justified, but this is not the issue here. The issue is whether the World Bank should be subject to the control of the US Congress as if it were an agency of the US government. If the World Bank and similar institutions of international economic cooperation are to remain meaningful then the answer to this question must be in the negative. As the major contributor to the Bank the US will inevitably have more influence within that institution than its other members who contribute less, and the Bank's weighted voting system reflects this; but *as a party to the Bank's Charter the US has accepted the obligation not to use this voting power for political purposes unrelated to the agreed goals of the Bank.*

This study formulates a preliminary "minimal" standard which embodies the limited consensus among Bank members on this matter, but in the long run the Bank will need better and more definite standards if it is to continue to function effectively. Even the preliminary standards set out here will occasionally be breached, however, and the identification of those occurrences can contribute to the development of better standards in this area. One hopes that in the future scholars from different fields will collaborate in order to achieve a greater understanding of the issues raised, and in particular of the way in which the politicization phenomenon can involve links between legal, political and economic considerations.

3. The Evolving Mandate of the World Bank, and the Need to Distinguish Politicization from Constructive Efforts to Reform the Bank

While the language of the World Bank's Charter provides the clearest indication of that organization's essential mandate, the possibility of and even the need for evolutionary development in that mandate must also be considered. Some of the important problems associated with economic development today were not anticipated by the negotiators at Bretton Woods, and yet the World Bank is now under pressure to take them into account.

The Bank should be able to adjust to changed circumstances such as these, but this can only be brought about through the initiative of the member states. Accordingly, it is entirely appropriate for members to propose constructive reform of the World Bank's lending policies so long as the reforms are consistent with the basic purposes and principles of that institution.

In this context we should note that not all aspects of US legislative policies towards the Bank have been politicizing and unilateralist. Recent changes in the environmental policy of the Bank provide a positive example of how needed changes in multilateral policy can be effectively promoted by the US. Until recently, the Bank did not attach a very high priority to the environmental impact of the development projects which it funded, and had only a few full time staff members assigned to deal with environmental issues. But soon after the passage of US legislation in 1985 calling for environmental reform of the Bank and other MDBs[2] the situation began to change for the better. Since then the Bank has created a new environmental department and has also established environmental units within each of its four (geographic) divisions. The Bank now has about 60 people who work full time on the environment, preparing environmental impact reports on Bank projects and integrating environmental issues into its discussions with borrowers on their economic programs and reforms.[3]

These changes cannot be attributed solely to US initiatives for environmental reform of the Bank, but those initiatives clearly helped to bring them about. What this demonstrates is that US efforts to influence Bank lending policy have at times had a salutary effect. Why is it that US efforts for the environmental reform of the Bank have been so much more successful than the efforts to politicize the Bank which were discussed in Chapter VI? For one thing, improving the environmental performance of the World Bank is in the interest of all of its members, and because of this a number of other members supported that US initiative. Furthermore, the Bank's ability to function and to fulfill its mandate has been enhanced by these reforms. It is true, of course, that the Bank's Charter never specifically mentions protecting the environment as one of that institution's purposes; nonetheless, this objective is very much consistent with the objectives set out in that Charter.[4]

There is a difference between injecting totally extraneous political matters into Bank lending decisions and considering the human rights or environmental implications of the lending pro-

2 For a complete reference see Annex B, item #28 where this legislative provision is also summarized in greater detail.

3 Overseas Development Council, *Policy Focus*, 1988, No. 3, at p. 8.

4 According to Article I of the Bank's Charter its purposes include "raising the standard of living and conditions of labor" on the territory of member states, (paragraph iii); and arranging "that the more useful and urgent projects, large and small alike, will be dealt with first" (paragraph iv). Projects damaging to the environment will adversely affect the "conditions of labor", and such projects should also be seen as less "useful" than alternative projects which are non-damaging.

jects themselves. To continue to ignore the possible negative impact of Bank funded projects upon human rights or the environment would not serve the interests of borrowing countries, nor would it serve the cause of international cooperation in general. To permit these considerations to affect decision-making would mean deviating from strict application of the principle that only economic considerations should be relevant to Bank decisions,[5] but would not significantly alter the parameters of cooperation within the Bank.

US legislation tending to politicize the Bank has often been motivated by good intentions such as the desire to fight the international trade in narcotics, to deny refuge to aircraft hijackers or to promote respect for internationally recognized human rights. Whatever its motivations the US Congress has been rather careless in its attempts to achieve these objectives through the Bank; apparently failing to appreciate the incongruity involved in injecting external conflictual elements into the Bank's cooperative context. Ultimately, this approach may represent not only an incongruity, but also a grave threat to the Bank's ability to function. To incur this risk seems foolish, particularly when one notes that the policy has yielded little effective result or positive benefit.

The US has more influence within the World Bank than any other member state but that influence goes a lot further when it is used for a purpose which other members consider to be a legitimate concern of the Bank. When the US acts constructively

5 From Article IV(10) of the Bank's Charter. It is interesting to note that the parameters of cooperation are defined differently for the newly created European Bank for Reconstruction and Development (EBRD). Article 1 of the EBRD Charter states that its purpose is "to foster the transition towards open market oriented economies and to promote private and entrepreneurial initiative in the Central and Eastern European countries committed to applying the principles of multiparty democracy, pluralism and market economics." The Preamble of the EBRD Charter specifically mentions that the EBRD is committed to "respect for human rights", and Article 2 paragraph 1(vii) states that one of its functions is "to promote in the full range of its activities environmentally sound and sustainable development". While at one time or another efforts to promote democracy, human rights, and environmental protection have all been controversial within the context of the World Bank; the EBRD begins its operations on the basis of a consensus that these are indeed legitimate objectives for the organization to pursue, and therefore presumably legitimate considerations in EBRD decision-making on loan proposals. Agreement Establishing the European Bank for Reconstruction and Development, *International Legal Materials*, Vol. 29, No. 5, (1990), at pages 1083–1107.

and in the spirit of cooperation, it strengthens its leadership position within the Bank as it has done by taking the lead in promoting the environmental reform of the Bank. If such a constructive approach is followed more consistently in the future the US may eventually have more success in getting the Bank to take account of other legitimate concerns such as the human rights implications of particular Bank lending projects.[6]

4. How Politicized Is the Bank?

a) The Lack of Access to Records of Bank Deliberations and the Possibility of Hidden Politicization

Like its sister institution the IMF, the Bank is privy to a great deal of sensitive economic information about its members, information which is not generally available to the public. Future access to accurate information of this kind may depend upon an ability to keep it confidential. Of course the Bank's preference for discretion goes beyond the confidentiality of economic reports such as these. It has long been the practice of the Bank not to allow outside access to minutes or other records concerning the deliberations of the Board of Executive Directors, and this complicates any effort to identify the extent of politicized decision-making on loan projects.

Although every loan the Bank makes must be presented to the Executive Directors and formally approved by them, the decision on each proposal is actually made by consensus before it is formally presented. Any loan presented to the Executive Directors for a vote will normally be approved, and details of

6 The Bank could justify considering the human rights implications of proposed projects by referring to those of its purposes enumerated in footnote 4, above. Apparently some consensus on the relevance of human rights considerations to World Bank lending decisions has been reached among the Group of Seven countries (US, Japan, Germany, Britain, France, Italy and Canada) who control a decisive bloc of voting power within the Bank. Soon after the government of China brutally cracked down on pro-democracy demonstrators in 1989 the G-7 countries decided that they would only support World Bank loans to China if those loans supported basic human needs. (This policy seems to reflect the same standard set out in the Harkin Amendment, discussed in Chapter VII, *supra*.) Approvals of World Bank loans to China were severely curtailed until the G-7 countries began to soften this stance in late 1990. Despite this broadening of support for a World Bank enforced policy on human rights it is unlikely that human rights considerations would be considered a legitimate criterion of decision by most members of the World Bank at this time.

these loans are published by the Bank. The Bank tells us nothing, however, about the loans which are discussed by the Executive Directors but not formally presented or approved.[7] Without more information about these behind the scenes discussions, it will be impossible to do a systematic study of politicization in the Bank's decision-making. But by focussing on actual legislation passed by the US Congress and signed into law it has been possible to get an idea of how the US government has attempted to influence that institution on a range of political and economic issues

In the course of this study we have also reviewed a number of anecdotal reports about deliberations among the Executive Directors. On the basis of these reports it is possible to identify only three separate cases in which it seems, *prima facie*, that a Bank member was deprived of the benefits of membership as a result of being a target of negative politicization.[8] In the 1950s Poland and Czechoslovakia were forced to withdraw from membership in the Bank after discovering that they, as Eastern Bloc states, had no access to the Bank's resources. This was part of the reality of the Cold War. In the early 1970s Allende's Socialist Chile got no new commitments of funds from the Bank, and

7 The Chile Case Study in Chapter VI, *supra*, paradoxically demonstrates the difficulty in identifying cases of successful negative politicization within the Bank. Between 1970 and 1973 Chile was the target of a concerted US Government effort to reduce or stop all international aid flows, both bilateral and multilateral. Normally, there would not be any publicly available record of the fact that the Bank was considering loans to Chile even as it withheld them during this period. It is only because of the subsequent coup d'état in Chile and the many accusations of economic warfare and intervention, that facts came out which provide a clearer than usual picture of Bank decision-making procedures. The Bank's own "White Paper", "Chile and the World Bank", (Appendix to SANFORD, J.E., "The Multilateral Development Banks and the Suspension of Lending to Allende's Chile", Foreign Affairs Division, Congressional Research Service, The Library of Congress, August 6, 1974, revised December 13, 1974), is particularly useful in this regard.

8 After pressure from the UN the World Bank has made no further loans to *apartheid* South Africa after 1966. On its face, this too might appear to be a case where politicization has deprived a World Bank member of the benefits of membership. Upon reflection, the economic arguments against support for an *apartheid* régime become apparent. As the Bank itself acknowledged back in 1947, "conditions of political instability or uncertainty in the borrowing country . . . must be taken into consideration" insofar as these affect the financial and economic prospects of the borrower. IBRD, *Second Annual Report*, Washington, 1947, at p. 17. On a more basic level it does not seem that the policy of *apartheid* constitutes a rational development policy worthy of the World Bank's financial support.

politicization of the issue (explicitly authorized by Nixon and Kissinger) probably contributed to this result. The last case study dealing with the negative politicization of the Bank is one of the most disturbing. What it involved was a successful attempt by the US Congress to subjugate and humiliate the Bank – all over the emotionally charged but economically trivial issue of potential loans to Vietnam.

In none of these three cases is it certain that the politicization which occurred actually prevented a country from receiving a loan, but legally significant politicization has nevertheless occurred. Since the US, as a member of the Bank and a party to its Charter, has agreed that the Bank is not to conduct political activities, it has accepted an obligation not to use its power in the Bank for political purposes unrelated to the agreed goals of that organization. With this standard in mind it appears that the US, due to its politicizing actions, has been responsible for material violations of the IBRD Charter on at least these three occasions.

While these cases are troubling, they are relatively few in number considering that the Bank has been operating for 40 years. Of course as long as the secrecy surrounding the deliberations of the Bank's Executive Directors isolates us from the real decision-making process, we cannot be sure that they are the only such cases. It is quite possible that there have been other completely unpublicized cases of successful negative politicization of the Bank.

b) The Ineffectiveness of US Negative Votes in the Bank, and the Purpose of such Votes

From October 1, 1979 to September 30, 1988 the US voted no 36 times and abstained 77 times on World Bank or IDA loans which were proposed to the Board of Executive Directors. Every one of these 113 loan proposals was nonetheless approved by the Bank's Board.[9] This simple statistic indicates that these "non-supporting" votes have had no direct effect on the final disposition of Bank loan decisions. In light of the possibility of

9 Source, US National Advisory Council on International Monetary and Financial Policies, *International Finance*, Annual Reports to the President and Congress for Fiscal Years 1980–1987.

"hidden" politicization which is discussed above, we cannot conclude on this basis that no effective and materially damaging politicization has occurred during this time. But the fact that formal US opposition votes have been 100% ineffective within the Bank[10] does suggest something about the nature of those votes.

While these 102 votes did not serve to prevent the proposed loans from being approved, they did communicate a message of concern to the MDBs and recipient governments.[11] At the same time, these votes served to placate certain domestic pressure groups in the US. Groups of this kind may lobby against MDB loans for any number of reasons ranging from sincere and altruistic concern about the environment or human rights violations, to an equally sincere (and self interested) opposition to any support for foreign producers with whom they are in competition. Though loans which these pressure groups oppose are generally approved in spite of the automatic US opposition which has been legislated, the US government can partially accommodate these groups by making a public statement to the effect that the US finds it impossible to support the disfavored loan.

At meetings of the UNGA and of other international political organs the representatives of member governments frequently read statements of this kind into the official record, but it is only relatively recently that such political posturing has been injected into the inner councils of the World Bank. The Bank itself does not release the minutes of its Board meetings nor does it even publicly report on negative votes or abstentions on its loan proposals. Perhaps this is because to do so might

10 Much the same could be said of all US negative votes cast (for whatever reason) in any of the MDBs. Since 1979 only a single one of the negative votes cast by the US in all the MDBs has resulted in the ultimate disapproval of the loan concerned. That vote was cast for what the US has said were "economic reasons on August 18, 1983. This was enough to block a IDB loan package for a rice irrigation project in Guyana. Part of the funds for the proposed project were to have come from the IDB's soft-loan program, the Fund for Special Operations (FSO). All projects funded by the FSO must be approved by Executive Directors holding 75% of the IDB's voting power. This leaves the US with an effective veto power over each proposal. Acting alone, the US does not have this much influence over any other MDB programs. Source, *loc. cit.*

11 SCHOULTZ, *op. cit.*, p. 565, note 70, makes this same point.

encourage the use of the Bank's Board meetings as a forum for political sermonizing.[12]

The practice of using the Bank as a forum for political statements is regrettable because this in itself represents a low level politicization of the Bank. Although it has had little detrimental impact upon the rights of Bank members thus far, and it cannot be said to constitute a material breach of the Bank's Charter, even this politicization could eventually build to the point where it would interfere with the Bank's ability to function. The US played a key role in founding the World Bank, and in setting its functional standards of decision-making, and now through negative votes and behind the scenes lobbying against certain countries it has demonstrated that it is willing to sacrifice those standards in pursuit of extraneous political goals. This is an ominous trend. But, looking at the bright side of the situation, one should note that when the opposition of the richest and most powerful member of the Bank does not generally prevent the Bank from making a loan, this says something positive about the soundness and functional autonomy of that institution.

c) Some Thoughts on How The Bank Manages to Function, Even Without Consensus on a Fundamental Legal Issue

The primary danger associated with politicization is that the injection of political issues into the technical work of an international organization might diminish or destroy its ability to function and to fulfill its agreed mandate. One practical test for determining whether serious and significant politicization has occurred is to ascertain the extent to which political issues have already impaired the functioning (or the membership) of the institution concerned. If we apply this test to the World Bank we must conclude that the level of politicization of that organization has not yet reached serious proportions.

Over the years, the Bank has functioned well, making more financial resources directly available to developing countries than has any other international organization. There is a

12 It is primarily through US National Advisory Council reports that details of US abstentions and negative votes are known to those outside of the Bank. The US government must publicize its own acts of politicization in order to reap the domestic political benefits.

tremendous coercive potential associated with control over resources such as these, but with the exception of a few cases which have been identified, it does not appear that any Bank member has been successful in causing the power of the Bank to be used abusively.

Nor can it be said that the Bank has remained totally aloof and indifferent to human rights abuses by its member governments. Although the Bank has not expressly acknowledged that South Africa's political system is relevant to its status as a potential borrower, the Bank has long since quietly ceased lending to the *apartheid* régime in that country.[13]

Through all of this the Bank has remained true to the essentially conservative economic principles upon which it is based. In its operations it has worked to promote those principles rather than to advance any particular political agenda. It has not hesitated to use its development loans as an incentive for promoting foreign investment and the growth of international trade, but these are both among the agreed purposes of the Bank as set out in its Charter.[14]

In Chapter II of this study we noted that the politicization of international organizations has sometimes been linked to an erosion of liberal principles in favor of a more statist approach to economic organization such as that reflected in the call for a New International Economic Order (NIEO). This has never been a problem within the Bank. In fact, one is hard pressed to find examples of the statist NIEO approach in the policies and operations of the Bank. Among the UN specialized agencies the Bank and the IMF remain as the last bastions of liberal economics. This is primarily because of the weighted voting system which applies within those institutions.

Many of the liberal economic principles upon which the Bank is based remain valid and relevant today, thus it would not be in the interest of any state to abandon them. Respect for such principles is to some extent necessary in order to keep the Bank solvent, and a bankrupt World Bank couldn't help anyone.[15]

13 See the case Study on Southern Africa, Chapter VI, *supra*.

14 IBRD Articles of Agreement, Article I(ii) and (iii).

15 Even though the Bank has had fewer problems collecting on its loans than many private commercial bank lenders to developing countries, the Bank has must still request additional funds from its richer members from time to time. This happens when the IBRD's members decide upon a general

Nonetheless, the Bank will need to make some adjustments and accommodations to changed circumstances in order to remain relevant to the problems and needs of its members.

Since the 1945 Bretton Woods Conference when the delegations of the US and of the UK first disagreed about whether Executive Directors should be subject to political control, there has never been a full consensus concerning this aspect of the Bank's management and operation. The US still keeps its appointed Executive Director under closer governmental control than other Bank members consider to be appropriate, and he is often required to oppose Bank loans for reasons which have more to do with domestic interest group politics in the US than with the Bank's purposes and mandate.

In spite of all this confusion, and notwithstanding the other problems cited in the case studies, the Bank continues to operate effectively. This is what we might refer to as the "functional bottom line." How is it that the Bank has managed to remain effective in the face of the politicizing actions and attitudes of its most influential member? It has been possible only because it is in the interest of all the Bank's members, including the United States, to maintain the institution's continued ability to function.

The Bank as an institution has not tended to go public with its legal case against American politicization. This is understandable, as it might have more to lose than to gain by bringing these issues to a head. From a practical point of view it is wiser for the Bank to concentrate on dealing with economic and political realities than to get involved in an extended debate on international legal issues. For the Bank, reality means dealing with political pressure from the US Congress, and all in all it has not done too bad a job of it.

---

capital increase (such as the one approved on April 27, 1988 and pending at the time of this writing), and on the occasion of the periodic voluntary "replenishments" of the IDA's soft loan fund. Renewed funding would not be possible if the Bank were to stray from the economic principles favored by these donors. The recent UN budget crisis suggests that one could make a similar point with regard to the general UN budget, but liberal economic principles are much more central to the technical mandate of the Bank than they are to the broader purposes of the UN.

B. OBSERVATIONS CONCERNING INTERNATIONAL ORGANIZATION AND THE INTERNATIONAL LEGAL SYSTEM

1. Beyond Legalistic Solutions

There are certain limitations upon the way a state may legitimately use its voting power in the World Bank, but from the very beginning nationalistic attitudes in the US have made it difficult to identify a clear consensus among Bank members on this question. These attitudes have most often been expressed through the US Congress. At the same time, the US Executive branch has tended to join in an underlying political–technical consensus among Bank members to the effect that the Bank should be able to operate without undue political interference. US Presidents have played a role in softening conflicts between the US Congress and the Bank, often using their discretion to avoid the broad application of Congressional directives sent to the US Executive Director in the Bank. This helps to explain why the Bank continues to work even though the troubling legal issues discussed here have not been resolved. But as the last of the case studies shows,[16] the President cannot always protect the Bank from bullying by Congress.

One conclusion of this study is that the use of voting power within the Bank for political purposes does violate the Bank's Charter. But as useful and important as it may be to identify the legal limits involved, there can be no purely legal solution to the dispute on this issue.

Even where the internal affairs of the US government are concerned the Congress rather frequently tests the constitutional limits of its power vis à vis the executive branch of the US government, occasionally passing legislation which proves to be unconstitutional. The US judiciary is always available to resolve the resulting disputes and clean up the mess.[17] Realistically, it cannot be expected that the US Congress will be any more restrained in challenging constitutional limits when international constitutional structures are involved, nor is it likely

16 See the Special Case Study on Restrictions, Chapter VI, *supra*.

17 *Immigration and Naturalization Service v. Chada*, 462 U.S. 919 (1983), which was briefly discussed in Chapter VII, *supra*, is one example of a case in which the US Supreme Court considered it necessary to invalidate certain aspects of legislation passed by Congress.

that it will fundamentally alter its approach to dealing with the World Bank merely because of questions about the "constitutionality" of that approach.

There is little prospect of the ICJ being asked to resolve any of these questions. The Bank's Charter specifically provides for any question of interpretation to be submitted to the Executive Directors for their decision.[18] Even if the Court were to rule on the issue, the two ICJ Admissions cases discussed in Chapter V illustrate that there may be no effective international legal remedy even where an illegal use of multilateral voting power has been conclusively established.[19]

In the final analysis, no legal rule or principle and no judicial mechanism can fully remedy a lack of consensus among the members of the World Bank or of any other international organization. Political progress is needed before the legal aspects of problems in this area can be clarified much further. In particular, what must be achieved is greater confidence on the part of all states in the ability of international organizations to deal fairly and effectively with the resources which are placed at their disposal. This is closely linked to the question of whether a more complete international consensus can be reached in each such organization concerning the goals it is to pursue and the means which it may legitimately use in the process.

2. International Organizations and The National Interest of the United States

Within the World Bank the same legal structure which operates to promote the common interests of the members in development should at the same time limit the way in which those members act (within that limited legal framework) to promote their individual interests.[20] Among other things, this means that

18 Article IX of the IBRD Articles of Agreement. See the discussion of this issue in Chapter IX.

19 See, "Conditions of Admission of a State to Membership in the United Nations", Advisory Opinion, *ICJ Reports* (1947/1948), at p. 57, and, "Competence of the General Assembly for the Admission of a State to Membership in the United Nations", Advisory Opinion, *ICJ Reports* (1950), at p. 4.

20 Georges Abi-Saab mentions the link between the role of law as a "facility" which can "enable the subjects to achieve collectively what they cannot undertake individually", and the role of law as a "constraint". ABI-SAAB, G., *The United Nations Operation in the Congo 1960–1964*, Oxford, Oxford University Press, 1978, at pp. 198–199.

the members should accept that there are legal limits upon the discretion they may exercise when using their voting power and acting as part of the organization. One cannot expect a state to abandon national interest analysis, thus it is incumbent upon the international legal scholar to demonstrate that international law serves the national interest. Of course it cannot serve the interests of all states in every situation, but generally it must continue to serve the interests of states or it will risk becoming irrelevant.

It is often suggested that the Bank promotes US foreign policy objectives by promoting economic development, international trade, international investment, and general international stability along the lines of a liberal international economic order; while at the same time drawing in outside money from other donor countries. This outside money is sometimes said to "leverage" the US contribution thus allowing it to produce "more bang for the buck" in the pursuit of US interests. But at the same time it is only by releasing control of what it contributes that the US can expect these effects to operate.[21] There is thus an inherent contradiction in the US attitude towards the Bank. It can easily be resolved if the US government will accept that the Bank can and should serve US interests only within the agreed parameters of cooperation. Expecting it to go much further, and to be readily adaptable to the service of all US interests is unrealistic and inconsistent with the whole idea of multilateral economic cooperation.

The legislation and policies reviewed in this study represent a potential threat to the autonomy of the World Bank, a real threat to the Bank's credibility (which depends to no small extent upon its perceived autonomy), and of course ultimately, a threat to the ability of the Bank to function and to fulfill its mandate.

The US rightfully prides itself upon its respect for "constitutionalism" and for the rule of law in its domestic affairs. But aren't the same principles also worthy of respect in the context of international cooperation? Some American policy-makers

21 The same reasoning applies to another of the major advantages of multilateral aid from the US point of view, i.e. the recognition that a multilateral organization can exert more influence on the policies of borrowers than can a US agency. See the discussion of the advantages of multilateral aid, in Chapter III, *supra*.

seem to doubt their applicability in this setting.[22] The actions which follow from such a viewpoint and attitude have fueled the passions of critical observers outside the US who attempt to depict it as an arrogant and aggressive state. They may claim with some justification that the US is not only opposed to progressive changes in the international system, but is even unwilling to respect the present rules of a system which was largely American inspired. This criticism does and should sting, since the image it evokes is contrary to the US self-image as a law-abiding state and a crusader for justice worldwide. The problem is that worldwide justice can best be furthered in accordance with a worldwide standard, not a "Made in USA" standard seen as reflecting the narrowly defined and changing interests of the US. The success which the US has had in promoting the environmental reform of the Bank demonstrates what can be accomplished when the US chooses to use its power within the Bank in a constructive way.

For some time now the US has complained of politicization in some of the organizations dominated by a Third World majority.[23] Clearly, US actions in the Bank undermine any US attempt to promote the rule of law in other intergovernmental bodies such as UNESCO or the UN General Assembly. It is the official policy of the US under the Kassebaum Amendment to promote the adoption of a weighted voting system, such as that used in the World Bank, by all international agencies.[24] This is intended to be part of a constructive effort to reform these agencies and minimize the ability of the Third World majority to politicize them. It is ironic that in direct opposition to this

22 When told that proposed restrictions on the contribution to the Bank would be illegal one US Senator reportedly replied "Let's forget about these legal niceties. Even if we're wrong, lets do it anyway." See, "Freeze on Vietnam Loans Ends Effort to Restrict U.S. Funds for World Bank", *Congressional Quarterly*, November 3, 1979, at p. 2504. This particular incident is described in context as part of the Special Case Study on Restrictions in Chapter VI, *supra*.

23 See GROSS, L., "On the Degradation of the Constitutional Environment of the United Nations", *AJIL*, Vol. 77 (1983) 3, at pp. 583.

24 The US Congress has passed the Kassebaum Amendment which requires the US to promote "the adoption by the United Nations and its specialized agencies of procedures which grant voting rights to each member state on matters of budgetary consequence . . . proportionate to the contribution of each such member state to the budget. "Foreign Relations Authorization Act, Fiscal Years 1986 and 1987", P.L. 99-93, Title I, Sec. 143, August 16, 1985, 99 Stat. 424, 22 USC 287e note.

goal certain short-sighted US policies within the Bank seem to demonstrate that weighted voting does not remedy politicization, but instead merely facilitates politicization by the US.[25]

What is needed is for American policy-makers to recognize a broader and less simplistically unilateral conception of the national interest.[26] Once they have done so, and once this is reflected in US policy towards international organizations, the interests of the United States will be better served.[27] Like a number of other "unilateralist" activities of the US, legislative policy towards that Bank has tended to be moralistic, unrealistic, ineffective and self-defeating. That policy fails to reflect a proper assessment of the needs and aspirations of other countries or the limits of US power.[28] Since these unilateral policies within the Bank have accomplished little, they cannot truly be in the interest of the US. It cannot serve US interests to protest in a manner which is both illegal and ineffective.

The present problems can in part be attributed to a pervasive attitude of fatalism with regard to international organizations. During the past two decades the US came to expect the worst from these organizations with changing majorities, and thus the idea that they should have a large degree of functional autonomy was no longer appealing to most Americans. At the same time many critics of US policies among the developing states of the Third World came to expect the worst from the US, and as a result, international majorities sometimes refused to acknowledge even the most legitimate interests of the US.

25 Williams, D., *The Specialized Agencies and the United Nations: The System in Crisis*, New York, St. Martins Press, (1987), at p. 68–69.

26 In accord see, Bloomfield, L., *In Search of American Foreign Policy*, Oxford Univ. Press, 1974, p. 165.

27 Stephen Schwebel, presently the American Judge on the International Court of Justice made the following comments about US policies within the ILO some years back, (SCHWEBEL, S. M., "The United States Assaults the I.L.O.", *American Journal of International Law*, Vol. 65, (1971), at p. 142):
"What is clear in this case of assault by the United States Congress on the I.L.O. is that a sense of proportion, of intelligent and practical purpose, of legality, has been lamentably lacking. It is to be hoped that this gross display of international insensitivity and illegality will have been reversed by the time these comments appear in print; the longer it is prolonged, the greater will be the damage to the I.L.O., to international law and organization, and to the interests of the United States."

28 See Theberge, L.J., "Unilateralism: The direct challenge to International Law", *California Western International Law Journal*, Vol. 9, (1979), pp. 553–562, where he discusses five (5) characteristics of unilateral US activities with consequences for the international system.

For too long the fatalistic attitudes of the two sides seemed to justify one another.

The only possible remedy for this regrettable state of affairs is more enlightened leadership on issues of international cooperation both within the US and in the international community at large. In recent years American political leaders have found it easier to accept and indulge the popular misconceptions about international law and organization than to educate the American public about the subject. A new attitude could be detected in 1990 when the President of the United States turned to the United Nations Security Council to authorize enforcement action to liberate Kuwait from Iraqi occupation. The Gulf Crisis may highlight the potential value of the United Nations in dealing with matters of security, but the value of the World Bank and other international economic organizations is still not fully appreciated.

Since the 1944 Bretton Woods Conference the US has resisted demands for radical changes in the international economic system by claiming that existing institutions, such as the World Bank, are the best means for dealing with the problems of the world's poor majority. In the face of the international debt crisis demands for change in international financial institutions are louder than ever. If the US wants to ensure the success of "conservative reforms" rather than the more radical programs favored by others, it must not undermine the legitimacy of the very institutions it is trying to defend and promote as part of its conservative program. Politicizing the World Bank could cripple it, and may already have made it less credible and appealing as an advisor to developing states. Neither the United States nor the international community can be served by such a development.

9

ANNEXES

ANNEX A

EXTRACTS FROM THE ARTICLES OF AGREEMENT OF THE INTERNATIONAL BANK FOR RECONSTRUCTION AND DEVELOPMENT

Article I
PURPOSES

The purposes of the Bank are:

(i) To assist in the reconstruction and development of territories of members by facilitating the investment of capital for productive purposes, including the restoration of economies destroyed or disrupted by war, the reconversion of productive facilities to peacetime needs and the encouragement of the development of productive facilities and resources in less developed countries.

(ii) To promote private foreign investment by means of guarantees or participations in loans and other investments made by private investors; and when private capital is not available on reasonable terms, to supplement private investment by providing, on suitable conditions, finance for productive purposes out of its own capital, funds raised by it and its other resources.

(iii) To promote the long-range balanced growth of international trade and the maintenance of equilibrium in balances of payments by encouraging international investment for the development of the productive resources of members, thereby assisting in raising productivity, the standard of living and conditions of labor in their territories.

(iv) To arrange the loans made or guaranteed by it in relation to international loans through other channels so that the more useful and urgent projects, large and small alike, will be dealt with first.

(v) To conduct its operations with due regard to the effect of international investment on business conditions in the territories of members and, in the immediate post-war years, to assist in bringing about a smooth transition from a wartime to a peacetime economy.

The Bank shall be guided in all its decisions by the purposes set forth above.

Article VI
OPERATIONS

Section 10. *Political Activity Prohibited*

The Bank and its officers shall not interfere in the political affairs of any member; nor shall they be influenced in their decisions by the political character of the member or members concerned. Only economic considerations shall be relevant to their decisions, and these considerations shall be weighed impartially in order to achieve the purposes stated in Article I.

Article V
ORGANIZATION AND MANAGEMENT

Section 3. *Voting*

(a) Each member shall have two hundred fifty votes plus one additional vote for each share of stock held.

(b) Except as otherwise specifically provided, all matters before the Bank shall be decided by a majority of the votes cast.

Section 4. *Executive Directors*

(a) The Executive Directors shall be responsible for the conduct of the general operations of the Bank, and for this purpose, shall exercise all the powers delegated to them by the Board of Governors.

(b) There shall be twelve Executive Directors, who need not be governors, and of whom:

(i) five shall be appointed, one by each of the five members having the largest number of shares;

(ii) seven shall be elected according to Schedule B by all the Governors other than those appointed by the five members referred to in (i) above.

(g) Each appointed director shall be entitled to cast the number of votes allotted under Section 3 of this Article to the member appointing him. Each elected director shall be entitled to cast the number of votes which counted toward his election. All the votes which a director is entitled to cast shall be cast as a unit.

Section 8. *Relationship to other International Organizations*

(a) The Bank, within the terms of this Agreement, shall cooperate with any general international organization and with public international organizations having specialized responsibilities in related fields. Any arrangements for such cooperation which would involve a modification of any provision of the Agreement may be effected only after amendment of this Agreement under Article VIII.

(b) In making decisions on applications for loans or guarantees relating to matters directly within the competence of any international organization of the types specified in the preceding paragraph and participated in primarily by members of the Bank, the Bank shall give consideration to the views and recommendations of such organization.

Article VII
STATUS, IMMUNITIES AND PRIVILEGES

Section 6. *Freedom of Assets from Restrictions*

To the extent necessary to carry out the operations provided for in this Agreement and subject to the provisions of this Agreement, all property and assets of the Bank shall be free from restrictions, regulations, controls and moratoria of any nature.

Article IX
INTERPRETATION

(a) Any question of interpretation of this Agreement arising between any member and the Bank or between any members of the Bank shall be submitted to the Executive Directors for their decision. If the question particularly affects any member not entitled to appoint an executive director, it shall be entitled to representation in accordance with Article V, Section 4 (h).

(b) In any case where the Executive Directors have given a decision under (a) above, any member may require that the question be referred to the Board of Governors, whose decision shall be final. Pending the result of the reference to the Board, the Bank may, so far as it deems necessary, act on the basis of the decision of the Executive Directors.

ANNEX B
TABLE OF SELECTED US LEGISLATION RELATIVE TO US POLICY WITHIN THE WORLD BANK AND SIMILAR INTERNATIONAL FINANCIAL INSTITUTIONS

Legislation not Applicable to the World Bank

Identifying Code: #1
Popular Name/Descriptor: Communist dictatorships
Effective Date: November 30, 1983
Applicable to US Participation in (Org.): *IMF only, not IBRD*
PL Reference: 98-181, Sec. 804, 97 Stat. 1270
Act and Section: Supplemental Appropriations Act of 1984
US Code Reference: 22 USC Sec. 286aa (a)
Summary: US ED shall oppose Fund credits to any "Communist dictatorship" unless three separate conditions are met. The proposed drawing must 1) provide basis for restoring a sustainable BOP position of the drawing state; 2) reduce constraints on labor and capital mobility or inefficient labor and capital supply rigidities and advance market-oriented forces in that country; and 3) be in the best economic interests of the majority of the people in that country.
Comment on its application and effectiveness: An economic justification is clearly presented as part of the legislation.

Identifying Code: #2
Popular Name/Descriptor: *Apartheid* regimes
Effective Date: November 30, 1983
Applicable to US Participation in (Org.): *IMF only, not IBRD*
PL Reference: 98-181, Sec. 804, 97 Stat. 1271
Act and Section: Supplemental Appropriations Act of 1984
US Code Reference: 22 USC Sec. 286aa (b)
Summary: Applies to any country practicing *apartheid* much the standards applied to communist dictatorships under 22 USC Sec. 286aa (a).
Comment on its application and effectiveness: An economic justification is clearly presented as part of the legislation.

Identifying Code: #3
Popular Name/Descriptor: Taiwan membership
Effective Date: November 30, 1983
Applicable to US Participation in (Org.): *ADB only, not IBRD*
PL Reference: PL 89-369, Sec. 27, as added PL 98-181, Sec. 1002, 97 Stat. 1285
Act and Section: ADB Act Sec. 25
US Code Reference: 22 USC Sec. 285x(c)
Summary: Expresses Congressional findings that the Republic of China (Taiwan) is a "model of economic success for other nations in Asia", that it should remain a full member of the Asian Development Bank and that the United States "will not countenance attempts to expel Taiwan" from the ADB.
Comment on its application and effectiveness: Perhaps at least in part because of this clearly expressed attitude the ADB now has both China's as members although neither the PRC nor Taiwan normally favors a "two China policy".

Legislation Applicable to the World Bank

Identifying Code: #4
Popular Name/Descriptor: Young Amendment
Effective Date: October 18, 1978 and June 3, 1980 (directive effective only a single time, but renewed once)
Applicable to US Participation in (Org.): IBRD, IFC, IDA, IDB, ADB, AfDF, AfDB

PL Reference: 95-481, Sec. 511, 92 Stat. 1602 & 96-259, Sec. 501(c), 94 Stat. 432
Act and Section: Int. Financial Institutions Act, Sec. 705
US Code Reference: 22 USC 262d, note
Summary: President is to instruct US Governors to these institutions to consult with other governors concerning the adoption of a Charter amendment in those organizations which would set human rights standards applicable to loan decisions.
Comment on its application and effectiveness: No mandatory action. Expressed Congressional frustration with argument that these matters are excluded from consideration by present Charters. Not binding in any way once the initial instruction has been given to the US Governors.

Identifying Code: #5
Popular Name/Descriptor: Int. consultations, basic human needs and human rights
Effective Date: October 3, 1977 (directive effective only a single time)
Applicable to US Participation in (Org.): IBRD, IDA, IFC, IDB, AFDF, ADB, AFDB
PL Reference: 95-118, Sec. 703, 91 Stat. 1070
Act and Section: International Financial Institutions Act Sec. 703
US Code Reference: 22 USC 262c, note
Summary: The US Secretaries of State and of the Treasury were to initiate consultations designed to develop a viable standard for meeting basic human needs and protecting human rights, and to insure that the results of international economic cooperation shall especially benefit those countries meeting such standards.
Comment on its application and effectiveness: Not binding in any meaningful way. A one time message sent from the Congress to the Executive about this one aspect of US foreign policy.

Identifying Code: #6
Popular Name/Descriptor: Harkin Amendment (modified form)
Effective Date: October 3, 1977

Applicable to US Participation in (Org.): IBRD, IDA, IFC, IDB, AFDF, ADB, AFDB
PL Reference: 95-118, Sec. 701, 91 Stat. 1069, as amended up through 98-181, Sec. 1004, 97 Stat. 1286
Act and Section: International Financial Institutions Act Sec. 701(a), (e) and (f)
US Code Reference: 22 USC Sec. 262d(a), (e) and (f)
Summary: US to channel funds towards countries other than those whose governments engage in a consistent pattern of gross violations of human rights, or provide refuge to individuals committing acts of international terrorism by hijacking aircraft. US EDs are authorized and instructed to oppose any loan or assistance to these (violating) countries unless the assistance is directed specifically to programs which serve the basic human needs of the citizens of that country.
Comment on its application and effectiveness: The determination of what constitutes a "consistent pattern of gross violations of human rights" leaves room for flexibility in the application of this standard. Subsection (e) does provide that in making this determination the US government is to consider the extent to which the appropriate international organizations have been permitted to investigate alleged violations of human rights in the country concerned.

Identifying Code: #7
Popular Name/Descriptor: Rangel Amendment
Effective Date: March 10, 1972
Applicable to US Participation in (Org.): IBRD, IDA, IDB, ADB
PL Reference: 92-247, Sec. 2, 86 Stat. 61 (IBRD and IDA)
Act and Section: IDA Act, Sec. 13
US Code Reference: 22 USC 284k (IBRD & IDA)
Summary: The Secretary of the Treasury is to instruct US EDs to oppose loans to countries failing to take adequate steps against the illegal traffic from or through their territory of narcotic drugs reaching either US territory or US personnel within the jurisdiction of such country.
Comment on its application and effectiveness: Application is entirely in the hands of the President, who alone determines the "adequacy" of any steps being taken.

Identifying Code: #8
Popular Name/Descriptor: Military equipment
Effective Date: September 22, 1967
Applicable to US Participation in (Org.): *IDB only, not IBRD*
PL Reference: 90-88, Sec. 2, 81 Stat. 227
Act and Section: IADB Act, Sec. 16(c)
US Code Reference: 22 USC Sec. 283m(c)
Summary: US to vote against any loan "which might assist the recipient country directly or indirectly to acquire sophisticated or heavy military equipment."
Comment on its application and effectiveness: MDB loans can never be used directly for such purposes, and any country acquiring this type of equipment might be indirectly aided in that enterprise by its IADB loans.

Identifying Code: #9
Popular Name/Descriptor: Long Amendment (repealed version)
Effective Date: August 14, 1974 – October 3, 1977
Applicable to US Participation in (Org.): IDA
PL Reference: 93-373, Sec. 3, 88 Stat. 445 (repealed by PL 95-118, Sec. 702, 91 Stat. 1070)
Act and Section: IDA Act Sec. 15
US Code Reference: 22 USC Sec. 284m
Summary: US to oppose concessional loans to countries which developed nuclear weapons and which had not signed the nuclear nonproliferation treaty.
Comment on its application and effectiveness: Invoked only against India; every loan opposed approved without US support.

Identifying Code: #10
Popular Name/Descriptor: Gonzalez Amendment
Effective Date: March 10, 1972
Applicable to US Participation in (Org.): IBRD, IDA, IDB, ADB, AFDB
PL Reference: 92-247, Sec. 1, 86 Stat. 60 (IBRD and IDA)
Act and Section: IDA Act Sec. 12
US Code Reference: 22 USC 284j (IBRD & IDA)
Summary: US to oppose loans to countries which have expropri-

ated US investments without taking adequate steps towards compensation.
Comment on its application and effectiveness: Application is in practice left to the discretion of the President who has some flexibility in determining whether arrangements or negotiations are adequate to forestall application.

Identifying Code: #11
Popular Name/Descriptor: Consultations with Congress
Effective Date: August 13, 1981
Applicable to US Participation in (Org.): All MDBs
PL Reference: 97-35, Sec. 1361(b), 95 Stat. 746
Act and Section: IFI Act Sec. 1201
US Code Reference: 22 USC Sec. 262g-3
Summary: Secretary of the Treasury or his designee shall consult with the ranking congressional leaders of the relevant committees in both houses of Congress both before and during any international negotiations involving potential increases in the contribution or subscription of the US.
Comment on its application and effectiveness: Intended to insure Congressional input in these negotiations from the start and thus to help reconcile US Executive and Congressional positions before any international agreement is reached on expected levels of future US funding of these institutions.

Identifying Code: #12
Popular Name/Descriptor: Mathis/Moore Amendment
Effective Date: October 3, 1977
Applicable to US Participation in (Org.): All MDBs
PL Reference: 95-118, Sec. 901, 91 Stat. 1071, & 97-35, Sec. 1371(b)(2), 95 Stat 746
Act and Section: IFI Act sec. 901
US Code Reference: 22 USC Sec. 262g
Summary: US EDs to oppose any loan or other financial assistance intended to establish or expand production for export of 1) palm oil, 2) sugar, or 3) citrus crops if such loan or assistance will cause injury to US producers of the same or competing agricultural commodity. Congress also declares that it is the policy of the US to use its voice and vote in the MDBs to combat

hunger and encourage development in developing countries by seeking to channel assistance for agriculturally related development to projects fulfilling the domestic food and nutrition needs and alleviating hunger in the recipient country.
Comment on its application and effectiveness: Intended to protect the narrow economic interest of US exporters of the listed commodities. The declaration of Congressional policy articulates a more humane formal objective.

Identifying Code: #13
Popular Name/Descriptor: Obey Amendment
Effective Date: December 29, 1981; renewed with various appropriations bills for the MDBs
Applicable to US Participation in (Org.): All MDBs
PL Reference: Various, most recently PL 99-190, Sec. 101(i) [Sec. 523], 99 Stat 1291, 1306
Act and Section: Various appropriations Acts, most recently the Foreign Assistance and Related Programs Appropriations Act, 1986
US Code Reference: 22 USC Sec. 262h
Summary: Secretary of the Treasury is to instruct US EDs to oppose any use of MBD funds for the production of any commodity for export if it is in surplus on world markets, and if the assistance will cause substantial injury to US producers of the same, similar or competing commodity.
Comment on its application and effectiveness: Determinations required concerning surplus and likelihood of "substantial" injury permit flexibility. This provision is *not* limited to agricultural commodities.

Identifying Code: #14
Popular Name/Descriptor: Helms Amendment
Effective Date: October 3, 1977
Applicable to US Participation in (Org.): All international financial institutions fostering economic development
PL Reference: 95-118, Sec. 704, 91 Stat. 1071
Act and Section: Int. Financial Institutions Act, Sec. 704
US Code Reference: 22 USC Sec. 262e
Summary: President is to direct US EDs to take all appropriate

actions to keep salaries and benefits of employees of these institutions to levels comparable to salaries and benefits of those in the private sector or in the US government who hold comparable positions.
Comment on its application and effectiveness: The passage of this legislation is indicative of the widespread belief within the US that international civil servants are overpaid. The effect is hard to gauge, but see the legislative provision mentioned next below.

Identifying Code: #15
Popular Name/Descriptor: US ED Salary Limitation
Effective Date: October 10, 1978, renewed with various appropriations bills for the MDBs
Applicable to US Participation in (Org.): all MDBs
PL Reference: Various, most recently PL 97-121, 95 Stat 1648
Act and Section: Various Appropriations Acts, most recently the Foreign Assistance and Related Appropriations Act, 1982 Title I, and others)
US Code Reference: Does not appear in the USC
Summary: No US contribution may be made to a MDB whose US ED or Alternate receives more than the amount referred to; thus US EDs salaries are to be limited according to the pay scale of US government employees.
Comment on its application and effectiveness: Has held down salaries of US EDs, who are simply paid a lower salary than other EDs in the same institutions.

Identifying Code: #16
Popular Name/Descriptor: US access to MDB documentation
Effective Date: December 29, 1981
Applicable to US Participation in (Org.): all MDBs
PL Reference: Various, e.g.PL 97-121, Sec. 519, 95 Stat 1656
Act and Section: Various Appropriations Acts (e.g. Foreign Assistance and Related Appropriations Act, 1982 Title V, Sec. 519)
US Code Reference: Does not appear in the USC
Summary: Since 1981 US legislative Acts appropriating funds for foreign aid state that: "None of the appropriated or other-

wise made available by this Act shall be available to any international financial institution whose United States representative cannot upon request obtain any document developed by the management of the international financial institutions."
Comment on its application and effectiveness: Is intended to insure US access to all documentation of these organizations. But since US EDs are answerable to the US Executive (the Secretary of the Treasury), they have often refused to grant Congress total access to these records.

Identifying Code: #17
Popular Name/Descriptor: US access to MDB financial records
Effective Date: October 31, 1977
Applicable to US Participation in (Org.): all MDBs
PL Reference: Various, e.g. PL 95-148, Sec. 505, 91 Stat 1239, and PL 97-121, Sec. 518, 95 Stat 1656
Act and Section: Various Appropriations Acts, originally appeared in Foreign Assistance and Related Programs Appropriations Act, 1978, Title V, Sec. 505; more recently in Foreign Assistance and Related Appropriations Act, 1982 Title V, Sec. 518,
US Code Reference: Does not appear in the USC
Summary: Since US legislative Acts appropriating funds for foreign aid state that: "None of the appropriated or otherwise made available by this Act shall be available to any international financial institution whose United States representative cannot upon request obtain the amounts and the names of borrowers for all loans of the international financial institution, or the compensation and related benefits of employees of the institution."
Comment on its application and effectiveness: Is intended to assure US access to all financial records of these institutions.

Identifying Code: #18
Popular Name/Descriptor: Basic human needs to be addressed
Effective Date: October 3, 1977
Applicable to US Participation in (Org.): IBRD, IDA, IFC, IDB, AFDF, ADB, AFDB

PL Reference: 95-118, Sec. 701, 91 Stat. 1069 as amended through 97-375, Sec. 211, 96 Stat. 1826
Act and Section: International Financial Institutions Act, Sec. 701(d)
US Code Reference: 22 USC Sec. 262d(d)
Summary: The US to use its voice and vote in the MDBs to seek to channel assistance to projects which address basic human needs of the people of the recipient country.
Comment on its application and effectiveness: A statement of policy considerations, not a mandatory vote.

Identifying Code: #19
Popular Name/Descriptor: US aid policy, the poor and basic human needs
Effective Date: October 6, 1978
Applicable to US Participation in (Org.): All Multilateral aid institutions
PL Reference: 95-425, Sec. 101, 92 Stat. 938 as amended through 96-55, Sec. 104(a), 93 Stat. 360
Act and Section: Foreign Assistance Act of 1961, as amended, Sec. 102(a)
US Code Reference: 22 USC Sec. 2151-1(a)
Summary: US bilateral assistance and US participation in multilateral institutions is to emphasize programs in support of countries pursuing development strategies designed to meet basic human needs and self-sustaining growth with equity. US participation should also emphasize the principle that the poor majority of people in developing countries should be involved in the process of development and economic growth.
Comment on its application and effectiveness: Little more than a formal statement of policy.

Identifying Code: #20
Popular Name/Descriptor: List of Considerations for US EDs
Effective Date: October 3, 1977
Applicable to US Participation in (Org.): IBRD, IDA, IFC, IDB, AFDF, ADB, AFDB
PL Reference: 95-118, Sec. 701, 91 Stat. 1069 as amended through 97-375, Sec. 211, 96 Stat. 1862

Act and Section: International Financial Institutions Act Sec. 701(b)(1)–(4)
US Code Reference: 22 USC Sec. 262d(b)(1)–(4)
Summary: Secretary of the Treasury to instruct US EDs to take into consideration: 1) actions by either the executive branch or Congress on individual bilateral assistance programs because of human rights considerations; 2) extent to which economic assistance would directly benefit the needy people in the recipient country; 3) whether the recipient country has detonated a nuclear device or is not a State Party to the Treaty on Non-Proliferation of Nuclear Weapons or both; and 4) for Vietnam, Laos and Cambodia, their responsiveness in providing a more substantial accounting of US servicemen missing in action from the war in Indo-China.
Comment on its application and effectiveness: A statement of policy considerations, not a mandatory vote.

Identifying Code: #21
Popular Name/Descriptor: Long Amendment
Effective Date: October 3, 1977
Applicable to US Participation in (Org.): All MDBs
PL Reference: 96-118, Sec. 801, 91 Stat. 1069 as amended through 97-375, Sec. 211, 96 Stat. 1862
Act and Section: IFI Act Sec. 801
US Code Reference: 22 USC Sec. 262f
Summary: US is to use its voice and vote in the MDBs to promote the development and utilization of light capital technologies.
Comment on its application and effectiveness: An extremely flexible and non-binding directive.

Identifying Code: #22
Popular Name/Descriptor: Integration of women
Effective Date: December 30, 1974
Applicable to US Participation in (Org.): All international organizations of which the US is a member, including all MDBs
PL Reference: 93-559, Sec. 54, 88 Stat. 1818 as amended by 94-161, Sec. 313(b), 89 Stat. 866 and 95-88, Sec. 118(b), 91 Stat. 540

Act and Section: Financial Assistance Act of 1961 (as amended) Sec. 305
US Code Reference: 22 USC Sec. 2225
Summary: The President is to instruct US representatives to carry out their duties so as to encourage and promote the integration of women into the national economies of member and recipient countries and into professional and policy-making positions within the organizations themselves. In making the US contribution to these agencies the President is to take into account the progress of these organizations on this score.
Comment on its application and effectiveness: Amounts to little more than a statement of policy preferences.

Identifying Code: #23
Popular Name/Descriptor: Annual reports to Congress
Effective Date: June 3, 1980
Applicable to US Participation in (Org.): All MDBs
PL Reference: 96-259Sec. 501(a), 94 Stat. 431
Act and Section: IFI Act, Sec. 701(c)
US Code Reference: 22 USC Sec. 262d(c)
Summary: US Secretary of State and Secretary of the Treasury are to report annually to Congress on progress towards achieving the legislatively declared goals of the US in the MDBs. The Secretary of the Treasury is to report quarterly, specifying certain details about all of the loans considered by the MDBs, "the vote of the United States Government", reasons for US government opposition, if any, the result of the vote, and if the US opposed the loan, whether the loan meets basic human needs.
Comment on its application and effectiveness: Allows Congress to monitor compliance with its directives by US EDs.

Identifying Code: #24
Popular Name/Descriptor: Quarterly reports to Congress, and consultations
Effective Date: June 3, 1980
Applicable to US Participation in (Org.): All MDBs
PL Reference: 96-259, Sec. 501(b), 94 Stat. 432 as amended 98-181, Sec. 1004, 97 Stat. 1286.

Act and Section: IFI Act, Sec. 701(g)
US Code Reference: 22 USC Sec. 262d(g)
Summary: The Secretary of the Treasury, in consultation with the Secretary of State, shall report quarterly to specified Congressional leaders, giving details whenever the US ED has opposed a loan because of human rights considerations. The report is to explain how the decision was made to oppose the loan, and how the action taken relates to US human rights policy in the country concerned. The Secretary of the Treasury is also to consult beforehand with these Congressional leaders, and inform them of prospective changes in policy direction towards countries which have or recently have had poor human rights records.
Comment on its application and effectiveness: Allows Congress to review compliance by US EDs with its human rights directives, and to participate in the US policy debate on MDB loans to individual countries.

Identifying Code: #25
Popular Name/Descriptor: US multilateral aid policy
Effective Date: October 6, 1978
Applicable to US Participation in (Org.): All multilateral aid institutions
PL Reference: 95-424, Sec. 103(a), 92 Stat. 943
Act and Section: Foreign Assistance Act of 1961, as amended, Sec. 103(b)(2)
US Code Reference: 22 USC Sec. 2151a(b)(2)
Summary: Where development requires major infrastructure projects, the US assistance should be furnished in a multilateral framework along with significant contributions of other donor countries. Infrastructure projects should be complemented by other measures to ensure that the benefits of the infrastructure reach the poor.
Comment on its application and effectiveness: Little more than a formal statement of policy, but helpful as an indication of the Congressional views on the utility of multilateral aid.

Identifying Code: #26
Popular Name/Descriptor: Assistance to the Private sector of El Salvador, Nicaragua and other Nations

Effective Date: October 7, 1980
Applicable to US Participation in (Org.): IBRD, IMF
PL Reference: 96-389, Sec. 8, 94 Stat. 1554
US Code Reference: 22 USC Sec. 286x
Summary: Expresses the "sense of the Congress that in providing assistance through loans or other means to any nation, in particular El Salvador and Nicaragua, the Fund and the Bank should encourage programs which assist the private sector to create an environment which will stabilize the economy of the nation". US representatives to the Bank and Fund are to promote the use of assistance by these organizations to encourage such programs.
Comment on its application and effectiveness: A non-binding policy statement coupled with a vague directive to the US ED. It seems superfluous for Congress to request that the Bank promote the private sector in these countries or in others, since the Bank frequently does this in any case. In essence this is a political statement by the US Congress that it would strongly prefer that any loans to Nicaragua not be granted to finance government owned projects. More significant than this legislation is the fact that the present US administration has pledged to oppose any MDB assistance to Nicaragua until that state adopts more conventional free market economic policies.

Identifying Code: #27
Popular Name/Descriptor: Criteria for US Voting in IFIs
Effective Date: August 15, 1985
Applicable to US Participation in (Org.): All MDBs and the IMF
PL Reference: 99-88, Title I, Sec. 502, 99 Stat. 330
Act and Section: Supplemental Appropriations act of 1985
US Code Reference: 22 USC Sec. 262K
Summary: 1) Declares that the US national objective of furthering the economic and social development of the nations of the world provides the basis for US participation in and contributions to the international financial institutions. Also declares that it is the intent of the US Congress that US contributions to these institutions "should be primarily directed to those projects that would not generate excess commodity supplies on world markets, displace private investment initiatives or foster depar-

tures from a market-oriented economy." 2) Requires the Secretary of the Treasury to instruct US "representatives" to these institutions to take into account the effects of country adjustment programs when reviewing loans or credits in order to (i) minimize any projected adverse impact upon individual industry sectors and international commodity markets which might be affected, and (ii) avoid whenever possible government subsidization of production and exports of international commodities without regard to economic conditions in the markets for such commodities. 3) Lists three separate criteria which are to be considered by the US ED when voting on any project proposal relating to mining, smelting, and fabricating of minerals and metal products, i.e. (i) Analysis showing that the project could be financed commercially on reasonable terms, (ii) Analysis by the US Bureau of mines of indicating that there would be surplus capacity in the industry for the primary product of the proposed project during half the period of that project's projected economic life; or (iii) Whether US imports of the commodity involved constitute 50 percent of the US domestic production of the primary product in cases where the US is the substantial producer of such commodities.
Comment on its application and effectiveness: A combination of non-binding elements. Includes two separate policy statements as well as a bewildering array of non-binding directives about how to cast the US vote in these organizations.

Identifying Code: #28
Popular Name/Descriptor: Environmental reform of MDBs
Effective Date: December 19, 1985
Applicable to US Participation in (Org.): All MDBs
PL Reference: 99-190, Sec. 101(i) [title V. Sec. 5540], 99 Stat. 1291, 1309
Act and Section: Foreign Assistance and Related Programs Appropriations Act, 1986
US Code Reference: 22 USC Sec. 2621
Summary: The US Secretary of the Treasury is to instruct the US EDs of all the MDBs "to vigorously promote" environmental expertise and sensitivity in the staff and operations of the development banks. The long list of actions to be taken includes steps to improve the staff of these banks and to call special

meetings of the EDs for consultations on the "environmental performance" of the MDBs. US EDs are to request reviews from the banks concerning their past environmental performance, and the Treasury department is to report to Congress on the steps taken to implement these directives.
Comment on its application and effectiveness: Sends a number of mandatory directives to the US EDs in the MDBs, but no "No" vote directives are involved. Primarily a policy statement, but also obliges US EDs to consult on these issues with other member countries. This has been very effective, and has done much to contribute to the recent environmental reform of the MDB's, especially the IBRD and the IDB, with the new attitude towards Brazilian rain forest projects as the best case in point.

Identifying Code: #29
Popular Name/Descriptor: Anti-Drug **Legislation**
Effective Date: October 27, 1986
Applicable to US Participation in (Org.): All MDB's
PL Reference: 99-570, Sec. 2005 and 2017, 100 Stat. 3207-61, 62 and 100 Stat. 3207-68, 69
Act and Section: Antidrug Reorganization Act of 1986
US Code Reference: 22 USC Sec. 2413, and 22 USC Sec. 2291, note.
Summary: The US Secretary of the Treasury is to instruct the US EDs of all the MDBs to vote against any loan or other utilization of funds for any major illicit drug producing country or major drug transit country, unless the President has determined that during the previous year that country has cooperated fully with the US, or has taken adequate steps on its own, to prevent drugs produced or processed in or transiting through that country from being sold to US personnel within the jurisdiction of such country or from being transported to the territory of the US, and to prevent and punish the laundering in that country of drug profits or drug related monies. An exception can be made in cases where the President certifies that the vital national interests of the US require that such assistance be given in any case.

Also requires the Secretary of the Treasury to instruct the US EDs to initiate discussions with other MDB Directors to propose that all possible assistance be provided for drug eradication programs in major drug producing countries, specifically including crop substitution programs.

Comment on its application and effectiveness: The President retains considerable discretion in preventing the application of the "no" vote directive. The order to initiate policy discussions is a perfectly appropriate mechanism for influencing MDB lending policy.

ANNEX C
ANALYTICAL CLASSIFICATION OF US LEGISLATION

MEANS THROUGH WHICH THE LEGISLATION ATTEMPTS TO AFFECT BANK POLICY

	I. Non-Binding statements of Policy and Policy Directives a. Policy Statements b. Vague Directives c. Obligations to Consult d. Obligations to promote a specific policy	II. "No" Vote Directives a. Presidential Discretion allowed for b. Effectively Mandatory	III. Declarations that none of the funds are to be used for certain purposes
TYPES OF CONSIDERATIONS REFLECTED	I.	II.	III.
Political Unilateral			
I) TYPE OF GOVERNMENT OF RECIPIENT		#1, #2 (a) (IMF only)	
II) COUNTRY SPECIFIC LEGISLATION	#3 (a) (ADB only)		
III) POLICY ON AMERICAN MIAs	#20 (b)		

	I.	II.	III.
Political, Related to Upholding International Norms			
IV) HUMAN RIGHTS VIOLATIONS	#4, #5 (c) #6 (a) £20 (b)	#6 (a)#6 (a) £20 (b)	
V) DRUG TRADE	#29 (d)	#29 (a) #7 (a)	
VI) POLICY TOWARDS HIJACKERS	#6 (a)	#6 (a)	
Political Military			
VII) PURCHASE OF HEAVY MILITARY EQUIPMENT		#8 (a)	
VIII) NUCLEAR WEAPONS POLICY		#9 (b)	
Economic, National/Unilateral			
IX) EXPROPRIATION OF US INVESTMENTS		#10 (a)	
X) US NATIONAL ECONOMIC CONSIDERATIONS	#11 (c) #12 (a)	#12 (b) #13 (a)	
XI) SALARIES OF BANK EMPLOYEES AND EDS	#14 (b)		# 15

	I.	II.	III.
Other Considerations			
XII) US ACCESS TO RECORDS/DOCUMENTS			#16, #17
XIII) BASIC HUMAN NEEDS	#18 (b) #19 (b)		
XIV) ENVIRONMENTAL REFORM OF MDBs	#28 (a),(b) & (d)		
XV) MISC.			
List of considerations	#20 (b)		
Further Criteria for US voting in MDBs	#27 (a) & (b)		
Light capital technologies	#21		
Integration of women	#22		
Promotion of the Private Sector, esp. in El Salvador & Nicaragua	#26 (a) & (b)		
Reports to Congress on US MDB Policy	#23, #24 (c)		
General Statements of US Aid Policy	#25 (a)		

10

BIBLIOGRAPHY

SOURCES

INTERNATIONAL SOURCES

Judicial Opinions

Permanent Court of International Justice, *Certain German Interests in Polish Upper Silesia, and the Factory at Chorzów*, (Merits), May 25, 1926, *P.C.I.J.*, Series A., No. 7, p. 4.

International Court of Justice, *Conditions of Admission of a State to Membership in the United Nations*, Advisory Opinion, 28 May 1948, *ICJ Reports* (1947/1948), p. 57.

International Court of Justice, *Competence of the General Assembly for the Admission of a State to the United Nations*, Advisory Opinion, 3 March 1950, *ICJ Reports* (1950), p.4.

International Court of Justice, *Nottebohm Case* (second phase), Judgment, 6 April 1955, *ICJ Reports* (1955), p. 4.

International Court of Justice, *Certain Expenses of the United Nations*, Advisory Opinion, 20 July 1962, *ICJ Reports*, (1962), p. 150.

International Court of Justice, *Barcelona Traction Light and Power Company*, Judgment, 5 February 1970, *ICJ Reports*, (1970), p. 3.

International Court of Justice, *Legal Consequences for States of the Continued Presence of South Africa in Namibia (South West Africa) Notwithstanding Security Council Resolution 276 (1970)*, Advisory Opinion, 21 June 1971, *ICJ Reports* (1971), p. 16.

International Court of Justice, *Military and Paramilitary Activities in and Against Nicaragua*, Judgment, 27 June 1986, *ICJ Reports*, (1986), p. 14.

Constitutive Agreements of Intergovernmental Organizations

Charter of the United Nations – entered into force 24 October 1945; as amended effective 31 August 1965; amended effective 20 December 1965 and amended effective 24 September 1974.

Articles of Agreement of the International Bank for Reconstruction and Development – entered into force 27 December 1945; as amended effective 17 December 1965.

Articles of Agreement of the International Monetary Fund – entered into force 27 December 1945, as amended effective 28 July 1969 and as amended effective 1 April 1978.

Articles of Agreement of the International Development Association – entered into force 24 September 1960.

Charter of the Organization of American States, done at Bogota, 30 April 1948, as amended effective 27 February 1967.

Agreements between Intergovernmental Organizations

Agreement Between the United Nations and the International Bank for Reconstruction and Development, United Nations Treaty Series, Vol. 16, (1948), pp. 346–357.

World Bank Publications

World Bank *Annual Reports*, Washington, D.C., 1970–1990: *Policies and Operations: The World Bank, IDA and IFC*, Washington, DC, (1969).

IDA International Development Association, Washington (1978), 48 pp.

The World Bank and International Finance Corporation, Washington (1983), 65 pp.

World Bank Documents

"United Nations Assembly Resolution 377 (V) Entitled 'Uniting for Peace' ", Resolution No. 64, Adopted on September 13, 1951 by the I.B.R.D. Board of Governors, in International Bank for Reconstruction and Development, *Summary Proceedings*: Sixth Annual Meeting of the Board of Governors, Washington D.C., September 10–14, 1951, at p. 26.

Statement of the IBRD General Counsel (Mr Broches) to the Fourth Committee of the UN General Assembly on 28 November 1966, as distributed to the Executive Directors of the Bank on 1 December 1966. Reproduced in *International Legal Materials*, Vol. VI (1967) pp. 150–153, paraphrased in UN GAOR 21st Session, 4th Committee, 1645th meeting, 28 November 1966 at pp. 317–318.

"Chile and the World Bank", White Paper prepared by the World Bank, undated (circa. 1974) Appendix to SANFORD, J.E., "The Multilateral Development Banks and the Suspension of Lending to Allende's Chile", Congressional Research Service, The Library of Congress, August 6, 1974 (Revised December 13, 1974).

Letter dated July 5, 1977 from Robert McNamara, President of the International Bank For Reconstruction and Development, to W. Michael Blumenthal, Secretary of the Treasury of the United States; reproduced in "Foreign Operations Hearings, 1979", (*op. cit., infra* under US Government Publications) at pp. 492–493.

Internal World Bank memorandum dated August 29, 1977 from Mr.

A. Broches, Vice President and General Counsel of the Bank, to Mr. Edward R. Fried, Executive Director (US appointed); (First Opinion on the possibility of restricted contributions reproduced in "Foreign Operations Hearings, 1979", (op. cit., infra), at pp. 537–538.

Internal World Bank memorandum dated September 28, 1977 from Mr. A. Broches, Vice President and General Counsel of the Bank, to Mr. Edward R. Fried, Executive Director (US appointed); (Second Opinion on the possibility of restricted contributions) reproduced in "Foreign Operations Hearings, 1979", (*op. cit., infra*), at pp. 539–540.

Letter dated November, 1, 1979 from IBRD President Robert McNamara to Clarence Long, Chairman of the Subcommittee on Foreign Operations and Related Agencies, of the Committee on Appropriations of the US House of Representatives; reproduced in the *Congressional Record*, (House), (December 3, 1979), at p. 34415.

Letter dated November, 1, 1979 from IBRD President Robert McNamara to G. William Miller, US Secretary of the Treasury. Reproduced in the *Congressional Record*, (House), (December 3, 1979), at p. 34415.

"Prohibition of Political Activities Under the IBRD Articles of Agreement and Its Relevance to the Work of the Executive Directors", Opinion by Mr. Ibrahim F. I. Shihata, Vice President and General Counsel of the Bank, (December 23, 1987, unpublished World Bank document).

Document Collections

Proceedings and Documents of the United Nations Monetary and Financial Conference, Bretton Woods, New Hampshire, 1–22 July 1944, Washington, D.C., US Government Printing Office, 1948.

MOSS, A. G. and WINTON, H. N. M. (compilers), A New International Economic Order, New York, United Nations Institute for Training and Research, (1976), in two volumes, vii–964 pp. (UNITAR Document Service No. 1).

MUTHARIKA, P. A., *The International Law of Development, Basic Documents*, Vol. 1, New York, Oceana Publications (1978), 646 pp.

Resolutions of the UN General Assembly

"Implementation of the Declaration on the Granting of Independence to Colonial Peoples and Territories", Resolution 2105 (XX) of 20 December 1965, UN GAOR 20th Session, Supplement No. 14, UN Document A/6014.

"Declaration on the Inadmissibility of Intervention in the Domestic Affairs of States and the Protection of their Independence and Sovereignty", Resolution 2131 (XX), 21 December 1965, UN GAOR, 20th Session, Supplement No. 14, UN Document A/6014.

"The Policies of Apartheid of the Government of the Republic of South Africa", Resolution 2054A(XX) 15 December 1965, UN GAOR 20th Session, Supplement No. 14, UN Document A/6014 (Invites specialized agencies to deny technical and economic assistance to the Government of South Africa).

"Declaration on Principles of International Law Concerning Friendly Relations and Cooperation Among States in Accordance with the Charter of the United Nations", Resolution 2625 (XXV), 24 October 1970, UN GAOR 25th Session, Supplement 28, UN Document A/8028.

"Charter of Economic Rights and Duties of States", Resolution 3281 (XXIX), 12 December 1974, UN GAOR, 29th Session, Supplement No. 31, UN Document A/9631.

UN Documents and Reports

United Nations Conference on International Organization Documents, Vol. 6, Doc. 784, I/1/27 (1945).

"Consultations with the International Bank for Reconstruction and Development", Secretary General's Report, UN GAOR, 22nd Session, Annexes, Agenda Item 66, UN Document A/6825, 15 September 1967, pp. 2–16.
(assembles together many relevant documents not listed separately here)

US National Sources

Constitutional

The Constitution of the United States of America, proposed by Convention, September 17, 1787; effective March 4, 1789; and as subsequently amended.

US National Legislation

The Bretton Woods Agreements Act, Public Law hereinafter ("PL") 79–171, approved July 31, 1945; as amended. Codified in Volume 22, United States Code ("USC") sections 286–286k-2.

The International Development Association Act, PL 86-565, approved June 30, 1960; as amended. Codified at 22 USC sections 284–284o.

The International Financial Institutions Act, PL 95-118, approved October 3, 1977; as amended. Codified at 22 USC sections 262c–262g-3.

US Executive Orders and Communications

Executive Order 11269 (National Advisory Council on International Monetary and Financial Policies) of February 14, 1966; as amended.

National Security Decision Memorandum (NSDM) 93, issued by Henry Kissinger on behalf of President Richard M. Nixon on 9 November 1970.

Letter dated 5 November, 1975 from Mr. Henry Kissinger, Secretary of State of the United States of America, to Mr. Francis Blanchard, Director General of the ILO, containing notice of intent to withdraw from the ILO, in *International Legal Materials*, Vol. XIV, No. 6, November 1975, at pp. 1582–1584.

Letter dated October 6, 1977 from Jimmy Carter, President of the United States, to Clarence D. Long, Chairman, Subcommittee on Foreign Operations, Committee on Appropriations of the US House of Representatives. Reproduced in the *Congressional Record*, (House), Vol. 123, (October 18, 1977), at p. 34093.

United States Government Publications

United States Department of the Treasury, *United States Participation in the Multilateral Development Banks in the 1980s*, Washington, US Government Printing Office (1982), 194 pp.

(US) National Advisory Council on International Monetary and Financial Policies, *International Finance*, Annual Report to the President and Congress for Fiscal Years 1980–1988.

United States House of Representatives, (hearings), "Foreign Assistance and Related Appropriations for 1979", (hearings), Ninety-fifth Congress, Second Session, before the Subcommittee on Foreign Operations and Related Agencies of the Committee on Appropriations of the US House of Representatives ("Foreign Operations Hearings, 1979"), Volume 1, 823 pp.

United States House of Representatives, (hearings), "US Economic Sanctions Against Chile", (Hearings), Ninety-seventh Congress, First Session, 10 March 1981, before Subcommittees on International Economic Policy and Trade and on Inter-American Affairs of the Committee on Foreign Affairs of the US House of Representatives, 86 pp.

United States House of Representatives, (hearings), "The Future of Multilateral Development Banks", (Hearings), Ninety-seventh Congress, Second Session, 15 June 1982, before the Subcommittee on International Development Institutions and Finance held jointly with the Subcommittee on International Trade, Investment and Monetary Policy of the Committee on Banking, Finance and Urban Affairs of the US House of Representatives, 605 pp.

United States Senate, (staff report), US Policy and the Multilateral Banks: politicization and effectiveness; Staff report to the Subcommittee on Foreign Assistance of the Committee on Foreign Relations, US Senate, Washington, US Government Printing Office (1977), 33 pp.

US Congressional Research Service

SANFORD, J.E., "The Multilateral Development Banks and the Suspension of Lending to Allende's Chile", Foreign Affairs Division, Congressional Research Service, The Library of Congress, August 6, 1974 (Revised December 13, 1974).

WORKS

Books

ABI-SAAB, G., *The Concept of International Organization*, Paris, UNESCO, 1981, 245 pp.

ABI-SAAB, G., *The United Nations Operation in the Congo 1960–1964*, Oxford and New York, Oxford University Press, 1978, xvi-206 pp.

ALEXANDROWICZ, C. H., *World Economic Agencies – Law and Practice*, New York, Praeger (1963), xvii–310 pp.

BALDWIN, D.A., *Economic Statecraft*, Princeton N.J., Princeton University Press, (1985), xiv–409 pp.

BEDJAOUI, M., *Fonction publique internationale et influences nationales*, London, Stevens & Sons, 1958, xv–674 pp.

BERGSTEN, C.F., *The Future of the International Economic Order: An Agenda for Research*, Lexington, Massachusetts, Lexington Books, 1973, xv–357 pp.

BOWETT, D. *Self-Defense in International Law*, Manchester, Manchester University Press, 1958, xv–294 pp.

BOWETT, D., *The Law of International Institutions*, 3rd edition, London, Stevens & Sons, (1975), vii–382 pp.

BROWNLIE, I., *Principles of Public International Law*, Oxford, Clarendon Press, (1979), xxxviii-743 pp.

BULL, H. (ed.), *Intervention in International Politics*, Oxford, Clarendon Press, 1984, VII–198 pp.

CALVO, C., *Le Droit international théorique et practique*, 4th ed., Vol. I, Paris, Guillaumin et Cie., 1887.

CARREAU, D., JUILLARD, P. and FLORY, T., *Droit International Economique*, 2nd edition, Paris, Librarie Générale de Droit et de Jurisprudence (1980), xix–631 pp.

CARREAU, D., *Souverainté et cooperation monétaire internationale*, Paris, Cujas (1970), x–531 pp.

CLAUDE, I. L.(Jr.), *Swords into Plowshares: The Problems and Progress of International Organization*, 4th edition, New York, Random House (1971), xii–514 pp.

CUNNINGHAM, G., *The Management of Aid Agencies: Donor structures and procedures for the administration of aid to developing countries*, London, Croom Helm (1974), vii–181 pp.

DAVIS, N., *The Last Two Years of Salvador Allende*, London, Tauris & Co., (1985), xv–480 pp.

de VATTEL, E., *Le Droit des gens ou principes de la loi naturelle*, Washington, Carnegie Institution, 1916 (reproduction of the edition of 1758), Vol. I, lix–541 pp.

DELAUME, G., *Legal Aspects of International Lending and Economic Development Financing*, New York, Oceana Publications (1967), xxiii–371 pp.

DIAMOND, W. and RAGHAVAN, V.S. (eds.), *Aspects of Development Bank Management*, Baltimore, The Johns Hopkins University Press, (1982), xiii–297 pp. (EDI Series in Economic Management, The World Bank)

DIEHL, P.F. (ed.), *The Politics of International Organizations: Patterns and Insights*, Chicago, Dorsey Press, (1989), x–468 pp.

FEIS, H. *Foreign Aid and Foreign Policy*, London, Macmillan & Co. Ltd., 1964, vii–246 pp.

FINGER, S. M., and HARBERT, J.R., (eds.), *U.S. Policy in International Institutions*, Boulder, Westview Press, (1982), xv–217 pp.

FINKELSTEIN, L.S. (ed.), *Politics in the United Nations System*, Durham NC, Duke University Press, (1988), xvi–503 pp.

FLORY, M., *Droit international du développement*, Paris, Presses Universitaires de France (1977), 336 pp.

FRIEDMANN, W. G., KALMANOFF, G. and MEAGHER, R. F., *International Financial Aid, New York, Columbia University Press*, (1966), xiv–498 pp.

FRIEDMANN, W., *The Changing Structure of International Law*, London, Stevens and Sons Ltd., 1964, xvi–410 pp.

GARDNER, R. N., *Sterling-Dollar Diplomacy in Current Perspective*, New York, Columbia University Press (1980), x/ix–423 pp.

GOLD, J., *The Rule of Law in the International Monetary Fund*, Washington D.C., The International Monetary Fund (1980), xiii-96 pp. (IMF Pamphlet Series No. 32).

HENKIN, L., *Foreign Affairs and the Constitution*, New York, Norton & Co. (1972), xi–569 p.

HIRSCH, F., DOYLE, M.W. and MORSE, E.L., *Alternatives To Monetary Disorder*, 1980s Project/Council on Foreign Relations, New York, McGraw-Hill, 1977.

HOLSTI, K.J., *International Politics: A Framework for Analysis*, Englewood Cliffs, N.J., Prentice-Hall, 1983, xiii–478 pp.

HURNI, B. S., *The Lending Policy of the World Bank in the 1970s:Analysis and Evaluation*, Boulder, Colorado, Westview Press (1980), xv-173 pp.

KAPLAN, J. J., *International Aid Coordination: Needs and Machinery*, Washington, The American Society of International Law (1978), ix–58 pp. (Studies in transnational legal policy; no. 16).

KAY, D., *The Functioning and Effectiveness of Selected United Nations System Programs*, American Society of International Law, (1980), ix–208 pp. (Studies in Transnational Legal Policy; no. 18).

KELSEN, H., *The Law of the United Nations: A Critical Analysis of its Fundamental Problems;* with supplement: "Recent Trends in the Law of the United Nations", (1951), xvi–994 pp.

KELSEN, H., *Principles of International Law*, 2nd edition, revised and edited by Robert W. Tucker, New York, Holt, Rinehart and Winston, 1966, 461 pp.

KEOHANE, R.O. and NYE, J.S., "World Politics and the International Economic System", a chapter in BERGSTEN, C.F., *The Future of the International Economic Order: An Agenda for Research*, Lexington, Massachusetts, Lexington Books, (1973) xv–357 pp.

KISSINGER, H., *The White House Years*, Boston, Little Brown, (1979), xxiv–1521 pp.

KNORR, K., *The Power of Nations: The Political Economy of International Relations*, New York, Basic Books (1975), 353 pp.

KRASNER, S.D. (ed.), *International Regimes*, Ithaca, New York, Cornell University Press (1983), x–372 pp.

KUDIN, S. J. (ed.), *Foreign Development Lending – Legal Aspects*, Leiden, A. W. Sijthoff (1971), 353 pp.

LASSWELL, H.D., *Politics: Who Gets What, When, How*, New York, Meridian Books, 1958, (Twelfth printing 1972), 222 pp.

LAUTERPACHT, H., *The Function of Law in the International Community*, Oxford, Clarendon Press, (1933), xxiv–469 pp.

LAVALLE, R., *La Banque mondiale et ses filiales: Aspects juridiques et fonctionnement*, Paris, Librarie Générale de Droit et de Jurisprudence (1972), 324 pp.

LILLICH, (ed.), *Humanitarian Intervention and the United Nations*, Charlottesville, University Press of Virginia, 1973, xii–240 pp.

LILLICH, R. B. (ed), *Economic Coercion and the New International Economic Order*, Charlottesville, Virginia, The Michie Company (1976), 401 pp.

LITTLE, I.M.D. and CLIFFORD, J.M., *International Aid*, London, George Allen and Unwin, 1965, 360 pp.

MACDONALD, R. St. J., and JOHNSTON, D.H., (eds.), *The Structure and Process of International Law: Essays in Legal Philosophy Doctrine and Theory*, The Hague, Martinus Nijhoff, 1983, vii–1234 pp.

MASON, E. S. and ASHER, R. E., *The World Bank Since Bretton Woods*, Washington, Brookings Institution (1973), xxiii–915 pp.

MASON, E.S., *Foreign Aid and Foreign Policy*, New York, Harper and Row, 1964, ix–118 pp.

MCDOUGAL, M. and FELICIANO, F. P., *Law and Minimum World Public Order: The legal regulation of international coercion* (1961), Yale University Press, 1961, xxvi–872 pp.

McNAIR, A.D. (Lord McNair), *The Law of Treaties*, London, Oxford University Press, 1961, xxi–789 pp.

MIKESELL, R.F., *The Economics of Foreign Aid*, Chicago, Aldine Publishing Co., 1968, xv–300 pp.

MITRANY, D. *A Working Peace System: An argument for the functional development of international organization*, 4th edition, London, National Peace Council (1946), 64 pp.

NINCIC, Miroslav, and WALLENSTEEN, Peter (eds.), *Dilemmas of Economic Coercion: Sanctions in World Politics*, New York, Praeger Publishers, 1983, 250 pp.

NURICK, L., "Certain Aspects of the Law and Practice of the International Bank for Reconstruction and Development", in SCHWEBEL, S. M. (ed.): *The Effectiveness of International Decisions*, Leyden Sijthoff, 1971, pp. 100–128.

OMER, A. U., *Le Financement international public du développement*, Genève, Librarie Droz (1979) xvii–219 pp.

PERARA, P., *Development Finance: Institutions, Problems, and Prospects*, New York, Praeger (1968), xiii–440 pp.

RENDELL, R. S. (ed.), *International Financial Law: Lending, Capital Transfers and Institutions*, London, Euromoney Publications (1980), 319 pp.

REUTER, P. *Institutions Internationales*, 5th ed. Paris, Presses Universitaires de France, (1967), 332 pp.

RIDEAU, J., *Juridictions internationales et contrôle et respect des traités constitutifs des organizations internationales*, Paris, Librarie Générale de Droit et de Jurisprudence, (1969), xv–382 pp.

ROTHSTEIN, R.L., *The Third World and US Foreign Policy: Cooperation and Conflict in the 1980s,* Boulder, Colorado, Westview Press (1981), xvi–271 pp.

SALMON, Jean, *Le Rôle des organizations internationales en matière de prêts et d'emprunts, Problèmes Juridiques,* London, Stevens & Sons Limited (1958), xiii–366 pp.

SANFORD, J.E., *U.S. Foreign Policy and Multilateral Development Banks,* Boulder, Colorado, Westview Press, (1982), xiv–279 pp.

SCHERMERS, H. G., *International Institutional Law,* Alphen aan den Rijn, The Netherlands, Sijthoff & Noordhoff, (1980), XXXII–1054 pp.

SCHWARZENBERGER, G., *Economic World Order? A Basic Problem of International Economic Law,* Manchester, UK, Manchester University Press (1970), xii–159 pp.

SCHWARZENBERGER, G., *International Law and Order,* London, Stevens & Sons, 1971, xxiii–298 pp.

SCHWEBEL, S.M. ed., *The Effectiveness of International Decisions,* Leyden, Sijthoff, (1971), 538 pp.

SPERO, J. E., *The Politics of International Economic Relations,* 2nd edition, London, George Allen and Unwin (1982), x–374 pp.

TAYLOR, P. and GROOM, A.J.R., eds., *International Institutions at Work,* New York, St. Martin's Press, 1988, vii-245 pp.

THOMAS, A.V.W. and THOMAS, A.J.Jr., *Non-Intervention: The Law and its Import in the Americas,* Dallas, Southern Methodist University Press, 1956, xvi–476 pp.

TUNKIN, G.I., *Theory of International Law,* London, George Allen & Unwin, 1974, xxv–497 pp.

WEINTRAUB, S. (ed.), *Economic Coercion and US Foreign Policy,* Boulder, Colorado, Westview Press (1982), xvii–234 pp.

WILLIAMS, D., *The Specialized Agencies and the United Nations: The System in Crisis,* New York, St. Martins Press, (1987), xvi–279 pp.

WOOD, R., *Law and Practice of International Finance,* London, Sweet & Maxwell (1980), xiii–462 pp.

ZOLLER, E., *La Bonne foi en droit international public,* Paris, Editions A. Pedone, 1977, xxvi–392 pp.

Les Resolutions dans la formation du droit international du développement, Genève, Institut Universitaire de Hautes Etudes Internationales (1971), 189 pp. (Etudes et Travaux de l'I.U.H.E.I. No. 13).

North–South: A Programme for Survival, Report of the Independent Commission on International Development Issues under the Chairmanship of Willy Brandt, London, Pan Books (1980), 304 pp.

Articles

ALSTON, P., "The United Nations Specialized Agencies and the Implementation of the International Covenant on Economic, Social and Cultural Rights'', *Columbia Journal of Transnational Law*, Vol. 18 (1979), pp. 79–118.

ANDREWS, S. C., ''US Trade Sanctions Against Uganda: Legality under International Law'', *Law and Policy in International Business*, Vol. 11, No. 3, (1979), pp. 1149–1191.

ASHERMAN, J., ''The IMF: a History of Compromise'', *New York University Journal Of International Law and Politics*, Vol. 16, No. 2, 1984, pp. 235–304.

BAADE, R. A., ''Economic Sanctions Against South Africa: Policy Options'', *Alternatives*, Vol. 4 (1979), pp. 487–505.

BALDWIN, D. A., ''The International Bank in Political Perspective'', *World Politics*, Vol. 18, (1965), pp. 68–81.

BALDWIN, D., ''The Power of Positive Sanctions'', *World Politics*, Vol. 24 (1971) pp. 19–38.

BALDWIN, D.A., ''Foreign Aid, Intervention and Influence'', *World Politics*, Vol. 21, (1968), pp. 425–447.

BALLADORE PALLIERI, G., ''Droit interne des organizations internationales'', *Recueil des Cours*, Vol. 127 (1969), pp. 1–37.

BERLIA, G., ''Admission d'un état aux Nations Unies'', *Revue générale de droit international public*, Vol. 53, (1949), pp. 481–502.

BETZ, J., ''Functions of the Multilateralization of Development Assistance'', *Law and State*, Vol. 18 (1978), pp. 40–71.

BILDER, R. B., ''Comments on the Legality of the Arab Oil Boycott'', *Texas International Law Journal*, Vol. 12, No. 1 (1977), pp. 41–46.

BITTERMAN, H. J. ''Negotiation of the Articles of Agreement of the International Bank for Reconstruction and Development'', *The International Lawyer*, Vol. 4 (1971), pp. 59–88.

BLEICHER, S. A. ''UN v. IBRD: A Dilemma of Functionalism'', *International Organization*, Vol. XXIV, No. 1 (1970), pp. 31–47.

BLUM, Y. Z., ''Economic Boycotts in International Law'', *Texas International Law Journal*, Vol. 12, No. 1 (1977), pp. 5–15.

BOORMAN, J. A. III, ''Economic Coercion in International Law: The Arab Oil Weapon and the Ensuing Juridical Issues'', *Journal of International Law and Economics*, Vol. 9 (1974), pp. 205–231.

BOWETT, D. W., and others, ''Economic Coercion: Past and Present'', A Symposium, *Virginia Journal of International Law*, Vol. 16 (1975-1976), pp. 233-295.

BOWETT, D. W., ''Economic Coercion and Reprisals by States'', *Virginia Journal of International Law*, Vol. 13, No. 1 (1972), pp. 1–12

BOYLE, F. A., ''The Irrelevance of International Law: the Schism between International Law and International Politics'', *California Western International Law Journal*, Vol. 10, No. 2 (1980), pp. 193–219.

BROCHES, A., ''International Legal Aspects of the Operations of the World Bank'', *Recueil des cours*, Vol. 98 (1959), pp. 297-409.

BROCHES, H., ''The Arab Oil Embargo and United States Pressure Against Chile: Economic and Political Coercion and the Charter of the United Nations'', *Case Western Reserve Journal of International Law*, Vol. 7, No. 1 (1974), pp. 3–35.

BROMS, B., "The Definition of Aggression", *Recueil des Cours* Vol. 154, No. 1 (1977), pp. 299–400.

CAHIER, P., "Le droit interne des organizations internationales", *R.G.D.I.P.*, vol. 67, 1963, at pp. 563-602.

CASSIN, V.; DEBEVOISE, W.; KAILES, H.; and THOMPSON, T. W., "The Definition of Aggression" *Harvard International Law Journal*, Vol. 16, No. 3 (1975), pp. 589–613.

CASTENADA, J., "La Charte des droits et devoirs economique des etats", *Annuaire Français de Droit International*, Vol. XX (1974) pp. 31–77.

CHIMNI, B. S., "Towards a Third World Approach to Non-Intervention: Through the Labyrinth of Western Doctrine", *Indian Journal of International Law*, Vol. 20, No. 2 (1980), pp. 243–264.

CLARK, W., "Robert McNamara at the World Bank", *Foreign Affairs*, Vol. 60, (1981), pp. 167–184.

CLAUDE, I.L. Jr., "Collective Legitimization as a Political Function of the United Nations", *International Organization*, Vol. 20, (1966), pp. 367–379.

COHN, T.H., "Politics in the World Bank Group: The Question of Loans to the Asian Giants", *International Organization*, Vol. 28, No. 3, (1974), pp. 561–571.

DAVID, E., "Quelques réflexiones sur l'égalite économique des Etats", *Revue belge de droit international*, Vol. x (1974), pp. 399–424.

DE LANIS, J. A., " 'Force' Under Article 2(4) of the United Nations Charter: The Question of Economic and Political Coercion", *Vanderbilt Journal of Transnational Law*, Vol. 12, No. 1 (1979), pp. 101–131.

DEMPSEY, P. S., "Economic Aggression and Self-Defense in International Law: the Arab Oil Weapon and Alternative American Responses Thereto", *Case Western Reserve Journal of International Law*, Vol. 9, No. 2 (1977), pp. 253–321.

DOBROCZYNSKI, M. "State Sovereignty in the World of Today", *Studies on International Relations*, Vol. 12 (1979), pp. 149–174.

DOMB, M. "Defining Economic Aggression in International Law: The Possibility of Regional Action by the Organization of American States", *Cornell International Law Journal*, Vol. 11, No. 1 (1978) pp. 85-105.

DOOSE, J. A., "The United Nations Definition of Aggression: A Preliminary Analysis" *Denver Journal of International Law and Policy*, Vol. 5, No. 1, (1975), pp. 171–199.

DOXEY, M., "Oil and Food as International Sanctions", *International Journal*, Vol. 36, No. 2 (1981), pp. 311–334.

EL KADIRI, A. K., "Reflexions sur la contrainte economique dans la société internationale", *Revue juridique politique et economique du maroc*, No. 7, (1980), pp. 11–24.

ENGEL, S., " 'Living' International Constitutions and the World Court", *International and Comparative Law Quarterly*, Vol. 16 (1967), pp. 865–910.

FATOUROS, A. A., "Le Rôle de la banque mondiale dans le droit international'', *Journal du droit international*, Vol. 104, No. 3 (1977), pp. 559–594.

FATOUROS, A. A., ''On the Hegemonic Role of International Functional Organization'', in *German Yearbook of International Law*, Vol. 23 (1980), pp. 9–36.

FAWCETT, J.E.S., (''Détournement de Pouvoir by International Organizations'', *B.Y.I.L.*, Vol. 33, (1957), pp. 311–316.

FEITH, D. J. ''The Oil Weapon De-mystified'', *Policy Review*, No. 15 (1981), pp. 19–39.

FELTON, J., ''US Role in the World Bank Faces New Tests'', *Congressional Quarterly Weekly Report*, Vol. 40, 27 February 1982, pp. 451-456.

FITZMAURICE, G. *Law and the Procedure of the International Court of Justice, British Yearbook of International Law*, Vol. 30, (1953), pp. 1–70.

FLORY, M. ''Souverainté des etats et cooperation pour le développement, *Recueil des cours*, Vol. 141 (1974), pp. 255–230.

FRANCK, T.M., and BOB, C.A., ''The Return of Humpty-Dumpty: Foreign Relations Law after the Chada Case'', *American Journal of International Law*, Vol. 79, No. 4, (1985), at pp. 912–960.

FREDMAN, S. J., ''US Trade Sanctions Against Uganda: Legality under International Law'', *Law and Policy in International Business*, Vol. 11, No. 3 (1979), pp. 1149–1191.

FRIEDMANN, W., ''Intervention and the Developing Countries'', *Virginia Journal of International Law*, Vol. 10 (1969-1970), pp. 205–222.

FRIEDMANN, W., ''Intervention and International Law'', at pp. 40–68 in *Intervention in International Politics*, JACQUET, L. G. M., (ed.) The Hague, Netherlands Institute of International Affairs, 1971.

GARDNER, R., ''The Hard Road to World Order'', *Foreign Affairs*, Vol. 52 (1974), pp. 556–575.

GARVEY, J. I. ''The UN Definition of 'Aggression': Law and illusion in the context of collective security'', *Virginia Journal of International Law*, Vol. 17, No. 2 (1977), pp. 177–199.

GHEBALI, V., ''The Politicisation of UN Specialized Agencies: A Preliminary Analysis'', *Millennium*, Vol. 14, No. 3, (1985), pp. 317-334.

GOLD, J., ''Political Considerations are Prohibited by Articles of Agreement when the Fund Considers Requests for Use of Resources'', *IMF Survey*, Vol. 12, No. 10, 23 May 1983, pp. 146–148.

GOLD, J., ''The Amendment and Variation of their Charters by International Organizations'', *Revue belge de droit international*, Vol. 9, No. 1, (1973), pp. 50–76.

GOLD, J., ''Weighted Voting Power: Some Limits and Some Problems'', *American Journal of International Law*, Vol. 68 (1974), pp. 687–708.

GORDON, E., ''The World Court and the Interpretation of Constitutive Treaties'', *American Journal of International Law*, Vol. 59 (1965), pp. 794–833.

GROSS, L., ''On the Degradation of the Constitutional Environment of the United Nations'', *American Journal of International Law*, Vol. 77, No. 3, (1983), pp. 569–584.

GROSS, L. "Maximizing Politics and Minimizing Law", *Harvard International Law Journal*, Vol. 12 (1971), pp. 436–451.

GUELKE, A., "Force Intervention and International Conflict", in NORTHEDGE, (ed.), *The Use of Force in International Relations*, London, Faber, 1974, 258 pp.

HAQ, I., "The Problem of Global Economic Inequity: Legal Structures and Some Thoughts on the Next 40 Years", in *Georgia Journal of International and Comparative Law*, Vol. 9, No. 3 (1979), pp. 507–518.

HARROD, J., "Problems of the United Nations Specialized Agencies at the Quarter Century", *Yearbook of World Affairs*, Vol. 28 (1974), pp. 187–203.

HEXNER, E. P., "Interpretation by Public International Organizations of Their Basic Documents", *American Journal of International Law*, Vol. 29, No. 2, (1975), pp. 469–485.

HEXNER, E.P., "Teleological Interpretation of Basic Instruments of Public International Organizations", *Law State and International Legal Order*, S. Engel (ed.), 1964, Knoxville, University of Tennessee Press, pp. 119–138.

HOLLY, D. A. "L'ONU: le system économique et la politique international", *International Organization*, Vol. 29, No. 2 (1975), pp. 469–485.

ILUYOMADE, B.O., "The Scope and Content of a Complaint of Abuse of Right in International Law", *Harvard International Law Journal*, Vol. 16, No. 1, (1975), pp. 47–92.

JACKSON, B. W., "Foreign Aid: Strategy or Stopgap?", *Foreign Affairs*, Vol. 41 (1962), pp. 90–104

JACOBS, S. and POIRER, M. "The Right to Veto United Nations Membership Applications: The United States Veto of the Viet-Nams" *Harvard International Law Journal*, Vol. 17 (1976), pp. 581–607.

JEKER, R. M., "Voting Rights of Less Developed Countries in the IMF", *Journal of World Trade Law*, Vol. 12, No. 3 (1978), pp. 218–227.

JENKS, C. W., "Coordination in International Organization: An Introductory Survey", *British Yearbook of International Law* (1951), pp. 29–89.

JENKS, C.W., "Some Constitutional Problems of International Organizations", *British Yearbook of International Law*, (1945), pp. 11–72.

JOHNSON, D. L. "Sanctions and South Africa", *Harvard International Law Journal*, Vol. 19 (1978), pp. 887–930.

JONES, G. J. "The Principle of Non-Intervention in the International Affairs of States, with Special Reference to the Implementation of Human Rights", *International Relations*, Vol. 5, Vol. 6 (1977), pp. 154–161.

KATZEN, L. "South Africa's Vulnerability to Economic Sanctions", *Review of International Studies*, Vol. 8, No. 2 (1982), pp. 89–98.

KNORR, K. "The Bretton Woods Institutions in Transition", *International Organization*, Vol. 2 (1948), pp. 19–38.

KRASNER, S. D. "Power Structures and Regional Development Banks", *International Organization*, Vol. 35, No. 2 (1981), pp. 303–328.

KRAUSE, L. B., and NYE, J. S., "Reflections on the Economics and

Politics of International Economic Organizations", *International Organization*, Vol 29, No. 1, (1974), 323–342.

LAUTERPACHT, E., "Gentleman's Agreements" in *International Law and Economic Order*, Essays in Honour of F. A. Mann on the Occasion of his 70th Birthday on 11 August 1977, Ed. by W. Flume and others, Munich, Verlag (1971), pp. 381–398.

LECKIE, S., "The Inter-State Complaint Procedure in International Human Rights Law: Hopeful Prospects or Wishful Thinking?", *Human Rights Quarterly*, Vol. 10, No. 2, (1988), pp. 249–303.

LEW, J. D. M., "Economic Coercion, Economic Cooperation and International Law", *New Law Journal*, Vol. 51, No. 3 (1975), pp. 358-371.

LIBBY, R. T., "International Development Association: A Legal Fiction Designed to Secure an LDC Constituency", *International Organization*, Vol. 29, No. 4 (1975) pp. 1065–1072.

LILLICH, R. B., "Economic Coercion and the "New International Economic Order": A Second Look at Some First Impressions", *Virginia Journal of International Law*, Vol. 16, No. 2 (1976), pp. 233–259.

LILLICH, R. B., "Economic Coercion and the International Legal Order", *International Affairs*, Vol. 51, No. 3 (1975), pp. 358–371.

LILLICH, R. B., "The Status of Economic Coercion under International Law: United Nations Norms", *Texas International Law Journal*, Vol. 12, No. 1, (1977) pp. 17–23.

LIPSON, C., "The International Organization of Third World Debt" *International Organization*, Vol. 35, No. 4 (1981), pp. 603–631.

LOWENFELD, A. F., " . . . Sauce for the Gander: The Arab Boycott and United States Political Trade Controls", *Texas International Law Journal*, Vol. 12, No. 1 (1977), pp. 41–46.

LUARD, E, "Functionalism Revisited: the UN Family in the 1980s", *International Affairs*, Vol. 59, No. 4, (1983), pp. 677–692.

LUTTIG, A. J., "Economic Coercions and South Africa, Part I", *South African Yearbook of International Law*, Vol. 3 (1977), pp. 119–135.

LYONS, G.M., BALDWIN, D.A. and MCNEMAR, D.W., "The Politicization Issue in the UN Specialized Agencies", in KAY, D.A. (ed.), *The Changing United Nations, Options for the United States*, New York, Praeger, 1977, at pp. 81–92.

MANI, V. S., "The Concept of Economic Coercion", *India Quarterly*, Vol. 33, No. 3 (1977), pp. 334–343.

MANI, V. S., "The 1970 Declaration on Friendly Relations: A Case Study in Law Creation by the UN General Assembly", *International Studies* (Bombay), Vol. 18, No. 3 (1979), pp. 287–321.

MANN, F. A., "The Interpretation of the Constitutions of International Financial Organizations", *British Yearbook of International Law*, Vol. 43, (1968-69), pp. 1-19.

MARMORSTEIN, V. E., "World Bank Power to Consider Human Rights Factors in Loan Decisions", *Journal of International Law and Economics*, Vol. 13, No. 1 (1978), pp. 113-136.

McDOUGAL, M. and FELICIANO, F., "International Coercion and World Public Order: The General Principles of the Law of War", *Yale Law Journal*, Vol. 67 (1958) p. 771.

McDOUGAL, M. and FELICIANO, F., "The Initiation of Coercion: A Multitemporal Analysis", *American Journal of International Law,* Vol. 52 (1958), pp. 241–259.

McDOUGAL, M. S. and FELICIANO, F. P., "Legal Regulation of Resort to International Coercion: Aggression and Self-Defense in Policy Perspective", *Yale Law Journal,* Vol. 68, No. 6 (1959), pp. 1057–1165.

McDOUGAL, M.S., and LANS, A., "Treaties and Congressional–Executive or Presidential Agreements: Interchangeable Instruments of National Policy", *Yale Law Journal,* Vol. 54, (1945), pp. 181–351.

MITRANY, D. "The Functional Approach to World Organization", *International Affairs,* Vol. 24 (1948), pp. 350–363.

MOORE, J.N., "The Control of Foreign Intervention in Internal Conflict", *Virginia Journal of International Law,* Vol. 9, (1969), pp. 209–342.

MORGENSTERN, F. "Legality in International Organizations", *B.Y.I.L.,* Vol. 48, (1976–1977), pp. 241–258.

MORGENTHAU, H., "A Political Theory of Foreign Aid", *American Political Science Review,* Vol. 61, (1962), pp. 301–309.

MUSHAT, M. "Principles Underlying the Developmental Assistance Machinery of the UN Family", *Verfassung und Recht in Ubersee,* Vol. 5 (1972), p. 175.

NANDA, Ved P., "Human Rights and Environmental Considerations in the Lending Policies of International Development Agencies – An Introduction", *Denver Journal of International Law and Policy,* Vol. 17, No. 1, (1988), pp. 29–38.

NAVARRO, C.K., "Cyprus and the UN: A case for non-military collective measures", *Indian Law Journal,* Vol. 54 (1978), pp. 125–163.

NEFF, S. C., "The Law of Economic Coercion: Lessons from the Past and Indications of the Future", *Columbia Journal of Transnational Law,* Vol. 20, No. 3 (1981), pp. 411–437.

OLSON, R. S., "Economic Coercion in World Politics, with a Focus on North–South Relations", *World Politics,* Vol. 31 (1979) pp. 471–494.

OPSAHL, T., "An 'International Constitutional Law'?", *International and Comparative Law Quarterly,* Vol. 10, (1961), pp. 760–784.

ORSONI, G. "Le retrait des Etats Unis et la crise de le B.I.T", *Revue générale de droit international public,* Vol.83, No.3, (1979), pp.689–746.

OSIEKE, O., "The Legality of Ultra Vires Decisions of International Organizations", *American Journal of International Law,* Vol. 77, No. 2, (1983), pp. 239–256.

PARRY, C. and others "Transnational Economic Boycotts and Coercion", *Texas International Law Journal,* Vol. 12 (1977), pp. 1–60.

PAUL, V. "The Abuse of Rights and Bona Fide in International Law", *Osterreichische Zeitschrift für Offentliches Recht und Völkerrecht,* Vol. 28, No. 112 (1977), pp. 107–130.

PAUST, J. J. "International Law and Economic Coercion: 'Force', the Oil Weapon and Effects Upon Prices", *Yale Studies* in *World Public Order,* Vol. 3, No. 1 (1976), pp. 213–227.

PAUST, J. J. and BLAUSTEIN, A. P., "The Arab Oil Weapon – A

Threat to International Peace", *American Journal of International Law*, Vol. 68, (1974), pp. 410–439.

PAUST, J. J. and BLAUSTEIN, A. P., "The Arab Oil Weapon: A Reply and Reaffirmation of Illegality", *Columbia Journal of Transnational Law*, Vol. 15 (1976), pp. 57–73.

PETERSMANN, "International Economic Theory and International Economic Law: On the Tasks of a Legal Theory of International Economic Order", in MACDONALD, R. St. J., and JOHNSTON, D.H., (eds.), *The Structure and Process of International Law: Essays in Legal Philosophy Doctrine and Theory*, The Hague, Martinus Nijhoff, 1983, at pp. 227–262.

PETERSMANN, E. U., "International Economic Development Law: Myth or Reality?", *Law and State*, Vol. 15 (1977), pp. 7–37.

PETERSMANN, E. U., "International Law and the New International Economic Order", *Law and State*, Vol. 17 (1978), pp. 7–20.

PETRAS, J. F. and LAPORTE, R. Jr, "Can We Do Business with Radical Nationalists? Chile No." *Foreign Policy*, Vol. 7 (1972), pp. 132–158.

PIERSON-MATHY, P., "L'action des Nations Unies contre l'apartheid", *Revue belge de droit international*, Vol. 7, No. 1, (1971), pp. 148–198.

PLANK, J. N. and others, "Legal and Policy Considerations of Non-relations with Cuba", *American Journal of International Law*, Vol. 66, No. 4 (1972), pp. 143–148.

POLAKAS, J., "Economic Sanctions: An effective alternative to military coercion?", *Brooklyn Journal of International Law*, Vol. 6 (1980), pp. 289–320.

RAMAN, K. V., " 'Aggression' – A description to Serve as a Definition", *India Quarterly*, Vol. 32, No. 1 (1976), pp. 42–48.

REICHER, H. , "The Uniting for Peace Resolution on the Thirtieth Anniversary of its Passage", *Columbia Journal of Transnational Law*, Vol. 20, No. 1, (1981), at pp. 1–49

RIPHAGEN, W., "Some Reflections on 'functional sovereignty' ", *Netherlands International Law Review*, Vol. 6, (1975), pp. 121–165.

ROLING, B. V. A., "Aspects of the Ban on Force", *Netherlands International Law Review*, Vol. 24, No. 1–2 (1977), pp. 242–259.

RUSTOW, W. V. and others, "Rules for Unarmed Conflict in the Intermediate Status between Peace and War", *Proceedings of the American Society of International Law*, Vol. 70 (1976), pp. 159–175.

SANFORD, J. and GOODMAN, M., "Congressional Oversight and the Multilateral Development Banks", *International Organization*, Vol. 29 (1975), pp. 1055–1064.

SCELLE, G., "Droit constitutionel international", in *Mélanges R. Carré de Malberg*, Paris, Sirey, 1933, pp. 501–515

SCHACTER, O., "The Evolving International Law of Development" in *Columbia Journal of Transnational Law*, Vol. 15, No. 1 (1976), pp. 2–16.

SCHEIBLA, S.H., "McNamara's Band Sour – Directors, Staff Critical of World Bank Operations", *Barrons*, December 3, 1979, at p. 1.

SCHMIDT, W. E., "Rethinking the Multilateral Development Banks", *Policy Review*, No. 10 (1979), pp. 47–61.

SCHOULTZ, L., "Politics, Economics, and US Participation in Multilateral Development Banks", *International Organization*, Vol. 36, No. 3 (1982), pp. 537–574.

SCHWEITZER, P. P., "Political Aspects of Managing the International Monetary System", *International Affairs*, Vol. 52, April 1976, pp. 208–218.

SCHWENNINGER, S. R., "The 1980s: New Doctrines of Intervention or New Norms of Non-Intervention?", *Rutgers Law Review*, Vol. 33, No. 2 (1981), pp. 423–434.

SCOTT, A., "Economic Warfare: how to play handball with the Russians", *Armed Forces Journal International*, Vol. 117 (1980), pp. 67–69.

SEIDL-HOHENVELDERN, "The United Nations and Economic Coercion", *Revue Belge de Droit International*, Vol. 18, (1984–1985 – 1), pp. 9–19.

SEIDL-HOHENVELDERN, I., "International Economic 'Soft Law' ", *Recueil des Cours*, Vol. 163 (1979), pp. 165–246.

SHIHATA, I. F. I., "Arab Oil Policies and the New International Economic Order", *Virginia Journal of International Law*, Vol. 16, No. 2 (1976), pp. 261–288.

SHIHATA, I. F. I., "Destination Embargo of Arab Oil: Its Legality under International Law", *American Journal of International Law*, Vol. 68 (1974), pp. 591–627.

SHIHATA, I. F. I., "The World Bank and Human Rights: An Analysis of the Legal Issues and the Record of Achievements", *Denver Journal of International Law and Policy*, Vol. 17, No. 1, (1988), pp. 39–66.

SHNEYER, P. A., "The Legality of the US Economic Blockade of Cuba under International Law", *Journal of International Law*, Vol. 13 (1981), pp. 451–482.

SIGMUND, P. E., "The 'Invisible Blockade' and the Overthrow of Allende", *Foreign Affairs*, Vol. 52 (1974), pp. 322.

SLATER, J., "The Limits of Legitimization in International Organizations", *International Organization*, Vol. 23, (1969), pp. 48–72.

SORENSEN, M., "Autonomous Legal Orders: Some Considerations Relating to a Systems Analysis of International Organizations in the World Legal Order", *International and Comparative Law Quarterly*, Vol. 32, (1983), at pp. 559–576.

STEINER, H. J. and others, "The American Response to the Arab Boycott", *Texas Law Review*, Vol. 54 (1976), pp. 1353–1438.

TAMMES, A.J.P., "The Member State as a Subject and as Organ", Chapter V of the course on Decisions of International Organs, *Recueil des Cours*, Vol. 94, (1958 II), pp. 344–359.

THIEBERGE, L.J., "Unilateralism: The direct challenge to International Law", *California Western International Law Journal*, Vol. 9, (1979), pp. 553–562.

THIELE, T. V., "Norms of Intervention in a Decolonized World", *New York University Journal of International Law and Policy*, Vol. 11, No. 1 (1978), pp. 141–174.

VIRALLY, M., "La Charte des droits and devoirs economique des etats", *Annuaire française de droit internationale*, Vol. XX (1974), pp. 57–77.

VIRALLY, M., "Panorama du droit international contemporain", (cours général), *Recueil des cours*, Vol. 183, (1983,V), pp. 1–382.

VIRALLY, M., "Review Essay: Good Faith in Public International Law", *American Journal of International Law*, Vol. 77, No. 1, (1983), pp. 130–134.

WALDE, T. W. "North–South Economic Cooperation and International Economic Development Law: Legal Process and Institutional Considerations", in *German Yearbook of International Law*, Vol. 23 (1980), pp. 59–90.

WASSERMAN, G., "The Foreign Aid Dilemma", *The Washington Quarterly*, Vol. 6, No. 1, (1983), pp. 96–106.

WILKINS, John R. "Legal Norms and International Economic Development: The Case of the Cuba Shipping Restrictions in the United States Foreign Assistance Act", in *California Law Review*, Vol. 55, No. 4 (1967), pp. 977–1019.

WRIGGINS, H., "Political Outcomes of Foreign Assistance: Influence, Involvement or Intervention", *Journal of International Affairs*, Vol. 22, (1968), pp. 217–230.

YOKOTA, Y., "Nonpolitical Character of the World Bank", *Japanese Annual of International Law*, No. 20 (1976), pp. 39–64.

ZAMORA, S., "Voting in International Economic Organizations", *American Journal of International Law*, Vol. 74 (1980), pp. 566–608.

ZEDALIS, R. J., "Some Thoughts on the United Nations Charter and the Use of Military Force Against Economic Coercion", *Tulsa Law Journal*, Vol. 17, No. 3 (1982), pp. 487–506.

Unattributed articles

"The Use of Nonviolent Coercion: A Study in Legality under Article 2(4) of the Charter of the United Nations", *University of Pennsylvania Law Review*, Vol. 122 (1974), pp. 983–1011.

"It's the World Bank", *The Economist*, Vol. 267, No. 7025, 22 April 1978, pp. 19–20.

INDEX